T0305227

Investing in the Homeland

Since 1980, there has been a 20-fold increase in foreign direct investment (FDI), particularly into developing countries, and a steadily growing global migrant population. Once viewed primarily through a negative lens as "brain drain," emigrants are increasingly recognized as an important resource for promoting economic development in migrant-sending countries. In *Investing in the Homeland*, Benjamin Graham finds diasporans— migrants and their descendants—play a critical role in linking foreign firms to social networks in developing countries, allowing firms to adopt social-tie-based strategies and flourish even in challenging political environments most foreign investors shun.

Graham's analysis draws on new data from face-to-face interviews with the managers of more than 450 foreign firms operating in two developing countries: Georgia and the Philippines. Graham finds that diaspora-owned and diaspora-managed firms are better connected than other foreign firms and they are more likely to use social ties in a variety of ways, including resolving disputes and influencing government policy. At the same time, Graham shows that diaspora-affiliated firms are no more socially responsible than their purely foreign peers—they are profit-seeking enterprises, not development NGOs. Graham identifies implications for both policymakers seeking to capture the development potential of diaspora investment and managers of multinational firms seeking to harness diasporans' capabilities as a source of sustained competitive advantage.

Benjamin A. T. Graham is Assistant Professor of International Relations at the University of Southern California and cofounder of the Security and Political Economy Lab.

Michigan Studies in International Political Economy

SERIES EDITORS: Edward Mansfield, Lisa Martin, and William Clark

Benjamin A. T. Graham
Investing in the Homeland: Migration, Social Ties, and Foreign Firms

Jana Grittersová
Borrowing Credibility: Global Banks and Monetary Regimes

Steven E. Lobell and Norrin M. Ripsman, Editors
The Political Economy of Regional Peacemaking

Leslie Johns
Strengthening International Courts: The Hidden Costs of Legalization

Yu Zheng
Governance and Foreign Investment in China, India, and Taiwan: Credibility, Flexibility, and International Business

Nathan M. Jensen, Glen Biglaiser, Quan Li, Edmund Malesky, Pablo M. Pinto, Santiago M. Pinto, and Joseph L. Staats
Politics and Foreign Direct Investment

Yoram Z. Haftel
Regional Economic Institutions and Conflict Mitigation: Design, Implementation, and the Promise of Peace

Ka Zeng and Joshua Eastin
Greening China: The Benefits of Trade and Foreign Direct Investment

David H. Bearce
Monetary Divergence: Domestic Policy Autonomy in the Post–Bretton Woods Era

Kerry A. Chase
Trading Blocs: States, Firms, and Regions in the World Economy

Edward D. Mansfield and Brian M. Pollins, Editors
Economic Interdependence and International Conflict: New Perspectives on an Enduring Debate

William Roberts Clark
Capitalism, Not Globalism: Capital Mobility, Central Bank Independence, and the Political Control of the Economy

William Bernhard
Banking on Reform: Political Parties and Central Bank Independence in the Industrial Democracies

Roland Stephen
Vehicle of Influence: Building a European Car Market

Andrew C. Sobel
State Institutions, Private Incentives, Global Capital

For a complete list of titles, please see www.press.umich.edu

Investing in the Homeland

Migration, Social Ties, and Foreign Firms

BENJAMIN A. T. GRAHAM

University of Michigan Press
Ann Arbor

Published in the United States of America by the
University of Michigan Press
Printed and bound by CPI Group (UK) Ltd, Croydon, CR0 4YY

First published January 2019

A CIP catalog record for this book is available from the British Library.

Library of Congress Cataloging-in-Publication Data

Names: Graham, Benjamin A. T., 1982– author.
Title: Investing in the homeland : migration, social ties, and foreign firms / Benjamin A.T. Graham.
Description: Ann Arbor : University of Michigan Press, [2019] | Series: Michigan studies in international political economy series | Includes bibliographical references and index. |
Identifiers: LCCN 2018039261 (print) | LCCN 2018049198 (ebook) | ISBN 9780472131150 (hardcover : acid-free paper) | ISBN 9780472124619 (ebook)
Subjects: LCSH: Investments, Foreign—Georgia (Republic)—Social aspects. | Investments, Foreign—Philippines—Social aspects. | Social responsibility of business—Georgia (Republic) | Social responsibility of business—Philippines. | Georgia (Republic)—Emigration and immigration—Economic aspects. | Philippines—Emigration and immigration—Economic aspects.
Classification: LCC HG5706.4.A3 (ebook) | LCC HG5706.4.A3 G73 2019 (print) | DDC 332.67/3094758—dc23
LC record available at https://lccn.loc.gov/2018039261

For Lynn

CONTENTS

Digital materials related to this title can be found on
the Fulcrum platform via the following citable URL:
https://doi.org/10.3998/mpub.10011255

ACKNOWLEDGMENTS

This project was a decade in the making and would not have been possible without the inspiration, mentoring, collaboration, and labor of many people. It will take me the rest of my career to pay forward the investments others have made and continue to make in my development as a scholar.

As an undergraduate, I interned for George Perkovitch at the Carnegie Endowment for International Peace. The intellectual engagement I experienced there convinced me I wanted to make social science my vocation. At Dartmouth, Steve Brooks coached me patiently through my somewhat bumbling performance as a research assistant on his book *Producing Security*; Anne Sa'adah challenged me intellectually and invested long hours advising my thesis, sharpening both my writing and my thinking; and Bill Wohlforth provided genial guidance along the way, made teaching look fun, and then gently unraveled the core of my argument during my thesis defense.

Miles Kahler chaired my dissertation committee at the University of California, San Diego (UCSD) and has been my foremost professional mentor. Miles is always warm but pulls no punches. I recall laboring for weeks on a revision of a dissertation chapter only to be met with the (accurate) assessment that "this draft appears to be a step backward in terms of coherence." And then he guided me through the process of fixing it. When push came to shove, Miles generously contributed funds from his own research account to ensure that the survey could be completed.

Lawrence Broz provided consistently insightful advice and warm support throughout my graduate career (and since). He deserves a good deal of credit for my current identity as an International Political Economy scholar, as I dabbled in comparative politics for some time.

Eddy Malesky and Craig McIntosh were both assistant professors when they served on my committee, and I did not fully appreciate then how extraordinarily generous they were with their time in spite of that fact. In addition to providing portions of my methods training directly, they did the hard work of reading repeated drafts of survey instruments and empirical analyses as I stumbled through my development as a quantitative scholar. Any methodological flaws that remain in this book reflect only my failure to live up to their instruction. Eddy in particular has remained engaged in shaping my work since—I aspire to emulate him as closely as possible in the way he mentors his many students.

Kaare Strøm brought me on board as his research assistant on the Inclusion, Dispersion, and Constraint project and we have collaborated extensively since. Kaare has provided me with much sound direct advice, but he has taught me most by example. He always keeps his eyes clearly on the theoretical core of a paper and never lets something go out the door until the argument is crystal clear.

Throughout this process, my collaborators have been my teachers. Indeed my greatest professional strength has been my ability to convince incredible scholars to work with me and to teach me through that work. I owe a great debt to all these collaborators: Cesi Cruz and Molly Bauer Racenberg; Erik Gartzke and Chris Fariss; Ben Horne and Kristy Buzard; Allison Kingsley and Noel Johnston; Scott Gates and Håvard Strand; Yonatan Lupu; Michael Miller; Simon Hug, Nils-Christian Bormann, Lars-Erik Cederman, and Julian Wucherpfennig; Prudenciano Gordoncillo, Jeanette Madamba, and Jewel Cabardo; Jacob Tucker; Suzie Caldwell Mulesky; Jonathan Markowitz; Kelly Zvobgo; Lynn Ta; Mona Vakilifathi; and Michael Kenwick. My coauthors not only made specific papers work, they each taught me how to be a better social scientist.

When I set to work to collect the data for this book, Jonathan Kulick was my first point of contact in Georgia. He arranged my affiliation with the Georgian Foundation for Strategic and International Studies (GFSIS) and provided wide-ranging advice that enabled successful completion of the survey. Logistical support from GFSIS, its director Alexander Rondeli, and his assistant Tata Tsereteli was indispensable.

The hard work of executing the Georgia survey was carried out by a team of talented and dedicated enumerators: Maya Baramidze, Amiran Chanchibadze, Anna Gogokhia, Anastasia Laitadze, Giorgi Mekerishvili, and Giorgi Tarkhan-Mouravi. I also received important consultation in Georgia from David Kokiashvili, Alexandre Kukhianidze, Maia Mestvirishvili, Anna Sekowska-Livny, Timothy Blauvelt, and Hans Gutbrod, and benefited from additional logistical support from both American Councils and the Caucasus Research Resource Center.

The survey in the Philippines was carried out in coequal collaboration with Cesi Cruz. She provided a unique combination of in-country connections, local knowledge, and technical expertise in survey design and implementation, and I am extremely grateful to have the honor of collaborating with her. Prudenciano (Dodong) Gordoncillo directed the survey in-country, handled myriad logistical and implementation difficulties with aplomb, and managed the wonderful team that executed the survey and cleaned the data. This survey team included professors Jeanette Madamba and Jewel Cabardo from the University of the Philippines, Los Banos, as well as Venice Anulat, Kristina Bienes, Rhae Cisneros, May Gordoncillo, Tessa Lyrene Lantican, Mel Habito, Amanda Porcheron, Lheid Regalado, Charis Mae Tolentino, and Laura Vossler.

One of the great joys in my time at the University of Southern California (USC) has been my engagement with the students in the Security and Political Economy (SPEC) lab, which I run with two wonderful friends and colleagues, Jonathan Markowitz and Megan Becker. Many lab students contributed to this book directly, including Anbar Aizenman, Rod Albuyeh, Therese Anders, Ashlie Benson, Miranda Bidwell, Molly He, Joey Huddleston, Xinru Ma, Suzie Caldwell Mulesky, Johanna Reyes, Jihyun Shin, Jacob Tucker, and Patrick Vossler. These students worked with me on data imputation, analysis, and visualization; reviewed hard-copies of survey forms; reviewed the literature; and read drafts of the manuscript. They were incredible.

This book also benefited from a manuscript review workshop hosted by the Center for International Studies at USC. Special thanks to all my USC colleagues who provided feedback, and particularly David Kang, who hosted the conference and served as a discussant. Layna Mosley flew in from the University of North Carolina to provide incredibly helpful comments in person, and Nate Jensen and David Leblang provided extensive written comments. Reading an entire book manuscript is no small ask, and their generous feedback inspired six months of much-needed revisions. Nate also hosted me at George Washington University for a presentation of the project, the feedback from which was extremely valuable.

Other important mentors who guided various stages of this project include Liesl Riddle, who brought me into the field of diaspora studies in the first place, and Jennifer Brinkerhoff, who has continued to guide this project through to the time of publication. Carol Wise, Pat James, Jonathan Markowitz, Steve Brooks, and Allison Kingsley provided key advice in the late stages of the project, especially helping me frame the contributions of the project, polish the prose, and navigate the publication process. I was also the beneficiary of warm, detailed, and helpful anonymous reviews through the University of Michigan Press, which pushed me to an important final set of revisions without which the book would be noticeably weaker.

Financial support for this project came from The Rohr Chair of Pacific International Relations, the USC Center for International Studies, and the Zumberge Research and Innovation Fund.

Finally and foremost among all those in need of thanks is my wife, Lynn Ta, to whom this book is dedicated. Her unfaltering support sustained this project, and me, from beginning to end. She read drafts, batted around ideas, and helped me understand not only how to answer questions more effectively but how to identify what is worth studying in the first place. Three little boys have joined our family in the course of this project, and Lynn shouldered more than her share of the child care for years of six-day work weeks and international travel, all while launching her own legal career with one hand effectively tied behind her back. This book is as much hers as it is mine. The first decade of our intellectual and family partnership has gone rather splendidly, and the next five or six decades of collaboration are ripe with possibility.

CHAPTER 1

Introduction

1.0. Prologue

Francis Laurel is a member of a prominent political family in the Philippines. His grandfather was president and his father was ambassador to Japan.[1] After finishing his BA in the Philippines, Mr. Laurel travelled to the United States to attend business school at Northwestern University. There he became close friends with Tadahiro Yoshida, whose father owned a zipper company in Japan. After graduation, the two young men launched what is now the YKK Fastenings Products Group, with operations in Japan and the Philippines. At the time the venture was launched in 1977, the Philippines was not a major destination for global manufacturers. Without the personal connection Mr. Laurel formed in graduate school, it is unlikely Mr. Yoshida would have chosen to invest in the Philippines, and without Mr. Laurel's personal and political connections in the Philippines, it is unlikely the venture would have survived. Today it can be hard to find a product with a zipper made by anybody else.

In 2015, Nina Aguas stepped down after a phenomenally successful run as Citibank's head of consumer banking in the Philippines.[2] Among other successes, Citi became the leading issuer of consumer credit cards in the Philippines during Ms. Aguas's tenure. Ms. Aguas had previously spent several years abroad forming relationships and gaining cultural fluency before launching an international business career back home in the Philippines. At Citibank, Ms. Aguas was able to establish trust and communicate effectively with headquarters personnel, and also navigate the complex regulatory politics of the Philippines, manage relationships with business counterparts, and tailor products to Filipino consumers.

Migrants like Mr. Laurel and Ms. Aguas have emerged as pivotal players in the global economy. They own and manage some of the world's largest multinational corporations and thousands of smaller firms around the globe. The core argument of this book is that diasporans, namely migrants and their descendants, have unique social ties—connections to friends, family, and classmates in the homeland and to colleagues and neighbors in their country of settlement—and these ties provide immense value to the firms diasporans own and manage. Diasporans are able to use their unique social ties to connect multinational firms based in their country of settlement, which might otherwise have no social connections in the diasporan's homeland, to business counterparts and political actors in that country. While potentially useful in all countries, I argue that transnational broker- age is likely to be particularly important in countries where formal institu- tions are weak and social ties play a larger role in both business and politics.

1.1. Why Diaspora Investment Matters

Across the world, migration is steadily expanding and foreign direct in- vestment (FDI) is overtaking trade as the most important driver of global economic integration and growth, particularly in developing countries. Trade has increased six-fold since 1980, but FDI has increased 20-fold. More than half of FDI flows in 2012 went to developing countries. During the same time period, the global stock of migrants has increased by over 60%, with a large and increasing share of that stock having migrated from poor countries to wealthy ones.[3] And these trends in migration and FDI are intricately linked.

Recent research has exploited bilateral data on global patterns of migra- tion and FDI to establish that diaspora populations (i.e., migrants and their descendants) increase FDI from diasporans' countries of settlement to their homelands (e.g., Kugler and Rapoport 2007; Leblang 2010; Javorcik 2011). Other scholars estimate that direct investment by diasporans accounted for more than 50% of FDI inflows to China during the 1990s (Huang 2003; Ye 2010)[4] and 20–30% of FDI flows to India during the same time period (Ye 2010). On a grand scale, diasporans are shaping global flows of capital. At the firm level, we know anecdotally that diasporans own and manage some important multinational firms, but our knowledge of how diasporans shape the capabilities and behavior of these firms largely stops with these anec- dotes. Are diaspora-owned and diaspora-managed firms common? Do diaspora-owned and managed firms behave any differently than other foreign firms? Given that almost all foreign firms hire local managers, do diaspora owners and managers deliver value to their firms that these local managers do not? How do diaspora-affiliated firms impact development?

I present new data showing that 16% of the foreign firms operating in the country of Georgia are diaspora-owned; the number in the Philippines is around 37%.[5] While the Georgia data do not include information on which firms have diaspora managers, in the Philippines about half of the foreign firms in my sample are diaspora-managed—in total almost two-thirds are diaspora-affiliated in some way. Diaspora owners and managers are not minor players affecting a few firms on the margins; rather, diaspora ownership and management is widespread among multinational firms and absolutely essential to the ability of these firms to thrive in developing countries.

Understanding how diasporans affect the firms they own and manage is critical for at least three related reasons. First, developing-country governments need to know how to capitalize on diaspora investment to better promote economic development. Similarly, because they don't understand the role of diasporans in multinational firms, governments in wealthy countries likely underestimate the positive economic impacts of inward migration on their own economies and the economies of migrant-sending countries. Lastly, multinational firms can benefit from an improved ability to engage diasporans to enhance profitability and penetrate new markets.

Developing and testing a theory of diaspora homeland investment contributes to two strands of academic literature—one on the relationship between political risk and FDI and the other on the relationship between migration and FDI. Political scientists and economists have credibly established that political risk deters FDI and that, under the right conditions, FDI can be an important driver of economic growth in developing countries.[6] But political risk does not deter all multinational firms, and it may not deter some at all. One of the contributions of this study is to disaggregate FDI—distinguishing between multinationals that are diaspora-owned or diaspora-managed and those that are not—and providing evidence that diaspora-affiliated firms have unusual abilities for managing political risk.

From both a theoretical perspective and a policymaking angle, simply knowing that diasporans increase FDI to their homelands is insufficient. We need to know how diaspora investment works—what types of firms are involved, how they behave in the market, and how they interact with host governments. The burning policy question for developing countries isn't whether they should let people emigrate, and thereby increase FDI a decade or two down the line. The question is, how do these governments leverage the diaspora populations they have now to increase FDI and promote economic growth *today*? Similarly, the question facing multinational corporations (MNCs) is how to leverage diasporans to make their investment strategies more effective. For both of these purposes, we need a fully developed theory of diaspora direct investment, one that can answer all the questions above about diaspora-affiliated firms—including their capabilities, strategies, and impact on homeland development.

1.2. The Argument in Brief: The Diaspora Difference

I argue that Nina Aguas and Laurel Francis are archetypal of the role that diasporans play facilitating FDI. Many diasporans have social ties that span multiple countries, and they use these personal ties to connect the multinational firms they own and manage (which are often based in their country of settlement) to valuable social networks in the homeland. In both diaspora-owned and diaspora-managed firms, I expect that diaspora-provided social connections are critical in allowing foreign firms to overcome challenges and seize opportunities in otherwise daunting market and political environments.

I contrast this transnational brokerage mechanism with an important alternative theory proposed (but largely untested) within the existing literature, which is based on diasporans' social and emotional motivations for homeland engagement (e.g., Gillespie, Sayre, and Riddle 2001; Riddle and Nielsen 2010). This theory argues that at least some diasporans invest in the homeland due to the same social and emotional motivations that have been shown to affect diaspora philanthropy.

When comparing this alternative theory with my own, two distinct scenarios emerge in terms of how developing-country governments and multinational firms should proceed. My theory of diasporans as transnational brokers implies that MNCs that are not already diaspora-owned can gain substantial advantages by integrating diasporans into their management or bringing in a diaspora co-owner. It also implies that diaspora-affiliated firms may have particular advantages in overcoming the challenges of doing business in less institutionalized environments. Thus diasporans may allow multinational firms to thrive in countries that they would otherwise avoid, facilitating the flow of investment to capital-starved economies.

Conversely, if diasporans' motivations are a powerful factor, diaspora-affiliated firms are likely to be more socially responsible and lean toward development-oriented projects in the homeland. However, diaspora managers or partners could be a potential liability from the perspective of multinational firms, as they may seek to divert firm resources in the promotion of their own social or political agenda in the homeland.

While this project presents a comprehensive theory of diasporans' role as transnational brokers, it also introduces new data. We don't understand the mechanisms that connect diasporans to FDI because we have little empirical knowledge about the firms diasporans own and manage. Thus one of the key contributions of this study is the introduction of two new surveys of foreign firms operating in developing countries, one in the country of Georgia and the other in the Philippines. The data from these surveys are actually the first available for enabling scholars to directly compare foreign firms owned and managed by diasporans to those that are not.[7] The analysis of these new firm-level data allows me to ask and answer the most compelling questions about how diaspora-affiliated firms behave and how they affect economic and political development in the homeland.

My primary task in this introduction is to situate this book with two big picture questions: (1) What is the relationship between FDI and development in the investment host country? (2) What is the broader relationship between migration and development of which diaspora homeland investment is a part? Before proceeding to these questions let me pause briefly to define the key term in this study, diaspora, and to distinguish diaspora homeland investment from the related phenomenon of remittances, or wages that migrants send back to their families in the homeland.

1.3. Defining Diaspora

My interest in diasporans stems from the unique social networks they possess and the related capabilities they may provide to the firms they own and manage. Thus when I define diasporans and diaspora-affiliated firms, I seek definitions that identify the people who I expect to have these unique social ties and the firms upon which I expect they convey unique advantages. I define diasporans as migrants and their descendants who retain identifiable ties to the homeland, and I include both diasporans who currently live abroad and those who have returned to the homeland (i.e., returnees). I define diaspora-affiliated firms as foreign firms that are either owned or managed by diasporans.

Ties to the homeland are central to any definition of diaspora. Gabriel Sheffer (1986: 3) defines diasporans as individuals "residing and acting in host countries but maintaining strong sentimental and material links with their countries of origin—their homelands." Any migrant or descendent of migrants who retains significant ties to the homeland is considered a diasporan.[8] If a migrant cuts homeland ties and fully assimilates into her country of settlement, she is not.[9] Because my theory focuses on diasporans' unique social ties, it applies most directly to those individuals who meet Sheffer's definition of a diasporan most clearly—individuals who retain strong social ties to the homeland.[10] However, I also extend my focus beyond diasporans who remain abroad and include diasporans who have returned to the homeland.

The central contrast in this book, both theoretically and empirically, is between foreign firms that enjoy the (potential) advantages of diaspora-affiliation and those that do not. I include returnees in my study because diasporans who own or manage multinational firms that invest in the homeland often return to live at least part-time in the homeland. In other research contexts, the distinctions between returnees and diasporans who remain abroad is a critical one. In this context, my theory makes the same predictions for both groups; I expect that firms owned and managed by returnees enjoy similar transnational brokerage benefits to those owned and managed by diasporans still living abroad. Therefore, as a shorthand, when talking about both current diasporans and returnees, I will refer to them as "diasporans," and I will refer to the firms they own and manage as firms that are "diaspora-affiliated."

The inclusion of diaspora-managed firms also bears note, as most past work on diaspora investment has focused exclusively on firms that diasporans own (e.g., Newland and Tanaka 2010; Riddle, Hrivnak, and Nielsen 2010). However, while there are potentially important differences between diaspora-owned and diaspora-managed firms, I expect that both types of firms enjoy similar advantages with respect to transnational brokerage.

1.4. Homeland Investment vs. Remittances

It is important to distinguish diaspora homeland investment from the more frequently studied capital flow with which diasporans are associated, which is remittances. Remittances are funds that migrants send back to the homeland, usually to family members. These funds can promote financial development in the migrant's homeland (e.g., Giuliano and Ruiz-Arranz 2009; Gupta, Patillo, and Wagh 2009), but while some remittances may be used for business investment, particularly in household-based micro-enterprises, most remittances are spent on household consumption (e.g., Jongwanich 2007; Ang 2007). While the theory I develop regards the behavior of the foreign firms that diasporans own and manage, I do not examine micro-enterprises. Rather, my focus is on the medium- and large-size firms that account for the majority of global flows of FDI. This means that I am looking at a phenomenon quite distinct from even that subset of remittances that are invested in small-scale family businesses.

This study fits closely with the literature on the causes and consequences of FDI to developing countries, and less with the remittances literature. However, this book is an important complement to the sophisticated literature that has evolved on the development impact of remittances (e.g., Taylor 1992; Kapur 2004; Haas 2005; Ratha 2005). When scholars seek to highlight the global importance of remittances, they often note that remittances are the second largest capital flow to developing countries after FDI (e.g., Maimbo and Ratha 2005). I show that diasporans also exert important influence as the owners and managers of multinational firms, and thus their role in transforming global capital flows extends far beyond remittances—diasporans shape global flows of FDI as well.

1.5. The First Big Picture: FDI and Development

Simple neoclassical models of economic growth predict that capital will flow from rich countries, where capital is abundant and land and labor are scarce, to poor countries, where land and labor are abundant. But instead it more often flows the other way.[11] In 2010, for example, the world's least developed countries received less than 5% of the world's foreign direct investment.[12] Why?

Governance. Poor countries aren't just poor in economic terms; they are often poorly governed as well. There are other factors, and poverty is a major deterrent to investment in its own right, but governance is the dominant factor (e.g., Alfaro, Kalemli-Ozcan, and Volosovych 2008). Much more so than their rich counterparts, poor countries are plagued by political instability, corruption, bureaucratic incompetence, and political violence—in other words, political risk. Political risk deters investment and promotes capital flight, which leads to low growth and economic stagnation (e.g., Henisz 2000; Li and Resnick 2003; Jensen 2006).

Most of the existing research, both on the relationship between political risk and FDI and that between FDI and economic growth, is conducted at the aggregate, cross-national level. Political risk is used to predict net FDI inflows, and net FDI inflows are used to predict economic growth rates, all at the country level (e.g., Borensztein, Gregorio, and Lee 1998; Jensen 2003; Alfaro et al. 2004). Unfortunately, cross-national analysis of the causes and effects of FDI masks important variation across different types of multinational firms, both in terms of their sensitivity to political risk and their impact on economic and political development in the homeland. In this book I argue that diaspora-affiliated firms are better able than other foreign firms to operate effectively in the face of certain types of political risk, but that, counter to much of the literature in economic sociology, diaspora-affiliated firms do not behave in ways more conducive to economic and political development in the homeland.

Despite a predominance of cross-national work conducted over the past 15 years, this book builds on early scholarship in political risk that explores variation in firms' vulnerability to political risk.[13] Indeed this book is part of a small firm-level renaissance in the study of political risk and FDI (Kingsley and Noordewier 2011; Jensen 2012; Johnston 2012; Kerner and Lawrence 2013; Shi 2013; Wellhausen 2013; Lee, Biglaiser, and Staats 2014). This return to firm-level analysis in the literature is motivated by, among other things, the fact that even the world's most dangerous and poorly governed states attract some inward investment. Clearly, at least some multinationals are able to succeed in these countries. For example, the global beverage giant SAB Miller has invested over US $70 million in a brewery in South Sudan, a project begun two years before the referendum on South Sudan's independence and enlarged twice since, despite ongoing violence and political turmoil. Similarly, following the lifting of US sanctions against Myanmar in 2012, GAP Inc. began producing clothes at several factories in the country, despite continued political instability.

The market upsides of these investments are obvious. Myanmar has low wages and had hosted a large number of garment factories prior to widespread sanctions that hammered the industry in 2003. This past experience meant there was latent domestic expertise for GAP to draw on when sanctions were finally lifted. In South Sudan, the complete absence of domestic competition in the beverage industry gives SAB Miller the opportunity to dominate the local market, competing only with imported products. However, the costs of investing in these climates are high as well; in addition to extreme policy uncertainty and a risk of violence in both cases, a lack of local infrastructure forced SAB Miller to create its own water, power, and sewer facilities.

Firms like GAP and SAB Miller demonstrate that some multinational firms can invest profitably even when governance remains poor. Their presence can bolster the economy in the short term and perhaps provide a window of opportunity for political reform (or in the case of South Sudan, political consolidation). This reform can then help attract new flows of inward investment, further boosting growth and enabling further improvements in the political environment. But what kind of firms can invest successfully in the face of political dysfunction? While diaspora-affiliated firms are not the only type of firms that can thrive in the face of political risk, my theory of diasporans as transnational brokers provides an important answer to that question.

The First Development Question: What kinds of multinational firms can operate successfully in the face of political risk?

By establishing the value of diasporans in addressing the challenges common to most emerging markets, my theory generates important insights for multinational firms. To preview some of the implications drawn in chapter 7, when firms are selecting locations for new investments, they should consider the diasporans they employ as a critical strategic resource. A firm with large numbers of Filipino workers and managers likely possesses important capabilities that should support successful expansion into the Philippines. Similarly, a firm committed to entering a new country should strongly consider recruiting diasporans into the management team that oversees the expansion; entrepreneurs considering the establishment of a new transnational venture should consider the role that a diaspora business partner might play in managing risks and seizing opportunities associated with the specific political context in which it will operate. Understanding diasporans' potential as transnational brokers allows multinational firms to make the best use of the diasporans they already employ and highlights the recruitment and promotion of diaspora managers as a potentially fruitful means of expanding firm capabilities.

From a development perspective, understanding how different types of firms manage and respond to political risk is critical for several reasons. First, it allows poorly governed countries to identify the types of firms they should recruit—it tells us what firms can fill that critical role of investing **before** governance improves. More broadly though, it helps us understand the link between a country's political conditions and the types of investment it attracts. This is crucial because the welfare effects of inward FDI vary not just according to the volume of investment but also according to the type of firms that undertake it.

The Second Development Question: What kinds of multinational firms operate in a manner conducive to promoting economic and political development in the host country?

To understand how firms vary in their development impact, it is helpful to think in a simple way about the "good" foreign firm and the "bad" foreign firm. The good foreign firm enters the host country, bringing with it cutting-edge technology and managerial expertise. The good firm hires and trains locals, purchases inputs from local producers, and pays taxes to the host government. In the short run, the hiring reduces unemployment and raises wages, the tax revenues allow for new government programs, and the purchase of goods from local producers boosts the domestic economy. In the longer run, some of the local employees trained by the good foreign firm move on to new jobs at domestic firms, bringing their expertise with them. Local firms that collaborate, or even compete with the good foreign firm, copy its behavior and improve productivity. The good foreign firm reinvests its profits in the host country, continuing to expand and create progressively larger positive spillovers for the host economy over time.

But not all foreign direct investments follow this pattern. The bad foreign firm hires mostly foreign workers, buys few inputs from domestic firms, and pays few domestic taxes, all of which limit the positive spillovers to the host economy. The bad foreign firm competes with domestic producers to sell products locally, inflicts extensive environmental damage, and perhaps even pays bribes to local officials, fueling corruption. The impact on the host economy and the domestic political system may be negative in both the short and long run.

The extensive literature on FDI and economic growth makes it clear that both of these scenarios occur in practice.[14] Some of this variation is driven by the sectors in which investment occurs: investments by mining firms may be less beneficial for growth than investments by semiconductor manufacturers. However, even within a given sector it is clear that some foreign firms produce much greater positive impacts on the host economy than others.

Governments in developing countries work hard to promote inward direct investment, and some of these efforts—reducing the topline corporate tax rate or reducing regulation—benefit a wide swath of foreign investors. Many other incentives are more narrowly tailored, targeting specific industries or even specific firms. For example, in 2013 the Philippines introduced a package of incentives that targets the assembly and import of electric, hybrid, and alternative-fuel vehicles. These incentives include everything from tax breaks for producers to priority application approval for commercial operators.[15]

Developing countries have limited budgets, however, and these types of investment incentives can misdirect spending away from crucial areas like education and public health. From a social welfare perspective, it is important that when governments employ these incentives, they actually succeed in increasing investment, don't overpay to entice investors, and attract the right type of firms—namely the "good" foreign firms instead of the "bad." So what does it take for developing-country governments to get this strategy right? It takes good answers to two key questions: (1) What types of foreign firms are willing and able to invest in host countries with high levels of political risk? and (2) What types of firms have the largest positive impacts on development in the host economy?

In this book I examine one type of foreign firm in particular that I expect to be willing and able to invest in countries with high levels of political risk and that many hope may also have large positive impacts on economic development: foreign firms owned and managed by diasporans and returnees, namely diaspora-affiliated firms. I contend that diaspora-affiliated firms are both more capable than other foreign firms—better able to operate profitably in the face of certain political risk—and possibly better for economic development in the host country—they tend to reinvest more of their earnings locally. This argument about the development potential of diaspora investment is actually more conservative than one that is sometimes made in the policy community to justify diaspora investment promotion efforts. The policy community has suggested in the past that diaspora-owned firms also produce larger pro-development spillovers than other

MNCs (e.g., Debass and Ardovino 2009; Foreign Services Institute 2010; Rodriguez-Montmayor 2012). In this book I examine that expectation and find no evidence to support it.

One of the key contributions of this work is to examine the development-related behavior of diaspora-affiliated firms empirically, identifying which types of optimism are warranted, and which are not.[16] Thus this book is situated not only in a big picture conversation about the types of foreign firms that can invest profitably in the face of political risk and the types of foreign firms that contribute most to economic growth in the host country but also in a conversation about the economic and political impacts of migration on development.

1.6. The Second Big Picture: Migration and Development

When we think of modern migration, we generally think of refugees fleeing from conflict or low-skilled workers slipping illegally into rich countries to work for low wages. We think of migrants as weak and impoverished, not as titans of global finance who move ideas, technology, and billions of dollars of capital across borders every year. But that view is starting to change as a new reality emerges. The intersection of migration and globalization in the early 21st century has spawned a new class of immigrant entrepreneurs, a group particularly dominant in the tech sector. Take Kunal Bahl, for example, who grew up in India, was educated at MIT and Penn, worked for Microsoft, and then returned to India to start Snapdeal, now valued at over US $700 million (Gooptu 2014). His Russian counterpart can be found in Serge Faguet, who was born and raised in Russia, studied at Stanford, worked at Google, and eventually returned to Moscow to launch Ostrovok, which became the dominant player in Russian online travel bookings (Butcher 2014).

Migration has been steadily increasing since World War II, with upwards of 3% of the world's population now living outside their birth country (United Nations 2011), and it is only the restrictive policies of migrant-receiving countries that prevent this number from soaring higher and faster. Within poor countries, 40% of adults report that they would emigrate permanently if they could—a number that tops 60% in some countries (Esipova, Ray, and Pugliese 2011).

The United States has always been a nation of immigrants. In 2009, 13%

of the US population was foreign born. In the last thirty years, Europe has rapidly caught up—Germany, Spain, Sweden, and Austria have all surpassed the United States on this measure (United Nations 2011). Looking one generation farther down the line, fully half of the babies born in London in 2013 were born to foreign mothers (McDermott 2014). Many of them will grow up and retain strong ties to the homeland of their parents; the share of the world's population that belongs in Sheffer's definition of a diaspora is growing steadily, and no slowdown is apparent.

So what impact do diasporans (and emigration) have on the countries from which all these migrants are departing? This question is of course the flipside of the tense debate Americans and Europeans are more familiar with—what impact do migrants have on the country that receives them? There is a great deal of passion and controversy on the migrant-sending side of the debate as well.

For decades, the conversation was dominated by fears of "brain drain," or the idea that the best and brightest workers from poor countries would race off to pursue new opportunities in rich countries, leaving their homelands poorer than ever (e.g., Bhagwti and Hamada 1974; Miyagiwa 1991).[17] This idea isn't entirely wrong, in the sense that there are indeed short-term costs to the loss of human capital, but more recent research has shown this perspective to be incomplete. The key is that migrants' relationships with their homelands don't end when they emigrate; for an increasing number, the relationship is only just beginning.

In no field is the fear of brain drain more acute than in medicine. The Nigerian government, for example, spends close to US $50,000 to educate each Nigerian physician at public medical schools. Some of those physicians then emigrate, taking their skills with them. This is a staggering loss for Nigeria, which loses both the financial investment in education and some of its brightest, most productive workers. In 2001, James Johnson, chairman of the Council of the British Medical Association, called recruitment of health professionals from Sub-Saharan Africa "the rape of the poorest countries."[18] And of course it is not just doctors, and it is not just Nigeria or Sub-Saharan Africa. Wealthy countries welcome highly skilled migrants in many fields, including engineers, scientists, and other skill-intensive occupations. Capital-rich economies are hungry for talent and lure away many of the most educated citizens from developing countries. It would obviously be so much better for developing countries if their brightest and most educated citizens remained at home. Or so it seems.

New evidence suggests the reverse. Clemens and Pettersson (2008) surveyed thousands of African-born members of the American Medical Association and the Canadian Medical Association and revealed a number of key facts. For example, they found that doctors trained in their home country worked an average of five years before emigrating, allowing the state to recoup much of its investment. More importantly, the average African-born physician working in North America sends more than US $6,000 annually back to her homeland in the form of remittances, more than US $130,000 over the course of a career.[19]

These remittances tell just part of the story. Because they were surveying doctors who were still members of North American medical associations, Clemens and Patterson did not capture doctors who had returned to the homeland—what is known as circular migration. There is in fact an entire literature (of which this book is part) that focuses on what happens when migrants return to the homeland, bringing with them skills, knowledge, social connections, and capital they acquired abroad.[20] Cross-national evidence suggests that doubling the number of migrants from a given homeland living in an Organization for Economic Co-operation and Development (OECD) country increases flows of FDI from the OECD country to the developing country by about 16% in US dollars (Leblang 2010).[21]

There is also a literature on diaspora trade, which focuses on the role of diasporans in promoting trade between their homelands and their countries of settlement (e.g., Rauch and Trindade 2002; Newland and Taylor 2010; Law, Genç, and Bryant 2013). As developing countries struggle to integrate successfully into the global economy—as they seek to access new markets and sources of capital without being eviscerated by new competition and volatility—diasporas are emerging as one their most valuable resources.

While the primary actors in my theory are skilled migrants like Nina Aguas and Francis Laurel, it is important to note that low-skilled migrants, too, are more powerful economic actors than previously thought. Early views held that emigration of unskilled laborers might benefit the sending country by reducing unemployment, but for a long time there was little consideration that these migrants might benefit the homeland through any means other than their absence. That, too, has changed.

In 2005, the World Bank released the first systematic estimate of global flows of remittances—wages that workers send back to their families in the homeland (Maimbo and Ratha 2005).[22] Official remittance flows back to the homeland were at least US $90 billion in 2003, with unofficial flows estimated to be much larger. And many of these remittances come from unskilled workers. If a Haitian migrates to the United States, her expected lifetime earnings increase more than six-fold (Clemens 2011), much of which is often sent back to Haiti to support family members who did not emigrate. Similarly, while the phenomena of diaspora trade, direct investment, and philanthropy are admittedly driven primarily by an elite subset of wealthy, well-connected diasporans, many of these diaspora elites now shaping global commerce were not wealthy or educated when they emigrated.

Despite this flood of new evidence on the positive effects that diasporans have on their homelands, the debate over whether emigration is good for the homeland remains contested. For many scholars, policymakers, and advocates, fears of brain drain continue to dominate. Ralph Nader is among those opposing recent efforts to expand the number of H1-B visas available to bring high-skilled workers to the United States, arguing that doing so deprives the host countries from which those workers are drawn. He writes, "Isn't it fortunate for the people of Bangladesh and others that a young Muhammad Yunus was not lured away to Wall Street and stayed in Bangladesh to start the now famous micro-credit movement in thousands of villages?" (Nader 2014).[23]

This ongoing controversy about the effects of skilled migration on migrant-sending economies is driven, at least in part, by a lack of knowledge. Although the economic and political effects of diasporans and returnees are exploding around us, academics and policymakers have been racing desperately to catch up—trying to understand phenomena that are transforming entire economies before our eyes. In countries like Liberia, Moldova, Kyrgyzstan, Haiti, and Nepal, remittances account for more than 25% of total GDP in some years.[24] In Tajikistan, that number topped 50% in 2013. More money was sent home by migrants working abroad than was earned by all the people working in the homeland itself.

But policymakers can't adapt to changes, and countries can't fully take advantage of new resources, until we understand those changes and resources. For that, we need data. Recall two of the new data points noted earlier: 16% of the foreign firms operating in the country of Georgia are at least part-owned by members of the diaspora. In the Philippines, diasporans or returnees own all or part of 37% of foreign firms in my sample. If we add in firms that are managed by diasporans or returnees, 60% of all foreign-owned firms surveyed in the Philippines are diaspora-affiliated.

These are large numbers, and in conjunction with the more detailed evidence I present about the advantages diasporans convey to the firms they own and manage, they help make the empirical case that brain drain fears are no longer justified in most cases. It is time to shift focus toward evaluating the best strategies for firms and governments to take advantage of diasporans as transformative actors in the political economy of developing countries.

1.7. Diasporans: A Threat as Well as a Resource?

Before moving on to a map of this book, I want to digress briefly about how the more political aspects of this migration and development debate look from the perspective of governments in migrant-sending countries. From the sending-country perspective, diaspora populations can be economically enticing and politically threatening at the same time. Diasporas often include political exiles and other regime opponents; as extreme examples, consider the Iranian or Cuban diasporas in the United States. Even when not directly opposed to the standing regime, the political preferences of diasporans may not be aligned with the government or the non-emigrant public in the home country. However, this sense of political threat is offset by remittances, diaspora investment, and diaspora philanthropy. Over the past 50 years, there has been a gradual evolution in government perceptions as the allure of economic benefits has gradually overtaken concerns about political threats.

Prior to 1990, and especially prior to 1960, when governments thought about the policy benefits of outward migration, their goal was generally to encourage (or force) the departure of problematic citizens. Governments hoped that the emigration of unskilled laborers would reduce domestic unemployment and that the departure of dissidents and potential dissidents would prevent domestic political unrest. Unemployed young men often fell neatly into both camps.

For example, during the colonial era, the French targeted their recruitment of Moroccan laborers toward those regions most prone to unrest. They hoped that by recruiting young men from rebellious regions they could both meet the labor demand in France and limit the risk of armed insurrection against French colonial rule. This policy of treating emigration as a "safety valve" continued after independence, with the Moroccan government encouraging outward migration from politically restive Berber-speaking regions in particular (de Haas 2007). It was only in the 1990s that government policy toward the Moroccan diaspora pivoted from a focus on preventing the emergence of an organized political opposition to promoting economic engagement.

As developing countries focus on the economic potential of their diasporas, they seek to engage them and to promote diasporan contribution to the homeland economy (e.g., Alonso and Mylonas 2017; Gamlen, Cummings, and Vaaler 2017). A 2005 survey by the International Organization for Migration revealed that more than 90% of countries have policies or programs in place targeting their diasporas for development purposes.[25] One of the objectives of this book is to provide those programs with deeper knowledge about the diaspora investors they seek to attract.

1.8. A Map of This Book

Chapter 2, "Diasporans as Transnational Brokers: A Theory of Homeland Investment," introduces my theory and an alternative explanation drawn from the literature. I argue that diasporans facilitate FDI into their homelands by serving as transnational brokers, connecting foreign firms to business counterparts and government officials in the homeland. Diasporans are uniquely effective brokers because of their own social networks, which often include strong ties to a community in the homeland, including extended family, childhood friends, and university classmates, as well as a community in the country of settlement, including friends, neighbors, and colleagues. Diasporans thus occupy powerful bridging positions between these two networks, connecting individuals and firms who would otherwise have no connection. Diasporans use their social ties to help the firms they own and manage to access information, establish trust, and enforce contracts with business counterparts, secure better outcomes in interactions with the homeland bureaucracy, and influence government policy in the homeland. I contrast my theory of transnational brokerage with an alternative theory based on diasporans' social and emotional motivations for homeland engagement.

Chapter 3, "Research Design and New Firm-Level Data," lays out my strategy for testing these two theories. This strategy involves testing of a wide array of hypotheses regarding how diaspora-affiliated firms differ from other foreign firms in terms of their capabilities, strategies, and development impact. Much of this chapter is devoted to introducing the new firm-level data from Georgia and the Philippines that makes these tests possible. After outlining the overall framework in which these tests are embedded, I discuss the nature of the Georgia and Philippines cases and compare them to other developing countries. I then describe the survey design and the nature of the inferences that are possible based on this new data.

Chapter 4, "Measuring Firms' Social Connectedness," shows that diaspora-affiliated firms are indeed more socially connected than their nondiaspora-affiliated peers. I compare the size and nature of the social networks in which diaspora-affiliated and nondiaspora-affiliated foreign firms are embedded and evaluate the subjective importance of social ties to those firms. I use data from the Philippines to assess the strength of firms' ties to peer firms, bureaucrats, and elected officials. I use data from both the Philippines and Georgia to examine the subjective importance of social ties to firm profitability.

Chapter 5, "How Do Diaspora-Affiliated Firms Use Social Networks?," continues and deepens the comparison between diaspora-affiliated and nondiaspora-affiliated foreign firms, evaluating firms' use of social ties for different business purposes: gathering information, establishing trust, enforcing contracts, accessing credit, renting/buying real estate, and improving government relations. I also test whether diaspora-affiliated firms are better able than other foreign firms to influence government policy in the homeland. I find strong evidence that diaspora-affiliated firms lean more heavily on social ties than do other foreign firms, providing them with marked advantages in resolving disputes, interacting with government officials, and influencing government policy.

Chapter 6, "The Development Impact of Diaspora-Affiliated Firms," evaluates the optimistic expectations that underlie some of the enthusiasm of NGOs and developing-country governments for promoting diaspora investment. I test whether diaspora-affiliated firms are more socially responsible, as the social and emotional motivations theory predicts, and find they are not. I then test a broader range of ways through which diaspora-affiliated firms might be associated with larger pro-development spillovers, and find only limited evidence that this is the case. Thus I argue that the most significant development-related characteristic of diaspora-affiliated firms is their ability to operate successfully in the type of capital-starved, institutionally weak developing countries that most other foreign firms avoid.

Chapter 7, "Conclusion: Implications for Governments and Multinational Firms," concludes the book, providing a summary of its empirical findings and their implications. I pay particular attention to the implications for three groups of actors: developing-country governments looking to capitalize on diaspora direct investment to catalyze economic development; wealthy country governments making decisions about the number and type of migrants to admit; and multinational firms, whom I argue often have much to gain by integrating diasporans into their management if they are not already diaspora-owned.

CHAPTER 2

Diasporans as Transnational Brokers

A Theory of Homeland Investment

2.0. Prologue: Marcus and Georg

Flying from Frankfurt to Tbilisi in 2010, I sat next to Marcus, a Swedish man on his way to check in on the Georgian affiliate of his recycling company. It turned out that this Georgian affiliate was co-owned by a member of the Georgian diaspora—a man named Georg.[1] Without Georg, Marcus never would have invested in Georgia. What a terrific story—a diasporan investing back in the homeland, bringing along his own capital, but also capital and expertise from other foreigners.

What was it that Georg brought to the table, I asked. Why couldn't Marcus have invested without him? Mostly it turned out to be information. Georg had lived and worked in Sweden for many years, and he knew the economics of the Swedish market for recycled aluminum. He knew Marcus and his firm. He also knew that there was a lot of scrap aluminum in Georgia that could be acquired cheaply. So the business plan was simple. Marcus and Georg teamed up to import Swedish recycling technology—furnaces, molds, and so on—into Georgia. Then they bought up cheap scrap aluminum, hired (relatively) cheap Georgian labor, and melted the scrap aluminum into ingots to be shipped back to Sweden.

So far, a very positive story of a diasporan contributing to development. Until we get to the crux of the business plan—why was it particularly profitable to do the recycling in Georgia? Environmental regulations. The environmental laws on the books are actually quite strict in Georgia, but Georg knew what most nondiaspora foreigners didn't—the air quality laws on the books were very weakly enforced. I visited their small recycling plant in a suburb of Tbilisi and saw the aluminum window frames, rubber seals and all, heading into the furnace and black smoke coming out of the top—no expensive filters for the smoke, no labor-intensive process to remove the rubber and plastic from the scrap before it went into the furnace—but to my untrained eye, some substantial air pollution.

2.1. Three Questions

The story of Georg and the aluminum recycling firm points toward the central empirical question of this book—how do diaspora-affiliated firms differ from foreign firms that are not diaspora affiliated? It also leads us toward two related questions that speak to these differences: what impact do diaspora-affiliated firms have on development in the homeland (i.e., investment host country) and what are the mechanisms through which diasporans induce capital to flow from their countries of settlement to their homelands? I selected Georg's story because it illustrates important aspects of the answers that I provide in this book:

1. Diasporans provide value to the firms they own and manage by serving as **transnational brokers** that connect firms based in their country of settlement to valuable networks in the homeland. Diaspora-affiliated firms differ from other foreign firms by relying more heavily on social ties, particularly to enforce contracts, interact with government officials, and influence policy.
2. Diaspora-affiliated firms contribute to development in the homeland by virtue of their ability to operate successfully in challenging environments, including high-political-risk environments, that often confound other foreign firms.
3. Thus an important mechanism through which diasporans shape global investment flows lies in the way they alter the behavior of the firms that they own and manage.

This theory of diaspora homeland investment is the central focus of this chapter. At the heart of this theory is the central proposition from which all three of the above answers flow: diasporans provide value by serving as transnational brokers.

The Central Theoretical Claim: Diasporans provide value to the firms they own and manage by serving as transnational brokers con-

necting firms based in their country of settlement to valuable networks in the homeland.

Diasporans are able to serve as transnational brokers primarily because
of their unique social networks. Many diasporans have strong ties to individuals in the homeland, including friends, extended family, and former
classmates. They often also have strong ties in their country of settlement,
particularly to friends and colleagues. This places diasporans in a unique
bridging position in their social networks, providing a rare connection between their network in the homeland and their network in the country of
settlement.[2]

Being connected to the right social networks is extremely valuable to
foreign firms in developing countries. While developing countries are diverse in the nature of their governance and the strength of their market-
supporting institutions, investors in many developing countries face at least
some of the following challenges: an unstable policy environment; bureaucratic corruption; local courts unable to resolve disputes fairly and efficiently; and a scarcity of market and political information due to a lack of
government transparency and a shortage of information intermediaries like
journalists and investment analysts. The right social networks can substitute for these shortcomings in important ways, providing access to information, establishing trust with business counterparts, enabling the enforcement of contracts, and providing a means to bypass bureaucratic corruption
and even influence government policy.

This chapter articulates how diasporans provide value to the firms they
own and manage and makes the case that nondiaspora-affiliated foreign
firms have difficulty creating that same value through other channels, such
as hiring local managers who have not previously lived overseas. My theory
draws on insights from across the social sciences: political science, economics, sociology, and international business. I begin by specifying how I
expect diasporans to differ from nonmigrants, focusing on diasporans'
unique networks. I then develop a theory regarding how these individual-
level differences in capabilities provide value to the firms that diasporans
own and manage.

The key comparison made in this study, both theoretically and empirically, is between diaspora-affiliated and nondiaspora-affiliated foreign
firms. While nondiaspora-affiliated foreign firms lack diaspora owners and
managers, almost all of them employ one or more local managers.[3] I argue
that local managers are poor substitutes for diaspora affiliation. I detail the

reasons for this later in this chapter, but the central claim is that while it is possible to hire a local manager with the right social ties in the investment host country, most local managers lack fluency in the culture of the headquarters country and ties to headquarters personnel. This makes trust between local managers and headquarters personnel more difficult to establish. A local fixer you can't trust is a local fixer you can't use, and thus diasporans provide value in ways few local managers can match.

This chapter presents my theory in detail, but it also contrasts my theory of diasporans as transnational brokers with an alternative theory, based on diasporans' social and emotional motivations for homeland engagement. These two theories have sharply divergent implications for how diaspora-affiliated firms behave and how they impact homeland development. The motivation-based theory is premised on the idea that diasporans have strong social and emotional ties to the homeland and that these ties motivate diasporans to invest in the homeland even when doing so might not be as profitable as investing elsewhere. Both theories predict that diaspora-affiliated firms behave differently than other foreign firms. However, each theory proposes a distinct mechanism by which diasporans affect the behavior of the firms they own and manage: shaping firm strategy and improving firm performance by serving as transnational brokers, or influencing the objectives and strategies of firms to reflect diasporans' multifaceted motivations for homeland engagement. Table 2.1 summarizes the contrasting implications of these two theories.

My theoretical expectation is that diasporans' capabilities as transnational brokers have a powerful effect on the behavior of the firms they own and manage. In particular, I expect diaspora-affiliated firms to use social

Table 2.1. My Theory and an Alternative

Description	Implication for Development
My Proposed Theory Diasporans provide value to the firms they own and manage by serving as **transnational brokers** and connecting firms based in the country of settlement to valuable networks in the homeland.	Diaspora-affiliated firms **are more capable**, but not more socially responsible than other foreign firms.
Alternative Theory from the Literature Diasporans have strong **social and emotional motivations** for homeland investment and these motivations induce diaspora-affiliated firms to pursue objectives beyond profitability.	Diaspora-affiliated firms **are more socially responsible** than other foreign firms and have a more positive impact on homeland development.

ties more than their nondiaspora-affiliated peers—gathering information, establishing trust with business counterparts, and interacting with government officials—and to gain value from doing so. In contrast, I expect that social and emotional motivations are not strong drivers of behavior in most diaspora-owned or diaspora-managed firms.

If my theory of diasporans as transnational brokers is correct, it implies that diaspora-affiliated firms are more capable than other foreign firms, and thus better able to operate successfully in the homeland in the face of political risk and other obstacles. It implies that the primary impact of diasporans on firm behavior is not to alter firms' objectives but to alter their strategies for achieving those objectives. Conversely, if the social and emotional motivations mechanism dominates, we would expect the diaspora investment to be an extremely powerful force for development. Diaspora-affiliated firms would not only be more likely to enter and continue operating in high-risk homelands, they would be more socially responsible and seek to promote homeland development. Because I expect that the transnational brokerage mechanism dominates, I expect instead that the most valuable way in which diaspora direct investment contributes to development is simply by succeeding in doing business in markets that often confound other foreign investors.

The theory in this chapter animates everything that follows. I structure my presentation of the theory to establish clear testable implications regarding differences between diaspora-affiliated and nondiaspora-affiliated foreign firms: how they gather information, enforce contracts, interact with governments, and ultimately affect political and economic development in the homeland. I then introduce the social and emotional motivations mechanism in a parallel, albeit less exhaustive, manner. The remainder of the book serves to design and execute empirical tests of the implications of these mechanisms and to discuss the policy and development implications of those results.

Throughout this discussion, I will illustrate the mechanisms in question with quotations from the managers of diaspora-affiliated firms in Georgia and the Philippines. Most of these quotations are drawn from responses to open-ended questions[4] on the surveys described in chapter 3; others are drawn from a series of focus groups my team ran during cognitive pretesting of the survey instrument in the Philippines.[5] These quotations provide some evidence of face-validity for my theory—at least some diaspora-affiliated firms are using social ties in the ways I expect. The empirical question, of course, is whether diaspora-affiliated firms have access to better/

larger social networks than other foreign firms and whether they are able to translate these networks into a competitive advantage. To establish this will require much more than illustrative quotes. It requires new data and a direct empirical comparison between diaspora-affiliated and nondiaspora-affiliated foreign firms, which I deliver in chapters 3–6.

Before presenting the theory itself, I take a brief step back to establish a general framework for understanding the types of firms that invest in countries with underdeveloped institutions and why social ties are of greater importance to investors in these countries than in wealthy, industrialized countries with strong political institutions.

2.2. Social Ties and Foreign Investment in Developing Countries

One of the core motivations of this project is to identify a way for developing countries, and particularly countries with underdeveloped political institutions, to overcome the difficulties they face in attracting and retaining investment by foreign firms. I examine the types of firms that are most willing and able to invest in poorly governed host countries, focusing on the role that social ties can play in allowing firms to manage political risk.

The fields of economics and international business have developed a good understanding of why firms invest in institutionally underdeveloped countries and what types of firms are able to do so successfully.[6] Some key points: (1) firms that invest overseas are more capable than firms that invest only at home;[7] (2) these capabilities are necessary to offset the disadvantages that foreign firms face relative to their domestic competitors, which are referred to collectively as the "liability of foreignness";[8] (3) some of these disadvantages are specifically related to the fact that foreign firms don't have the necessary social ties, referred to as the "liability of outsidership";[9] and (4) social ties are more important for conducting business in developing countries than in wealthy countries, and they are most important in countries with low levels of institutional development.

Firm Capabilities

Helpman, Melitz, and Yeaple (2004) argue that, within a given home country, the least productive firms serve the domestic market exclusively, more productive firms export, and the most productive firms engage in outward

FDI. In their model, there are fixed costs associated with each stage of the internationalization process. All firms must pay a fixed cost to operate in the home market, but only some firms choose to export, which requires paying the fixed cost associated with forming a distribution and servicing network in a foreign country. Still fewer pay the additional fixed cost necessary to establish a foreign subsidiary (i.e., to engage in FDI). More productive firms have lower marginal costs of production and can thus afford to pay the fixed costs associated with exporting and FDI.

But what makes some firms more productive than others? The resource-based view of the firm provides a framework for organizing the factors that make some firms more productive than others. In this context, "resources" are tangible and intangible assets tied semi-permanently to the firm (Wernerfelt 1984: 172) and include everything from brand names and patents to skilled employees, technical knowledge, and social connections.[10] Resources provide firms with sustained advantages over their competitors when those resources are: (1) valuable; (2) rare; (3) difficult to imitate; and (4) difficult to replace with substitutes (Barney 1991). In countries with low levels of institutional development, the right social ties can provide firms with exactly this type of sustained advantage.

The Liability of Foreignness

In the international business literature, "the liability of foreignness" serves as a catch-all term for the ways in which operating a subsidiary in a foreign market is difficult. The liability of foreignness takes many forms: language barriers, cultural differences, differences in laws and regulations,[11] and the costs associated with managers traveling back and forth to foreign subsidiaries, among other things. Much of this chapter deals with the ways in which diaspora owners and diaspora managers can help foreign firms reduce these liabilities. I argue that diasporans themselves are not fully foreign, and that they shape the capabilities and strategies of the firms they own and manage such that these firms are, in many respects, also not fully foreign. In other words, diasporans can help the foreign firms they own and manage enjoy some of the advantages of domestic firms.

There is evidence in the existing empirical literature consistent with my argument that diasporans can reduce the liability of foreignness that firms face. For example, Blonigen and Wooster (2003) find that when an American firm hires a foreign-born CEO, it becomes more likely to engage in investment overseas. Similarly, Herrmann and Datta (2006) find that managers with more international experience are more likely to opt for Greenfield entry into new markets, which they argue requires more local information than entry via merger or acquisition. The potential value of diasporans in limiting the liability of foreignness is also reflected in the rise of "inpatriate management," a practice in which multinational firms bring host-country managers from foreign affiliates to work in the headquarters office—in other words, encouraging their managers to migrate instead of simply trying to hire diasporans as managers.[12]

However, before turning to the capabilities of diasporans, I want to extend the general theoretical discussion of how one specific type of firm resource, social ties to other firms, allows firms to manage one specific liability of foreignness, the liability of outsidership.

The Liability of Outsidership

The liability of outsidership refers to those drawbacks associated with insufficient connections to appropriate social networks (Johanson and Vahlne 2009). While even a domestic firm can find itself outside of the right networks, the problem is particularly acute for foreign firms.

I break this idea apart in more detail as the chapter proceeds, but being connected to the right actors in the local economy (e.g., peer firms and government officials) allows firms to gather information, establish trust with business counterparts, resolve disputes, and access credit.[13] The interfirm ties that position firms within these crucial networks generally begin as personal ties between owners and managers at one firm and the owners and managers of other firms. Friends, family members, business school classmates, and long-standing professional acquaintances are all valuable business resources that firms can exploit. Foreign firms are at a distinct disadvantage when it comes to forming these networks. The social ties of foreign owners and managers exist primarily, if not exclusively, within a firm's home country. The investment host country, however, is *terra nova*, and many foreign firms make their initial entry into a new country weakly connected to the networks necessary for business success.[14]

Where Social Ties Are Most Valuable

Investing overseas is inherently difficult; the liability of foreignness applies any time a firm steps outside its home market. But developing countries are particularly difficult—this is why the Lucas Paradox exists. Capital is scarce in developing countries, so the return to capital should be high, but firms avoid investing in developing countries because the perceived risks and difficulties associated with those countries often outweigh the potential returns. In many (though certainly not all) developing countries, markets are undeveloped, public information is scarce, corruption is high, bureaucratic competence is low, and policymaking is weakly institutionalized.[15] Under these conditions, profitable investment is difficult, and social ties in particular are much more important to firms than in rich industrialized countries. In high political risk countries, the liability of outsidership looms particularly large.

While diasporans' capabilities are likely to have at least some value in any context, I expect them to be most valuable in developing countries, and particularly in contexts where political institutions are underdeveloped and the liability of outsidership is high. Thus my theory of diasporans as transnational brokers applies specifically to these environments—developing countries with weakly institutionalized political systems—and may not extend to advanced industrialized democracies or developing countries with strong formal political institutions. In these more institutionalized contexts, the role of social ties in business is likely to be smaller and the strategic value of diasporans' social ties is likely to be lower.

2.3. The Diaspora Difference

Diasporans' social ties and cultural fluency provide sustained competitive advantages to the firms they own and manage. Not only are their ties valuable, but nondiaspora-affiliated foreign firms have difficulty creating this same value in other ways, such as hiring local managers. In the language of the resource-based view of the firm, diasporans' social ties are unique, rare, difficult to imitate, and difficult to replace with substitutes. Thus this section grapples with the following questions: Do most diasporans have the necessary social ties? Can they use these personal ties to benefit the firms they own and manage, and if so, how do they do this? What does this imply for the role of diaspora-affiliated firms in the economic and political development of their homeland?

Transnational Brokers: Strong Social Ties in Two Countries

> *In Georgia, just like in other developing countries, [friendship and family] relations are crucially important. You will always be in a winning position if you have the right friends.*[16]

What really sets diasporans apart from the rest of us is their social networks, namely the web of relationships that connects them to family, friends, classmates, and colleagues. Diasporans' networks are unique because they are rooted in not one country but in two—the homeland and the country of settlement. In the latter, diasporans develop social networks that include both fellow diasporans and native-born citizens: friends, family, colleagues, and neighbors.[17] However, most diasporans also retain strong ties to individuals in the homeland, including family members, former classmates, and childhood friends (e.g., Gillespie et al. 1999; Riddle and Brinkerhoff 2011; Duanmu and Guney 2013). Diasporans leave the homeland physically, but they remain connected to it in many other ways.

Diasporans' relationships with people in the homeland are unusual because they are intimate ties to individuals who are physically distant. These ties became strong initially through repeated in-person interaction when the diasporan lived in the homeland, and after emigration they are maintained by internet, phone, and visits back to the homeland (e.g., Portes, Guarnizo, and Landholt 1999; Vertovec 2009). While these ties are generally strongest for first-generation migrants, even second-generation migrants often retain strong homeland ties, making trips back and remaining in close contact with extended family (e.g., Levitt and Waters 2002; Haller and Landholt 2005; Haikkola 2011).

Diasporans' social networks are thus composed of strong ties to clusters of individuals in two different countries, intimate connections that serve as bridges between their community in the homeland and their community in the country of settlement (e.g., Boyd 1989; Ryan 2009).

Decades of social network theory emphasize the power of this type of bridging network.[18] While I will emphasize the role of this bridging network in facilitating the flow of capital from the country of settlement to the homeland, an extensive literature on chain migration highlights the importance of these transnational networks in facilitating additional migration from the homeland to the country of settlement (e.g., McDonald and McDonald 1964; Banerjee 1983; Massey 1990). I do not have data that allow me to directly map the personal networks in which diasporans in my survey are embedded, but this literature provides insight into the type of value diasporans are able to create for the firms they own and manage.

Much of the early academic work on social networks was focused on identifying which individuals are "central" to a given network. A person is central in a network to the extent that she lies on the shortest path possible between other individuals in that network (e.g., Bavelas 1948). Being central in a network provides a person with power. If information needs to flow through the network, odds are it has to pass through an individual with high levels of what is often called "betweenness centrality" (Freeman 1977).

In recent decades, scholars have been increasingly sophisticated in their ability to analyze networks, allowing us to do an ever better job of mapping how information flows through networks, identifying which individuals control that flow of information and understanding the power that networks provide to the individuals who occupy particular positions in particular types of networks. Within certain network structures, there exist many different paths through which information may flow, and no one individual has the ability to control or block that flow. No one individual holds a critical position, and thus power is distributed broadly across individuals and not concentrated in any one person. In other network structures, a single person may hold a central position that forces all information to flow through her, concentrating power rather than distributing it.

Structures that concentrate power emerge when two large and distinct networks have only a very limited number of connections between them. These networks confer great power on the individual(s) through which these scarce connections run. Burt (1992, 2000) refers to the space between distinct social groups as structural holes and writes that these holes "create a competitive advantage for an individual whose relationships span the holes. . . . Structural holes are thus an opportunity to broker the flow of *information* between people, and *control* the projects that bring together people from opposite sides of the hole" (2000: 353).

Figure 2.1 provides a stylized illustration of diasporans' position in the structural hole between their homeland network and their country of settlement network (e.g., Boyd 1989; Portes 1995; Ryan et al. 2008). Of course, not all diasporans have social networks with this structure. In particular, some migrants never learn the language of the country of settlement and never expand their social networks in that country beyond the diaspora community (e.g., Wierzbicki 2004; Ryan 2007, 2011).[19] However, this styl-

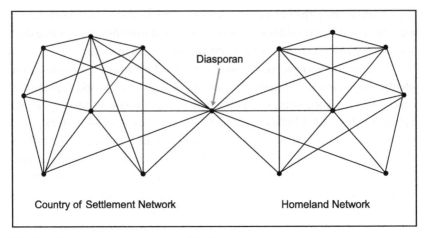

Fig. 2.1. *Diasporans as Transnational Brokers*

ized depiction is useful for understanding the value that well-connected diasporans can create.

A diasporan's homeland network and country of settlement network are distinct from one other: there are many ties within each network but very few ties that connect them. Diasporans create value (and exercise power) by linking two networks that would otherwise remain unconnected. But this concept of bridging, while powerful, still undersells just how rich diasporans' networks can be. Social networks provide the greatest information access when they connect an actor to diverse others, rather than to like actors (Schilling and Phelps 2007), and when they consist predominantly of ties between social groups rather than ties within social groups (e.g., McEvily and Zaheer 1999). Thus transnational ties—ties between individuals who reside in different places, different communities, different cultures—are unusually valuable for exposing individuals to novel information.

Exposure to novel information is at the core of what Granovetter (1973) refers to as the "strength of weak ties." Strong ties, such as those between family members or close friends, are often between individuals who live close to one another, who are similar to one another, and who have overlapping networks (e.g., share many mutual friends). Weak ties, such as ties between acquaintances, are more likely to exist between individuals who live far apart, in different communities, and with networks that overlap very little. Thus weak ties are often sources of novel information because they are likely to connect individuals who are distant from one another—physically, culturally, and otherwise.[20]

Trust, on the other hand, is best facilitated by networks with a high degree of closure, namely by dense networks of strong ties (e.g., Coleman 1988; Gulati 1995). Relational trust emerges from high-closure networks as a direct effect of tie strength in a given dyad, and as an indirect effect of the redundant connections between individuals. Individuals trust each other more when the tie between them is close, such as to family members and longtime friends, and when they share ties to many of the same individuals, such as when they are members of the same tight-knit community where everyone knows everyone else. This is pretty intuitive—you trust people when you know them well and when other people you know well can vouch for them.

Strong ties and networks with a high degree of closure have the added benefit of facilitating the collective sanctioning of misbehavior (Granovetter 1992; Jones, Hesterly, and Borgatti 1997). The social cost of misbehavior is to be punished or shunned by other people who are aware of your misbehavior. Within tight-knit communities, everyone quickly becomes aware of misbehavior, and being shunned has high costs. Thus strong ties and high-closure social networks are extremely effective tools for policing the behavior of members of those networks.

The key characteristic of diasporans' social networks is that they consist of strong ties to two geographically distant communities, allowing diasporans to enjoy the benefits of strong and weak ties simultaneously. Levin and Cross (2004) refer to ties that combine these benefits as "weak ties you can trust." McFayden, Semadini, and Camella (2009) refer to them as "strong ties to disconnected others." I believe these unique ties provide the key advantage enjoyed by diasporans as the owners and managers of multinational firms.

Each of the three uses of social networks I have identified in this section—accessing information, establishing trust, and sanctioning or deterring misbehavior—is related to the ability of firms to use social ties to overcome institutional and informational voids in developing countries. Achieving all three of these benefits requires combining two characteristics of social networks that do not frequently coexist: strong ties (which facilitate trust and the sanctioning of misbehavior) and connections to communities in two different, often distant, countries (which facilitates access to novel information). It is this unique combination that empowers diasporans as transnational brokers connecting foreign firms to essential social networks in the homeland, allowing capital to flow into politically challenging developing countries.

To summarize, diasporans' social networks are unique in that they possess strong ties to two nonoverlapping networks, spread across two different countries—the homeland and the country of settlement. Individuals in a diasporan's homeland network have few direct ties to individuals in a diasporan's country-of-settlement network, meaning that diasporans' ties between these groups are rarely redundant. Residing in different countries, individuals in a diasporan's homeland network also possess vastly different sets of information than individuals in his/her country-of-settlement network—they are both physically and culturally distant. In other words, diasporans often have strong ties, characterized by high levels of trust, that also possess the critical community-bridging traits associated with weak ties.

Language and Cultural Fluency

While diasporans' social networks are paramount in my conception of diasporans as transnational brokers, it is important to acknowledge that diasporans also possess language skills and cultural knowledge that other foreigners do not. Even second-generation migrants are often raised speaking the native language of the homeland and immersed (albeit partially) in its culture (e.g., Levitt and Waters 2002; Soehl and Waldinger 2012). Of course, diasporans also develop language skills and acquire cultural knowledge in their country of settlement. Thus just as diasporans possess social networks that bridge two countries, they are also fluent in multiple languages and cultures, further augmenting their bridging abilities. As anyone who has ever conducted a conversation via translator can attest, fluency in a shared language is essential to effective, efficient communication. Second languages are costly to learn, and thus the additional language(s) that diasporans are forced to acquire are valuable assets in international business. However, while language fluency is difficult to acquire, cultural fluency is more difficult still.

Cultural fluency is critical in the context of international business because the literal meaning of the words being said, which is what one understands if one is fluent in a language, often fails to capture the full meaning of what is being communicated (Samovar, Porter, and Jain 1981; Gudykunst and Kim 1984). Cultural fluency thus involves the ability to encode and decode meanings in tone, gesture, and expression that go beyond the literal meaning of the words spoken (Beamer 1992). It requires both a thorough understanding of the cultural context in which language is embedded and the nonverbal means of communication that accompany the language. While business schools and firms invest heavily in training employees in the art of cross-cultural communication, diasporans have a built-in edge that is difficult for nonmigrants to overcome.

The idea of cultural fluency is perhaps best articulated by example—here are a couple drawn from responses to open-ended questions in the Philippines survey. An American firm reported, "In the past my Western colleagues have been very straightforward, which can lead others to perceive them and their actions as insulting or mean when they honestly thought that they were pointing out a problem in the most efficient and direct manner in order to resolve it. . . . It's about understanding social cues."[21] According to another firm in the Philippines, "We need to have people who can speak to [our subcontractors] both in their same language and on the same level. . . . I import most of my managers from India and it is very hard for them because they don't get the Filipino mentality."[22]

Phrases like "the Filipino mentality" or "Asian business culture" show up frequently in conversations with firm managers in the Philippines. In Georgia, managers talk about "the Georgian mindset" in the same way. Each culture is characterized by different modes of nonverbal communication and by different sets of shared knowledge and shared assumptions that underlie how new information is understood. Cultural fluency is the ability to understand and be understood in a given cultural context—something that is difficult to achieve by any path other than extended immersion. In other words, cultural fluency is difficult to achieve for any foreigner who is not a diasporan.

Cultural fluency is particularly essential to sharing the types of information that are communicated most effectively in nonverbal form—such as expressions of trust, gratitude, or affection (e.g., Kinlock and Metge 2014: 12). And those types of information are at the core of one's ability to found and maintain social ties. Thus one of the ways cultural fluency benefits diasporans is that it extends the core advantage they already have in hand: extensive social networks in both the homeland and country of settlement. Not only do diasporans enter new business ventures with better networks in place, but also, because of their cultural fluency, their ability to develop new ties and exploit those ties for business advantage exceeds that of their non-migrant peers.

2.4. Connecting Individuals to Firms

I now move to connect the capabilities of diasporans—their social ties, their abilities, their motivations—to the strategies and performance of diaspora-affiliated firms. In particular, I explain why I expect the advantages conveyed by diaspora managers to be similar to, if possibly slightly weaker than, those conveyed by diaspora-owners. Before proceeding further, I present a short case that helps illustrate the role diaspora managers can play in multinational firms.

Sophia Ramos, Diaspora Manager

Sophia Ramos grew up in the Philippines and earned a bachelor's degree in marketing at De La Salle University in Manila.[23] At age 27, she emigrated to the United Arab Emirates to work at a paint company. Over the next several years she changed jobs a few times and eventually moved to Singapore, where she began working for Spyrea Singapore, a 3-D modeling and animation company.

Speaking in 2014, Ms. Ramos recounted what she had learned from various bosses and coworkers in her years abroad: the Danish boss who taught her to be more open-minded like a European; the Syrian-Canadian supervisor who taught her how to navigate the fine print of a contract and avoid "deep water"; and the Lebanese colleague who demonstrated the value of loyalty. These skills helped her thrive at Spyrea Singapore, and her boss there eventually sent her back to the Philippines to work as the marketing manager of the firm's affiliate in Manila.

Back in the Philippines, Ms. Ramos serves as the public face of the company, managing relationships with the firm's Filipino clients. Talking about doing business with Filipinos, she says, "There are times that you cannot really be honest with them because you might strike a nerve or two. You have to be very very careful with the way you use your words. Exercising authority has to be done in such a way that there's *lambing* [affection]. . . . With foreigners, you can be straightforward and it's not taken personally against you." That is difficult for her Singaporean supervisor. "He's very,

very good on the technical side, but then he doesn't like really talking to people, dealing with his [Filipino] employees or with supply-end. He has to course everything through someone. He's very uncultured with that." Someone has to bridge the gap.

Bridging the gap is Ms. Ramos's specialty. She has a close personal relationship with her Singaporean supervisor, developed during her time in Singapore. She considers him a friend as well as a boss. They trust each other and communicate effectively. Ms. Ramos, in turn, guides her boss's relationships with their Filipino employees and clients. While a local manager is likely to share Ms. Ramos's ties in the Philippines and understanding of Filipino business culture, it is much less likely that a local manager can match her cultural fluency in Singaporean business culture or her close personal tie to her Singaporean boss.

Diaspora-Owned Firms

I expect that the advantages conveyed by diaspora ownership and diaspora management are very similar. However, there are several reasons to expect that owners' networks may be slightly more valuable to firms than managers' networks. First, owners are the residual claimants of value they create for the firm, whereas managers are not. If a manager creates value for a firm, she may be rewarded for this with a raise or a bonus, but firm owners will retain much of the value created. To the extent that exploiting social networks on behalf of the firm requires risking personal credibility or incurring social debts, owners may be more willing than managers to bear the costs necessary to use their social ties effectively on behalf of the firm. Thus even if diaspora managers are as well connected as diaspora owners, they may be somewhat less willing to use those connections on behalf of the firm.

> Even if it's a small favor, they always expect something in return. They'll say "we risked our neck for you for this" even if they didn't actually risk much of anything.[24]

Second, diaspora firm owners may be more likely to view the use of social networks in business as appropriate and productive. This is more likely to be a factor in North-South FDI, namely cases where a firm's headquarters is located in a country that has strong rule of law and norms against the use of social networks in business while the investment host country (homeland) has weak rule of law and a norm of substituting for weak formal institutions with reliance on social networks. A norm against the use of social networks in business deters nepotism and corruption and, in the context of a strong rule of law, may impose few costs on firms. However, in developing countries where rule of law is weak, an unwillingness to integrate the use of social networks into firm strategy may be a substantial liability.

When asked about the role of social networks in their business, one Japanese firm operating in the Philippines reported, "We have a code of ethics. The employees are not encouraged to publicly show social activities [sic], this is a traditional Japanese attitude. The marketing department is the one in charge of social networks."[25] In that sort of a business culture, more common in countries with a strong rule of law, social ties have a reduced role.

Nondiaspora owners are likely to have internalized the norms of the firm's home country, while diaspora owners have earlier and longer exposure to the cultural norms of the homeland. Thus, particularly in the case of Western multinationals investing in countries in which the use of social ties in business is more accepted, nondiaspora owners may be less likely than diaspora owners to ask their managers to use social ties on behalf of the firm. In these cases, nondiaspora owners may simply be less acculturated to social-tie-based means of doing business, and thus be less likely to encourage their managers to use their ties on behalf of the firm.

In the empirical chapters, I focus on the comparison between foreign firms that are diaspora-affiliated and those that are not. I focus on this distinction because the type of transnational brokerage capabilities that I expect diaspora owners and managers to provide are fundamentally the same. Diaspora owners may be somewhat more willing than diaspora managers to incur the costs of using their ties on behalf of the firm, but this is a difference in degree rather than a difference in kind. With respect to the types of social ties I expect firms to have access to and the ways in which I expect them to use those ties, my predictions with respect to diaspora-managed and diaspora-owned firms are the same. Thus it makes sense to pool these two categories together empirically and to focus on the distinction between foreign firms that are diaspora affiliated and foreign firms that are not.

In the Georgia data, I only have information on diaspora ownership and not on diaspora management. Thus in the analysis based on the Georgia data I analyze only the effects of diaspora ownership. In the analysis based on the Philippines data, I focus primarily on the estimated effect of diaspora affiliation (i.e., ownership or management) but also separately estimate the effect of diaspora ownership, allowing an apples-to-apples comparison between the Georgia and Philippines results.

While I expect that diaspora-owned and diaspora-managed firms are similar in their transnational brokerage capabilities, there are important differences with respect to *how* firms become diaspora owned and diaspora managed. Diaspora-owned firms are generally diaspora-owned from their founding. In contrast, if established firms are seeking to add additional capabilities for transnational brokerage, hiring a diaspora manager can be done at any time. In chapter 7, the implications that I draw for multinational firms focus primarily on the potential for these firms to enhance capabilities through diaspora management. However, the implications for developing-country governments involve the recruitment of investment by diaspora-affiliated firms more broadly.

Diaspora Managers vs. Local Managers

Almost all foreign firms hire local managers.[26] Thus when I compare diaspora-affiliated firms to nondiaspora-affiliated firms, I am usually comparing diaspora-affiliated firms to foreign firms with at least one local manager.

Diasporans and nonmigrant locals both have language and cultural fluency in the homeland and extensive homeland social networks. Where they differ is in their social ties in the headquarters country of the firm that employs them, in the cultural distance between themselves and headquarters personnel, and in their general fluency in international business culture. For those diasporans who have lived in the headquarters country of the multinational firm for which they now work, they have (at least some degree of) cultural fluency in that country's culture, and they may have social ties to firm owners and headquarters personnel. In particular, many diaspora managers work in the headquarters office before returning to work in the homeland, allowing them to establish particularly strong and relevant ties.

However, even in cases where a diaspora manager lived in a country other than the headquarters country of the firm she is now working for, international experience of any kind is likely to reduce the cultural distance between that manager and headquarters personnel. For example, many of the advantages that Ms. Ramos believes she enjoys as a diasporan come not from her time spent in the headquarters country of the firm for which she now works (i.e., Singapore) but in other countries that she lived and worked in previously where she gained a fluency in international business culture more broadly.[27]

How important are social ties and cultural distance between affiliate managers and headquarters personnel? Is it not possible for foreign firms to simply hire well-connected local managers? As Holburn and Zelner (2010: 1292) write, "Using the market to access political resources is hazardous: just as potential entrants lack detailed knowledge of the identity and preferences of key host-country political actors, so too do they lack knowledge of who the best local agents are to provide advice or assistance, a problem compounded by the fact that such agents may misrepresent themselves or—if they have their own political agendas—deploy their superior local knowledge and ties against an MNE's interests *ex post*." Henisz (2000) makes a similar argument with regard to the vulnerability of foreign firms to exploitation by joint venture partners in institutionally underdeveloped host countries. Relying heavily on local partners and local managers can be a risky strategy—at the same time local managers and partners provide the foreign firm with valuable connections in the investment host country, they also open up the firm to a new risk of opportunistic behavior. In the absence of social ties between headquarters personnel and local parties, this risk can be prohibitively high.

The fundamental economic rationale for the existence of multinational enterprises is to concentrate transactions inside a single organization in order to reduce their costs (e.g., Williamson 1975; Rugman 1981). The interpersonal interactions between individuals within the firm and the social network within which those ties are embedded are fundamental to the ability of a multinational firm to achieve lower transaction costs within the firm than could be achieved in the market (Manev and Stevenson 2001). Without strong ties between headquarters personnel and a politically connected manager in the host country, the risk of opportunistic behavior remains too high for the transactions between the headquarters and the foreign affiliate to be efficient.

The importance of managers' social ties to headquarters personnel is recognized by multinational firms, many of whom actively recruit "inpatriate" managers as part of a global human resources strategy. Inpatriate managers are host-country nationals recruited to work permanently or semipermanently in the headquarters country. Inpatriate managers begin as local managers: they possess knowledge of the host-country market and

social ties to individuals within the firm and outside of it, including customers, suppliers, and other stakeholders in the host country. By transferring local managers from the investment host country to the headquarters
country, the multinational firm endeavors to provide inpatriate managers
with knowledge of the firms' global operations and to help them develop
social ties to headquarters personnel. This then positions the inpatriate
manager to bridge the divide and facilitate the flow of information between
headquarters and subsidiary (Reiche 2006, 2011; Harvey, Speier, and Novicevic 2000). This helps the firm improve organizational control and achieve
global coordination in establishing goals, monitoring performance, and
taking corrective action when necessary (e.g., Kiessling and Harvey 2006).

When firms recruit local managers to serve as inpatriate managers, they
induce migration and turn a local manager into a diaspora manager. Because inpatriate managers develop strong social ties in their firm's home
country while retaining strong ties in the homeland, I expect that they possess the same transnational brokerage capabilities as other diaspora managers. Indeed these brokerage abilities may even be greater because the social
ties that inpatriate managers form in their firm's host country are developed
intentionally, and are thus likely well-tailored to their professional needs.

The value added by moving local managers to the headquarters
country—both in terms of broadening managerial outlooks and developing
specific relationships—are illustrated nicely in the case of Sophia Ramos.
After Ms. Ramos emigrated, she developed her professional skills and out-
look working under supervisors from a wide range of nationalities. She
then forged a strong relationship with a specific supervisor, her boss at Spyrea Singapore, who later sent her back to her homeland to run the firm's
Philippines operations. At the time she began managing Spyrea Philippines,
Ms. Ramos had the benefits of both her broad international experience and
her strong social ties to her direct supervisor and other headquarters personnel at Spyrea Singapore.

The social networks of a manager produce value for a foreign firm when
they connect the firm to relevant parties in the investment host country.
Thus a manager's social ties in the investment host country (homeland) are
only valuable to the extent that the manager also has strong ties to the firm
(i.e., to the firm owners and headquarters management). In the international business literature, this is often discussed in terms of trust between
local managers and headquarters personnel. Establishing trust between local managers and overseas headquarters has been shown to be a significant

challenge for multinational firms, particularly in developing countries (Child and Möllering 2003; Li et al. 2006).

Nonmigrant local managers, while often well-connected in the homeland, are not well connected in the headquarters country, lacking both social ties and cultural familiarity. While the following quote comes from the manager of a domestic firm in the Philippines, it highlights shortcomings that I expect are common among local managers. "For our firm, at the manager level . . . they aren't well traveled and they haven't had a lot of exposure to different cultures. Especially when it comes to dealing with foreign clients, they lack the ability to reach out to those clients."[28] And of course it is not just foreign clients who are difficult to interact with effectively—it is also owners and managers at the firm headquarters overseas.

Child and Möllering (2003) argue that developing trust with local managers is particularly difficult when headquarters managers lack faith in the political institutions in the country in which the subsidiary is operating.[29] Institutions provide norms that local staff will follow—trust in those institutions induces trust in local staff and vice versa. This means that establishing trust between headquarters personnel and local managers is likely to be particularly difficult in countries where political institutions are less developed. This is unfortunate because, as I argue in section 2.2, the trust and information provided by firms' social networks are most valuable in countries in which political institutions function poorly. This implies that trust is most difficult to establish with local managers in precisely the countries in which local managers' networks would otherwise be most valuable.

In sum, I am skeptical about the degree to which multinational firms in institutionally underdeveloped countries can make effective use of the social ties of their local managers. Compared to diaspora managers, I expect the social ties of local managers to provide less value and thus be used less heavily by multinational firms in these countries. It is quite difficult to substitute for the social ties that diasporans bring with them.

Purely Local Firms

The theoretical and empirical focus of this book is on the comparison between diaspora-affiliated and nondiaspora-affiliated foreign firms. However, because I make the argument that diaspora-affiliated firms are "less foreign" than nondiaspora-affiliated foreign firms, it is useful to also contrast diaspora-affiliated firms with purely local firms.

Access to private information about local market and political conditions is an advantage that local firms generally have over foreign firms (Kingsley and Graham 2017). Locals have the same, if not better, access to network-based sources of information as diasporans. Similarly, local firms based in institutionally underdeveloped countries are fully accustomed to informal, social-tie-based modes of doing business. I therefore expect social ties to play a large role in the business strategy of local firms. Placed on a continuum, I expect the greatest use of social ties by domestic firms, followed by diaspora-owned firms, who use ties more than diaspora-managed firms, who use ties more than other foreign firms.

I expect local firms to reap substantial competitive advantage from their positions within, and willingness to use, social networks. However, compared to multinationals, domestic firms tend to possess less knowledge, less managerial expertise, and less proprietary technology.[30] Thus most domestic firms in developing countries are simply less productive than their foreign counterparts. It is only the liability of foreignness that, by hindering foreign competitors, allows some of these less-productive domestic firms to survive. In that way, the liability of foreignness acts as a barrier to inward direct investment, shielding domestic firms from competition. If diaspora-affiliated firms are able to overcome that liability of foreignness, the effect is akin to a partial removal of formal restrictions on inward investment, with the same accompanying mix of economic benefits and dislocation of domestic firms.

2.5. Transnational Brokerage and Competitive Advantage

The preceding sections describe the nature of diasporans' social networks and discuss the relative willingness of owners and managers to exploit these networks to create value for firms. The unique social ties of diasporans increase the social connectedness of diaspora-affiliated firms, which in turn increases the use of social ties by these firms. Use of social ties improves the performance of diaspora-affiliated firms, increases their political influence, and may potentially shape their development impact (i.e., if diaspora-affiliated firms are able to use social ties to substitute for formal political institutions, then these firms may be more willing than other foreign firms to invest in poorly governed host countries). Figure 2.2 displays the core components of this theory graphically.

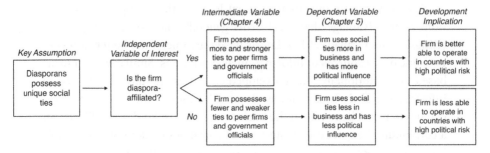

Fig. 2.2. *Diasporans as Transnational Brokers*

The next step is to articulate that theory in sufficient detail to generate the hypotheses I will test in the empirical portion of the book. To generate such hypotheses, it is necessary to be explicit about the precise mechanisms through which diasporans' social ties provide value to the firms they own and manage. The three primary mechanisms through which I expect these ties to affect firm performance are: access to information; trust and social contracting; and government relations. The following sections discuss each mechanism in detail.

Access to Information

Information about the local business environment can usefully be divided between private information and public information.[31] Local public information is that which is readily available but is only relevant locally, and thus often published or broadcast solely in local sources and/or in the local language. Thus, although this information is public, it is not easily accessible to most foreign investors. Local private information is that which is not published or broadcast at all. This includes truly confidential information, such as the private conversations of policymakers, as well as information that is simply unavailable to the public, such as unpublished views of local experts or business leaders. Often such views are shared only informally with circles of friends, family, and colleagues, even if they are not entirely secret.

Local public information tends to be scarce in countries with low levels of institutional development because government transparency is low (little top-down information) and there are few information intermediaries in the market, such as business journalists and professional analysts (little bottom-up information).[32] Thus firms without sources of local private information (i.e., most foreign firms) lack the necessary information about political and economic conditions and about other firms in the market, making it difficult to identify opportunities, assess risks, and screen potential customers, suppliers, and partners.

When public information about local business and political conditions is scarce, capable firms are able to substitute for local public information by relying on private sources to fill the void (Solinger 1989; Ronnas 1992; McMillan 1997; Portes and Rey 2005; Albuquerque, Bauer, and Schneider 2009). Social ties are critical resources here, as they connect firms to sources of private information they can trust (e.g., Burt 1992, 2000; Coleman 1988, 1990; Gulatti 1995).

Theoretically, I identify three mechanisms that provide diaspora-affiliated firms with an advantage in managing a scarcity of local public information: (1) diasporans' social networks provide them with local private information about the homeland and the ability to assess the credibility of the local public information that does exist; (2) diasporans' language skills give them an advantage accessing and evaluating both types of local information in the homeland; (3) diasporans' social ties to headquarters personnel and fluency in the culture of the headquarters country allow them to share information effectively across different units within the firm.

The foundation of the firm [in Georgia] was caused by the advice of the Georgian friend of the [German] owner.[33]

If I did not have friendship contacts here I could not have started my business in Georgia. Nobody can help you, there is an information lack, the embassy of Georgia has no info and there is a language problem too.[34]

The unique social networks of diasporans are tailor-made for gathering local private information about market and political conditions in the homeland that is either confidential or limited in circulation. The strength of ties, and specifically the high level of trust intrinsic to strong ties, allows the network to transmit information efficiently.[35] The physical distance between the homeland and country-of-settlement networks means that diasporans connect two distinct networks with non-overlapping sources of information. The local private information that diasporans' homeland contacts have at hand is not known to the diasporans' country-of-settlement contacts and vice versa. Thus I expect that diasporans wield power as brokers of local private information.

Diasporans also have an edge when it comes to monitoring local public information, particularly when that information is in the local language or when the reliability of publicly available information is highly varied or in question. Diasporans' edge in processing this local public information begins with their language skills, but knowledge about what sources of local public information can be trusted, or what biases are likely in each source, is itself private information. Diasporans obtain this knowledge both through long personal experience of following news of the homeland and through their social networks—friends and family members who share observations about the reliability of different sources. Thus diasporans' social ties play a role in granting access to local public information as well as local private information.

> We have a general manager who has hired 50 engineers from her alma mater . . . to get skills we use our networks.[36]

> Most of our clients are obtained through social [networks].[37]

Local managers share many of diasporans' advantages in gathering and evaluating local information. The key difference is diasporans' ability to disseminate the information they gather throughout the firm in ways that headquarters personnel can understand and trust. Both the literature on cheap talk and the literature on intrafirm movements of information are useful in understanding diasporans' advantage in this area.

The cheap talk literature (e.g., Cooper et al. 1992; Crawford 1998; Ozer, Zheng, and Chen 2011) identifies conditions under which accurate information can be sent, received, and believed by rational actors. Key features that enhance the credibility of information shared between diasporans and headquarters personnel include sufficient past interaction to establish a (nonbinding) commitment to communicate honestly and a preexisting common language about the meanings of particular commitments. Diasporans' cultural fluency provides a common language with headquarters personnel regarding the meaning of commitments. Particularly for diasporans who have worked for a firm in the headquarters country before returning to the homeland, there is ample opportunity to establish mutual expectations for honest communication. Thus diasporans are more credible transmitters of local information than are local managers.

There is a related business literature that argues that social ties are absolutely critical to the effective transfer of information between different parts of a firm, such as between headquarters and an overseas subsidiary (Kogut and Zander 1992; Hedlund 1994). This type of intra-organizational knowledge transfer is particularly difficult when it must occur between individuals who are geographically and/or culturally distant from one another (e.g., Bartlett and Ghoshal 1989; Szulanski 1996) and when it involves knowledge that is tacit, rather than explicit and easily codifiable (e.g., Nonaka 1994; Morris, Zhong, and Makhija 2015). Tacit knowledge is much more valuable than explicit knowledge precisely because it is difficult to imitate and difficult to transfer (e.g., Polanyi 1966; Grant 1996). It is transferred most readily between individuals who share a social tie characterized by a high level of trust (Collins 2001; Holste and Fields 2010). Diasporans' unique social networks position them to help firms with the most difficult and valuable type of intrafirm knowledge transfer—transfer of tacit knowledge between geographically distant parts of the firms.

I am not the first scholar to argue that diasporans are valuable conduits of business-relevant information (e.g., Bandelj 2002; Freinkman 2002; Rauch and Casella 2003; Saxenian 2006), and there is some existing evidence that supports diasporans' ability to play this role. Wang (2014), for instance, finds that diasporans are effective at transferring knowledge within firms, particularly when they are strongly embedded in social networks in both the home and host country. Similarly, Filatotchev et al. (2011) find that returnee entrepreneurs produce knowledge spillovers to other firms in the homeland—namely bringing knowledge from the country of settlement to the homeland; Choudhury (2010) finds that returnee managers increase the R&D productivity of employees in the homeland, which he argues is due to returnees' ability to transfer knowledge resources from the headquarters.[38] What remains empirically untested is whether diaspora-affiliated firms enjoy any information-related advantages over other foreign firms, almost all of whom employ local managers.[39] Thus an important contribution of this book is to test directly whether, when accessing information, diaspora-affiliated firms are more likely than other foreign firms to rely on social ties.

Trust and Social Contracting

The law and investment literature suggests that formal contracting institutions and social networks are substitutes. Firms can rely on formal institutions to enforce contracts and protect them from opportunistic behavior, or they can rely on social networks and personal relationships to play these same roles. In practice, many firms do both.

There are two related mechanisms through which social networks may be used to substitute for formal contracting institutions. The first is by providing a direct means of enforcing contracts and sanctioning opportunistic behavior. The second is by establishing trust between diaspora-affiliated firms and potential business counterparts, reducing the likelihood that diaspora-affiliated firms are victimized by opportunistic behavior.

Consider a hypothetical dispute between a diaspora-affiliated firm and a domestic firm that has received a shipment of goods but refuses to pay. If the court system in the homeland is efficient and reliable, the diaspora-affiliated firm can bring suit against the domestic customer and eventually win payment of its claim. If the domestic courts are slow, expensive, and/or unreliable, it might be more profitable for a well-connected diaspora-affiliated firm to rely on informal means to enforce the contract. For example, if the diasporan and a counterpart at the domestic firm are friends or share family ties, they may opt for informal mediation of the dispute by another friend or family member to avoid rupturing the social bond between them. If the diasporan has friendship or family ties with counterparts at a large number of other firms in the same industry, she can encourage these firms to refuse to do business with the customer until the debt is paid. In either scenario, the social ties of the diasporan facilitate the informal, rather than the judicial, resolution of the dispute. While potentially useful in any institutional environment, these informal contract enforcement and dispute resolution mechanisms are most valuable when formal contracting institutions are weak.

It is also possible for diasporans to use social networks as a more indirect substitute for, or even a complement to, formal contracting institutions. By seeking out business counterparts with whom they have social connections, firms can reduce the risk that they will be victimized by opportunistic behavior in the first place.

And the beautiful part about this is that when ten people answer for him, that's the credibility you give this person. It's not just, "Oh I have a contact that [can] supply this," and who knows who this Tom, Dick, and Harry is that I'm gonna buy this from. Is he gonna support my sale? Is he gonna support me five years down the line if I have a problem?[40]

The role of relational trust in reducing transaction costs and increasing economic efficiency is well-established at the cross-national level (e.g., Knack and Keefer 1996; Zak and Knack 1999) and at the firm level (Sako 1992; Barney and Hansen 1994; Chow and Holden 1997).[41] Reputation, trust, and norms of reciprocity are important factors in determining the duration and stability of exchange structures between firms and individuals (e.g., Granovetter 1985; Larson 1992; Adler 2001). In short, social relationships increase firms' incentives to resolve disputes amicably, and they provide the tools to do so effectively.

> *When we run into problems with clients, we try to salvage the relationship rather than going directly to the legal route. . . . If you push someone to court, you don't just lose them as a client, you lose their entire network.*[42]

If diasporans retain social networks in the homeland, they do not start from scratch in forming important business relationships. Consistent with the theory outlined above, social ties are expected to infuse trust into relationships beyond those that exist between a diasporan and his/her family and friends. Individuals with whom a diasporan shares a direct social tie can serve as ambassadors, providing introductions and vouching for the diasporan and the firm she owns or manages, helping form trusting relationships with people the diasporan has never met.[43] Thus diasporans' social networks in the homeland are far-reaching. These ties increase the degree to which diaspora-affiliated firms can use social trust to lower the likelihood that they fall prey to opportunistic behavior.

Government Relations

> *We try to follow the rules and act above board so that who we know becomes negligible in the outcome. . . . But of course if you run into trouble, we have people, you know?*[44]

It is useful to think separately about firms' ability to influence the behavior of government bureaucrats and their ability to influence elected politicians. While there is some overlap, especially at the local level, elected officials tend to set the rules of the game (i.e., write the laws), while bureaucrats control how those rules are applied to a given firm.[45] Altering the rules of the game usually involves seeking pro-business policy changes that benefit entire groups of firms. Influencing bureaucrats, however, is more likely to focus on securing a favorable application of the rules to a particular case, which is more likely to benefit only a single firm.

This mirrors a distinction in Graham (2015) between bureaucratic risk, which is related to corruption and low state capacity, and policy risk, or risks related to policy instability and opportunistic or predatory government behavior at the national level. Bureaucratic risk is something that capable firms are likely to be able to mitigate on their own, gaining an advantage over other firms. Policy risk is less amenable to this type of active mitigation by single firms—antibusiness policy changes are best avoided by groups of firms acting collectively.

Thus I expect firms to employ different types of social ties to influence each type of political actor. Ties to peer firms should be particularly important for mitigating policy risk and affecting favorable policy change at the national level because they increase a firm's ability to work collectively. For example, foreign firms might band together to encourage the government to invest in a port expansion or other infrastructure improvements (Olson 1965).[46] However, firms also often seek private goods from government, and in these instances collective action and the ties to peer firms that facilitate it are less important. Instead, social ties that connect firms directly to bureaucrats and elected politicians are likely to be most useful (Hansen, Mitchell, and Drope 2005; Cruz and Graham 2017).

Influencing the Bureaucracy

Bureaucratic risk is one of the dominant characteristics of institutionally underdeveloped countries and a major deterrent to inward FDI. In countries far down on the World Bank's Ease of Doing Business rankings, firms face demands for bribes and delays every step of the way: at customs, regulatory agencies, tax authorities, and in the courts. While it may be outside the power of individual firms to promote pro-market institutional reforms and the reduction of bureaucratic risk, capable firms can certainly act to reduce their own losses. I expect that social ties are key here, particularly ties directly to bureaucrats.

I do have a friend in [the Bureau of Internal Revenue] and in the past I've asked for favors and they came through. But in a way the favor asking was a way to circumvent corrupt practices. Basically, we were getting the runaround

at the front desk where the clerk was citing all sorts of penalties and fees . . .
and it was outrageous because here I was trying to actually submit my taxes
and I was being penalized for it. So I called the friend and it was suddenly
done in two hours and with no fee.[47]

According to the respondent at one diaspora-managed firm, when his American counterparts run into problems with the government officials, he must work to repair the relationships that his American counterparts have inadvertently damaged. This is critical because, for his firm, "A project must have buy-in from local officials to ensure sustainability."[48]

Respondents at other firms talk of using "fixers" to figure out how much of a bribe must be paid and to whom. But employing a fixer is difficult: to be useful the fixer must have close ties to the bureaucracy, and if the fixer is to be trusted, he/she must also have close ties to the firm.

A fixer that cannot be trusted is a fixer that cannot be used.

Influence over Government Policy

From a focus group of firm managers in Manila:

Speaker 1: *I mean you've gotta hire people and, you know, pay them so they*
    would know people inside depending on which city. Some sort of magic,
    you know?

Speaker 2: *That's what they call it. The connections.*

Speaker 3: *The fixers.*

Interviewer: *The fixers?*

Speaker 3: *Yeah, I mean actually, fixers are everywhere in all government*
    agencies, whether it be the LTO, which is the equivalent of the DMV or, I
    mean everywhere. A passport even–

Speaker 4: *Three months just to get the certificate of product registration. . . .*
    So, I have a license for one of my products. It took so long and they gave
    us so many, they kept coming back with saying "Oh you have to amend
    this part. . . ." So I kept having to amend everything until the original
    certificate of product registration expired, and I have to go through all
    the–

Interviewer: *All that stuff again? Wow*

Speaker 4: *Yeah! Another three months.*

Speaker 2: *All because he don't pay.*

[Laughter]

Speaker 3: *You have to pay.*
Speaker 2: *You've gotta pay.*

While generally not able to vote, and in many countries banned from making direct campaign contributions, foreign investors wield political influence in both democracies and nondemocracies.[49] This may or may not be a good thing for the investment host country. Foreign investors generally prefer policies that are favorable to economic growth, but they also, of course, prefer policies that are favorable to themselves (and perhaps not to citizens of the host country). Just as foreign firms vary in their impacts on the host economy, they also vary in their impact on host country politics (Kobrin 1987; Vaaler 2008)

Relative to other foreign firms, I expect diaspora-affiliated firms to possess more and stronger ties both to peer firms and to government officials. Strong ties to peer firms allow diaspora-affiliated firms to coordinate with their peers to pursue policy outcomes that benefit entire groups of firms. Strong direct ties to government officials, both bureaucrats and policymakers, allow firms to pursue policy outcomes that mainly benefit themselves, as well as outcomes that benefit whole groups. Thus I expect social ties to play a larger role in the political strategies of diaspora-affiliated firms and I expect diaspora-affiliated firms to be more successful in managing their relationships with government officials and achieving the policy outcomes they seek.

Can All Diasporans be Transnational Brokers?

I expect that most diasporans, and particularly most wealthy, educated diasporans, have social networks with the characteristics pictured in figure 2.2. Most have strong ties to both a community in the homeland and one in the country of settlement. In most cases there are few other ties that link these two communities. Thus many diasporans are well positioned to serve as transnational brokers. However, diasporans vary significantly both in their level of connectedness and in the economic significance of the communities they connect.

Multinational firms are not owned and managed by just any diasporans. From the perspective of firms, the most valuable transnational brokerage occurs between relatively wealthy and educated populations in the country of settlement, namely the owners and managers of firms considering or already engaged in overseas investment, and relatively wealthy and educated populations in the homeland, including the owners and managers of domestic firms, government officials, and other economic and political elites. Thus it is wealthy and educated diasporans who are most often positioned to provide the type of transnational brokerage that provides value to multinational firms. Those diasporans who have few social ties, or whose social ties are irrelevant to business, are unable to serve effectively as transnational brokers.

In thinking about variation in diasporans' connections, one useful contrast is between a well-connected middle-class diasporan, like Sophia Ramos, and a true member of the political elite, like Francis Laurel. Both types of diasporan can serve as valuable transnational brokers, but their connections are quite different. Ms. Ramos has ties to local businesspeople and to lower-level government officials. These ties, along with fluency in multiple languages and cultures, allow her to provide value to her firm with respect to critical day-to-day relationships and operations. She is a manager in the true sense of the word. Someone like Mr. Laurel, however, can offer more than day-to-day management, because he also offers connections to the political elite in the Philippines—to legislators, governors, and even the president. When it comes to influencing national level policy or securing large-scale government contracts, firms need the type of brokerage that only a member of the political elite can provide.

My expectation is that middle-class diaspora managers are far more common than politically elite diaspora managers, and I expect that that middle-class diasporans account for most of the diaspora-affiliated firms analyzed in the empirical sections of the book.[50] However, politically elite diasporans play critical roles in the strategies of many multinational firms. The role of politically connected "princelings" is particularly well documented in the financial sector in China and other emerging economies in Asia (e.g., Garnaut 2010; Viswanatha 2016). Some of these princelings are simply hired as a favor to their powerful parents and are expected to do little work; others more actively create value for the firm by using their political connections to secure business and protect the firm from adverse government action. Empirically, this book focuses on the comparison between foreign firms that are diaspora-affiliated and those that are not, but there is much future work to be done exploring the variations that exist within diaspora-affiliated firms, particularly with respect to which types of diasporans are able to provide which types of transnational brokerage.

Lastly, it is important to note that some diasporans who are neither wealthy nor well educated when they emigrate subsequently obtain education and (at least moderate) wealth in the country of settlement, and then proceed to fill roles similar to diasporans who were already middle class when they emigrated. Among even the most destitute group of refugees there are those who manage to rise into elite circles in the country of settlement, developing valuable social ties there. One can think of that small subset of the Lost Boys of Sudan who have gone on to earn graduate degrees and rise to management positions in large American firms.[51] While their social ties in the homeland may not be to the well-connected, they may still be able to use those ties to gain valuable market and political information and to achieve a level of understanding of the local investment climate that would be difficult for an unconnected foreigner to achieve. Similarly, it is important to note that while we generally think of multinational firms as very large firms, many small firms engage in foreign investment as well, such that not all owners and managers of foreign firms are wealthy.

2.6. Diaspora Downsides?

My theory of diasporans as transnational brokers focuses primarily on the positive implications of diaspora affiliation. It is my expectation that the net effect of diaspora affiliation on firm performance is positive and large. However, one should not be naïve. Not all aspects of diaspora identity will benefit the firms diasporans own and manage.

Firms may experience liabilities related to diaspora affiliation in countries where diasporans are resented, such as when locals have endured civil wars or other hardships that diasporans avoided by living abroad. Also, just as diasporans' political connections may provide value to a firm, a diasporan with the wrong political affiliations—such as ties to political groups opposed to the government—may just as easily become a liability. Diaspora-affiliated firms also take on the risk that their diaspora managers may have interests in the homeland—political interests, philanthropic goals, or family commitments—that do not align with firm objectives. As with any manager or business partner, there is a risk that diasporans will use firm resources to pursue their own objectives.[52]

When I test the implications of my theory in the empirical sections of the book, some of the hypotheses I test make predictions regarding expected positive effects of diaspora affiliation on firm performance. For example, I predict that diaspora-affiliated firms are more likely to report that social ties are important for firm profitability. These are hypotheses about the net effects of diaspora affiliation—the effect of the positive channels identified earlier in this chapter minus any potential downsides. If these downsides are powerful, it makes it less likely that I will observe the positive effects that I am predicting. However, if I do observe the expected positive effects, it will provide evidence not only that the positive channels I identify earlier in the chapter are indeed in operation but also that those effects are strong enough to subsume the potential liabilities associated with diaspora affiliation. Additionally, in chapter 5 (sec. 5.6), I examine respondents' answers to open-ended questions about the effects of owners' and managers' social ties and find no evidence of these sorts of negative effects are common.

2.7. The Social and Emotional Motivations Mechanism

Here I transition from presenting my own theory of diasporans as transnational brokers to contrasting this theory with the key alternative theory offered within the literature, which is based on diasporans' social and emotional motivations for homeland engagement. Diasporans have strong ties to individuals in the homeland, but they also have loyalty to the homeland itself and to the community of conationals with which they identify. This broader affinity is not entirely distinct from the social ties that link diasporans to individual people, such as friends and family, back in the homeland. Indeed transnational kinship and friendship networks are the bedrock of this homeland loyalty, but loyalty to the homeland often goes beyond direct relationships between individuals (e.g., Schiller and Fouron 1999). Diasporans belong to transnational communities in a much deeper and broader sense, and these communities link diasporans not just to the homeland but also to coethnics in other countries around the world.

Transnational diaspora communities are one of the most fascinating social responses to the dislocations wrought by globalization.[53] Cohen (1997: 515) and Brinkerhoff (2009: 29–30) offer useful characterizations of the shared values and beliefs that bond these transnational communities together, and I adapt their lists here. Members share:

- A collective memory and myth about the homeland.
- An idealization of the ancestral home.
- A strong ethnic group consciousness.
- A sense of empathy or solidarity with members of their community in the homeland and in other countries of settlement.

The size and strength of these transnational communities has exploded in the 21st century, not just in response to the rapidly growing number of migrants that exist globally but also as a result of the growing ease with which transnational relationships can be maintained. E-mail, websites and online forums, long-distance calling cards, Skype, and the declining cost of international travel all allow today's diasporans an ease of connectedness that previous generations lacked. Ease of communication and ease of travel facilitate not just individual relationships but collective relationships and indeed collective action in both the social and political sphere.

Community membership comes with obligations, and these obligations provide a means of understanding many of the ways in which diasporans engage with the homeland. When diasporans send remittances back to the homeland, the funds are sometimes a direct repayment of informal loans that the diasporan received to finance her emigration. Sometimes the funds fulfill a family obligation to support parents, siblings, and other relatives the diasporan left behind. And sometimes remittances are sent to fulfill broader obligations to the transnational community of which the diasporan is a part (e.g., Sana 2005).

One can also view diaspora philanthropy through the same lens. Diaspora philanthropy is booming, with rapid growth of both diaspora foundations, like hometown associations, and independent giving (Johnson 2007; Brinkerhoff 2014; Licuanan, Mahmoud, and Steinmayr 2015). It is a reasonable next step to ask, if affinity for the homeland induces diasporans to engage in philanthropic activity there, what related behaviors should we expect from diaspora-affiliated firms? In the following section, I explore the relationship between affinity for the homeland and philanthropic behavior at the individual level and the expected behavior of diaspora-owned firms. I examine diaspora-owned firms in particular because diaspora managers may have more limited control in this area. I focus on corporate social responsibility and corporate philanthropy and also explore whether these motivations may cause diaspora-owned firms to be more tolerant of certain political risks. Figure 2.3 provides a graphical summary.

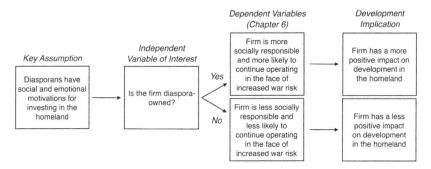

Fig. 2.3. *Alternative Theory from the Literature—Social and Emotional Motivations*

Motivations and Firm Objectives

Diasporans belong to transnational communities. There is substantial empirical evidence that the complex web of social ties and emotional attachments that characterize community membership sometimes lead diasporans to invest financial resources toward social and philanthropic goals in the homeland. Billionaire Kirk Kerkorian stands out among diaspora philanthropists—between 1989 and 2011 he gave more than US $1 billion in charitable contributions to Armenian causes. His early giving was focused on reconstruction following a 1989 earthquake in the homeland. In the early 1990s, Kerkorian's spending on infrastructure development helped offset the inability of a fledgling Armenian government to make necessary investments in the future of the post-Soviet economy (Beilock 2003). But many nonbillionaire diasporans give to the homeland on a smaller scale, both individually and via diaspora associations. Philanthropically oriented diaspora organizations have proliferated in recent years, as groups often organize around online platforms that accommodate a globally dispersed membership (e.g., Johnson 2007; Brinkerhoff 2007; Newland, Terrazas, and Munster 2010).

Homeland governments and international organizations often seek to steer diaspora philanthropy, so as to both amplify its effects on development and channel funds toward government priorities. For example, in 1980 the Commission on Filipinos Overseas (CFO) created a platform called Linkapil to channel diaspora donations toward government development priorities—the organization's efforts are currently focused on the Millennium Development Goals. Linkapil processed roughly $40 million in diaspora donations between 1990 and 2010, though it appears to be more successful in channeling giving by organizations than giving by individuals (Licuanan, Mahmoud, and Steinmayr 2012).

Existing theory suggests a variety of motives for diasporans to engage in homeland philanthropy: simple altruism, exchange (e.g., donations in return for care of relatives by the receiving community), and securing elevated social status or community membership rights more broadly (e.g., Luecke, Mahmoud, and Peuker 2012; Garchitorena 2007). If social and emotional ties to the homeland lead diasporans to engage in philanthropy in the homeland, might these same motivations shape the behavior of diaspora investors? Might they lead diaspora-owned (and possibly even diaspora-managed) firms to engage in more socially responsible behaviors?

Social Responsibility

The idea that diaspora investors might behave in a more socially responsible manner than other foreign investors is rooted in solid research on the motivations of those investors (Gillespie et al. 1999; Gillespie, Sayre, and Riddle 2001; Nielsen and Riddle 2009). Investment in the homeland by a diasporan is, in some cases, not just an economic act but also an emotional, social, and political act (Bandelj 2008). In addition to the desire to earn a profit, diasporans may invest for social reasons, such as raising their standing in the diaspora community in their country of settlement, or for emotional reasons, such as patriotism (Aharoni 1966; Schulte 2008; Nielsen and Riddle 2009). Empirically, surveys of US-based diasporas have shown that diasporans' self-reported interest in homeland investment is greatest among those diasporans with the strongest emotional ties to the homeland, as well as the strongest social ties to their diaspora community in the United States (Gillespie et al. 1999; Gillespie, Sayre, and Riddle 2001; Raveloharimisy, Riddle, and Nielsen 2010). This supports the idea that social and emotional motivations shape the behavior of potential diaspora investors.

These findings of nonpecuniary investment motivations have motivated further theorizing about the potential of diaspora investors as sources of social and economic development in the homeland. If diaspora investment in the homeland is motivated by the desire to increase social standing in the diaspora community in the country of settlement and to engage positively with a homeland to which the investor has strong emotional ties, it is reasonable to expect that diaspora-owned firms will engage in behaviors consistent with these goals. Specifically, the economic sociology literature theorizes that diaspora-owned firms may rely more heavily on local labor and local inputs, pay above-market wages, and strive to provide a high quality of life for their employees. Some may seek to protect the local environment and generally strive to promote the development of the homeland (Nielsen and Riddle 2009).

This argument, that the motivations of diaspora owners might serve as causes of socially responsible firm behavior, is consistent with the general literature on the reasons firms adopt corporate social responsibility (CSR). This literature suggests that the personal motivations of top management are important causes of CSR (Hemingway and Maclagan 2004; Juholin 2004), and that philanthropic, rather than strategic, CSR is particularly prevalent in the developing world (Jamali and Mirshak 2007). This is sound and compelling theory—not just optimism flying in the face of reason.[54]

The prospect of socially and emotionally motivated diaspora investment has generated substantial optimism in the policy world (e.g., Debass and Ardovino 2009; Foreign Service Institute 2010; Rodriguez-Montemayor 2012). While diaspora investment is solicited by host governments for a variety of reasons, the expectation that diaspora investment may produce pro-development spillovers that are larger than the spillovers from other types of FDI shows up frequently in the rhetoric of policymakers when they launch diaspora investment promotion initiatives. Many nonprofit initiatives seeking to increase diaspora investment do so specifically in the context of promoting "impact investment," namely investment with the express purpose of facilitating social change and/or economic development.[55]

Anecdotal evidence suggests that FDI is sometimes used as a vehicle for diasporans and returnees to pursue social goals in the homeland (Brinkerhoff 2004; Nyberg-Sørensen 2007; Riddle, Hrivnak, and Nielsen 2010). Socially responsible investment is particularly desirable in developing countries where the ability of the government to restrain rapacious firms and provide social insurance is low.[56] While exposure to the global economy is associated with greater welfare spending in rich countries, the reverse is true in the developing world (Wibbels 2006; Rudra 2002). Developing countries often open their economies to foreign direct investment to spur development, but their very openness prevents large social programs that might expand the benefits of growth to larger segments of the population (Kaufman and Segura Ubiergo 2001; Reuveny and Li 2003). Against this backdrop of limited government welfare capabilities, social responsibility among foreign investors is all the more salient.

If the social and emotional motivations mechanism outlined above operates as theorized, these motivations should be reflected in the behavior of diaspora-owned firms. This expectation of greater social responsibility is not directly in conflict with the implications of my theory of diasporans as transnational brokers. However, in the empirical analysis in chapter 6, I find no evidence that diaspora-owned firms are more socially responsible than other foreign firms, which suggests that diasporans' social and emotional motivations are not important drivers of firm behavior in this particular domain. This finding is an important contribution to the literature because, prior to this study, scholars had been unable to test the central implications of the social and emotional motivations theory directly.

Risk Tolerance of Diaspora Firm Owners

One of the most intriguing findings of the early research on diasporans' motivations for homeland investment comes from a survey of the Palestinian diaspora living in the United States. The survey was conducted in two waves, one in 1994 and one in 1998. Self-reported investment interest among these respondents was not only high but it remained so as the economy deteriorated and the respondent-perceived level of political risk increased between 1994 and 1998 (Gillespie, Sayre, and Riddle 2001). Altruistic intentions are important predictors of respondents' interest in investment, indicating that profit is not the only or necessarily even the primary motive, for diaspora investment in this context. This hints at a compelling possibility that nonpecuniary motivations may lead diaspora investors to be less deterred by the risk of political violence and other forms of risk than are other foreign investors (Riddle and Nielsen 2010).

This question of whether diasporans are more tolerant than other foreigners of political risk in the homeland because of nonpecuniary motivations is closely related to the question of whether diasporans' social ties may provide them with capabilities (e.g., access to information, ability to enforce contracts, ability to influence policymakers) that make some forms of political risk less costly to diaspora-affiliated firms. Both theories discussed above—brokerage and motivations—may lead diaspora-affiliated firms to be more likely to invest in host countries with high levels of political risk. However, the theoretical mechanisms are distinct, as are the implications for firm strategy.

In the empirical portion of the book, I exploit data from Georgia—which experienced a brief war with Russia shortly before I conducted my survey—to assess firms' sensitivity to the risk that war may reoccur. I examine not only whether war risk has had a lesser effect on the strategy of diaspora-owned firms (I find that it has), but I try to get at why that is the case. In particular, I test whether diaspora-owned firms perceive themselves to be less likely to suffer decreased profitability should it occur, which would be consistent with my theory of transnational brokerage. In contrast, the social and emotional motivations theory implies that diaspora-affiliated firms will be less likely to adjust their strategy in response to war risk, even if they are no more capable than other foreign firms of mitigating those risks.[57] I find that diaspora-affiliated firms are indeed less sensitive to war risk, but also that these firms are less likely to expect that a return to war would damage their profitability. This lack of sensitivity is most likely driven by capabilities rather than motivations.

2.8. Summary of Empirical Expectations

Faced with two plausible theories linking diaspora affiliation to firm behavior, and faced with a large divergence in development implications depending on which mechanism is dominant, it is time to move from theory to empirics and assess the explanatory power of each theory. Chapter 3 introduces new data and lays out the research design through which these expectations are tested. The design centers on direct comparisons between diaspora-affiliated and nondiaspora-affiliated foreign firms with regard to both the social ties that firms have access to, the ways that firms use these ties in business, and the impact they have on development in the homeland. Chapters 4–6 present the specific empirical hypotheses to be tested and present the results of the empirical analysis.

To preview the empirical chapters, tables 2.2 and 2.3 summarize the theoretical expectations of my theory of transnational brokers and the theory based on diasporans' social and emotional motivations, respectively. These tables also list the specific observable implications that are used to evaluate these expectations empirically and the number of discrete statistical tests performed for each expectation. The hypotheses are explained and stated formally in the empirical chapters, but these tables summarize the overall structure of the empirical analysis.

Table 2.2. Testable Implications of Transnational Brokerage

Theoretical Expectation	Observable Implications	Number of Tests
Diaspora-affiliated firms have more and stronger social ties than other foreign firms	Compared to nondiaspora-affiliated foreign firms, diaspora-affiliated firms: 1. Report interacting **more frequently** with peer firms and government officials 2. Report **stronger** ties to peer firms and government officials 3. Report **more** direct ties to government	11
Diaspora-affiliated firms view social ties as more important to firm performance than do other foreign firms	Compared to nondiaspora-affiliated foreign firms, diaspora-affiliated firms: 1. Report that their social ties are **more** important to firm performance	6
Diaspora-affiliated firms use social ties in business more than other foreign firms	Compared to nondiaspora-affiliated foreign firms, diaspora-affiliated firms are **more** likely to report: 1. Using social ties to gather information 2. Using social ties to resolve disputes 3. Extending credit to customers and receiving credit from suppliers 4. Using social ties to rent/purchase real estate 5. Using social ties to improve government relations 6. Attempting and succeeding in influencing government policy	13
Diaspora-owned firms are less likely to expect that violent conflict will alter their business strategy or decrease their profitability	Compared to nondiaspora-affiliated foreign firms, diaspora-affiliated firms are: 1. **Less likely** to expect that a return to war would change their business strategy 2. **Less likely** to expect that a return to war would damage their profitability	2

Table 2.3. Testable Implications of Social and Emotional Motivations

Theoretical Expectation	Observable Implications	Number of Tests
Diaspora-owned firms are more likely than other foreign firms to engage in socially responsible behavior	In comparison to other firms in their sector, diaspora-owned firms are: 1. **More likely** to report offering higher salaries 2. **More likely** to report providing employees a higher quality of life 3. **More likely** to report providing employees opportunities for professional development 4. **Less likely** to report focusing narrowly on profit 5. **Less likely** to report working to minimize labor costs 6. **More likely** to report prioritizing local employment 7. **More likely** to report **a low** environmental impact 8. **More likely** to report making donations to charity	8
Diaspora-owned firms are more likely to continue operations in the homeland when war breaks out, even if war damages their profitability	Compared to other foreign firms, diaspora-owned firms are: 1. **Less likely** to expect that a return to war would change their business strategy 2. **Equally likely** to expect that a return to war would damage their profitability	2

2.9. Conclusion

The transnational brokerage and social and emotional motivations for homeland engagement each serve as possible drivers of the behavior of diaspora-affiliated firms. However, these theories imply two quite different sets of answers to the big picture questions that I raised in the introduction. Much of the hope attached to diasporans as economic development *wunderkind* relies on the expectation that their social and emotional motivations shape the behavior of diaspora-owned firms. If the effect of these motivations is strong, then it is reasonable to expect that diaspora-owned firms are both less deterred by political risk and more socially responsible than their nondiaspora-affiliated peers.

If, instead, diasporans serve as transnational brokers, using their unique social ties as substitutes for poorly functioning formal political and economic institutions, this implies that diaspora-owned and diaspora-managed firms may be better able than other foreign firms to operate in developing countries in which governance is poor. This does not mean, however, that these firms will be more inclined than other companies to engage in pro-development behavior when they arrive. Rather, diaspora-affiliated firms contribute to development by increasing the *volume* of inward investment, something particularly valuable for their more poorly governed and weakly institutionalized homelands where other foreign firms struggle to operate successfully.

CHAPTER 3

Research Design and New Firm-Level Data

As noted in the introduction, FDI into emerging markets is booming and global migrant populations continue to grow. These two phenomena are linked. Cross-national studies of migration and FDI show that diaspora populations increase FDI from their country of settlement back to their homeland (e.g., Kugler and Rapoport 2007; Leblang 2010; Javorcik 2011; Burchardi, Chaney, and Hassan 2016), and there is anecdotal evidence that diaspora-affiliated firms are an important part of this story. Unfortunately, little is known about how prevalent these diaspora-affiliated firms are or how they differ from other foreign firms in terms of their capabilities, priorities, strategies, and impact on development.

The central empirical question of this book is, how do diaspora-affiliated firms differ from foreign firms that are not diaspora affiliated? Both of the theories introduced in chapter 2 predict that diasporans affect the behavior of the firms they own and manage, but their predictions diverge as to what those effects are. My theory of diasporans as transnational brokers predicts that diasporans exploit their unique social ties to augment the capabilities of the firms they own and manage. The alternative theory I present predicts that diasporans' social and emotional motivations for homeland engagement cause diaspora-affiliated firms, and particularly diaspora-owned firms, to embrace objectives beyond profitability and, among other things, behave in a more socially responsible manner. This chapter articulates the research design and introduces the new datasets I will employ to test these two theories.

The Central Empirical Question: How do diaspora-affiliated firms differ from foreign firms that are not diaspora affiliated?

The hypothesis testing work in this book is done at the firm level, where I exploit two single-country, firm-level survey datasets that were collected specifically for this project. These new data are the first to offer information on the strategies and capabilities of diaspora-affiliated firms and to allow direct comparison between diaspora-affiliated and nondiaspora-affiliated foreign firms. Without them, the theories introduced in chapter 2 would be impossible to test.

3.1. The Need for New Firm-Level Data

Empirically, this project sits at the intersection of two literatures, one on diaspora homeland investment and one on political risk and foreign investment. Both are theory-rich and data-poor. The literature on diaspora investment features a number of high-quality, inductive, theory-building papers, but rigorous theory testing has been hindered by the lack of data in general, and most critically by a lack of firm-level data that allow for direct comparison between diaspora-affiliated and nondiaspora-affiliated foreign firms. Despite some recent innovative work (e.g., Kerner and Lawrence 2013; Johns and Wellhausen 2017; Malesky, Gueorguiev, and Jensen 2015), the political risk and foreign investment literature continues to rely almost exclusively on analyses of country-year data on net FDI inflows to developing countries, which pools across all types of direct investors.[1] Thus the field has lagged in formulating and testing theory with regard to variation across different types of firms, in terms of both the causes of FDI and the effects of FDI on development.

Important data have been previously collected on diaspora investors—including by Portes and Guarniza (1990), Gillespie et al. (1999, 2001), Schulte (2008), and Raveloharimisy, Riddle, and Nielsen (2010). These data provide valuable descriptions of diaspora-affiliated enterprises, and I thus draw on this work in developing my theory. However, these studies only collect data on diaspora investors, which means that one cannot use their data to test for differences that may set diaspora-affiliated firms apart from their nondiaspora-affiliated peers. We need data that allow for a direct comparison between foreign firms that are diaspora-affiliated and those that are not.

Prior studies have established, for example, that some diaspora-affiliated firms use social networks to gather information (e.g., Liu et al. 2015). In and of itself, this doesn't tell us much. Among the firms my colleagues and I surveyed in the Philippines, including both firms that are diaspora-affiliated and those that are not, 80% report using networks in this way and 29% say networks are their most important source of information.[2] The question is not whether diaspora-affiliated firms use networks in this way—almost all firms use networks in this way occasionally—it is whether they use networks in this way *more than* other foreign firms. For that, we need data on both diaspora-affiliated and nondiaspora-affiliated foreign firms, and we need to compare them head-to-head. Only one study exists that collects data on both diaspora-affiliated and nondiaspora-affiliated foreign firms, allowing for such a comparison, but unfortunately these data do not include the other information of interest in this project.[3]

Thus one of the most significant contributions of this book is the introduction of two new firm-level data sets that allow precisely this type of direct comparison between diaspora-affiliated and nondiaspora-affiliated foreign firms. These are rich datasets that capture not only basic firm characteristics like size and sector but also information regarding how connected firms are, how they use social ties, and how they affect economic and political development in the investment host country (i.e., the homeland). Thus this data allows me to test a wide variety of hypotheses derived from my theory, subjecting multiple aspects of it to detailed scrutiny.

With regard to my theory of diasporans as transnational brokers, I conduct 31 distinct tests of 11 hypotheses. First, I evaluate whether diaspora-affiliated firms are indeed more socially connected than other foreign firms and whether these social ties are more important to their profitability (chapter 4). I then examine firm strategy to see whether diaspora-affiliated firms are more likely to use social ties across a range of tasks, including gathering information, enforcing contracts, and interacting with government officials, and whether diaspora-affiliated firms report more success areas where social ties are expected to be important—for example, whether they are better able to influence government policy or secure credit from suppliers (chapter 5).

With regard to diasporans' social and emotional motivations, I evaluate eight tests of one central hypothesis. These tests capture various firm behaviors related to social responsibility, evaluating whether diaspora-owned firms are indeed more socially responsible than other foreign firms. I also assess a range of hypotheses evaluating whether diaspora-affiliated firms are more likely to engage in behaviors like exporting and reinvesting earnings that would produce particularly large pro-development spillovers, and whether diaspora-owned firms are less sensitive to the risk of violent conflict (chapter 6).

While any individual hypothesis test has weaknesses, the strength of my empirical evidence derives from the accumulation of evidence across a large number of tests. In 31 tests of my theory of diasporans as transnational brokers, I find differences between diaspora-affiliated and nondiaspora-affiliated foreign firms that are in the expected direction in 29 of the tests. In 13 of those tests, the results are statistically significant ($p <$ 0.05) and eight more barely miss this threshold with p-values between 0.05 and 0.1.[4] It is possible that one or several of these results can be attributed to the influence of an omitted variable or to an error in measurement. However, as I argue in more detail in chapter 7, the consistency of these results across such a large and diverse array of tests makes is extremely difficult to explain unless the underlying theory is broadly correct.

3.2. Two New Firm-Level Datasets

Both of the theories presented in chapter 2 make predictions regarding differences in capabilities, motivations, strategies, and political influence between diaspora-affiliated and nondiaspora-affiliated foreign firms. Detailed firm-level data are scarce precisely because this type of information is costly and difficult to collect. First, firms are reticent to reveal information that may be used against them by rivals or regulators or that may damage their reputation. Second, individuals with broad knowledge of a firm's capabilities, strategies, and performance, such as high-level executives, are extremely busy and often reluctant to make time for conversations with those outside of the corporate world, such as researchers (e.g., Welch et al. 2002). These two constraints place limits on the type of information researchers can seek from firms and make it difficult to successfully implement random-sampling strategies with a high response rate.[5]

In both Georgia and the Philippines, I worked with teams of local researchers to conduct 40-minute face-to-face interviews with firm managers (including owner-managers).[6] The objective was to speak with someone high enough in the firm hierarchy to understand overall firm strategy. While most managers were, themselves, multilingual, I employed bi- and tri-lingual enumerators such that respondents could take the survey in the language in which they were most comfortable: English or Tagalog in the Philippines and English, Georgian, or Russian in Georgia.

In Georgia, my survey was facilitated by institutional support from the Georgian Foundation for Strategic and International Studies, which was run at the time by Alexander Rondeli, a widely respected political figure in the country. Mr. Rondeli's name and the support of the foundation's staff were key factors for convincing the Georgian government to share its list of all the foreign firms registered to do business in the country, and they helped establish my team's credibility with potential respondents.

In the Philippines, I conducted the survey alongside a coprincipal investigator, Cesi Cruz, who had previously run a number of successful surveys of households and government officials in the Philippines. We also worked with three local scholars in the Philippines, Prudenciano Gordoncillo, an economist who served as the field director of the project, and Jeanette Madamba and Jewel Carbardo, business school professors who helped us gain access to business elites.[7] Convincing firm managers to respond to our interview requests was extremely challenging in the Philippines.

By relying on local expertise and labor-intensive techniques, my colleagues and I were able to gather rich, high-quality survey data in both countries, but due to the high costs we were able to conduct surveys in only two countries, not dozens. The following two sections first situate Georgia and the Philippines relative to other developing countries and then describe the surveys themselves.

Case Contextualization: Georgia and the Philippines

The big picture questions regarding the relationship between migration, FDI, and development that motivate this book, and the two theories under consideration, are primarily concerned with foreign investment in developing countries, rather than in rich industrialized countries.[8] Diasporans' role as transnational brokers is likely to be most valuable in countries with low levels of institutional development, most of which are developing countries. The social and emotional motivations mechanism is also likely to operate more strongly in developing countries, as here the desire of diasporans to promote economic development may be stronger than in wealthier homelands.

Because this study draws data from only two countries, humility is necessary regarding the scope of inference that is possible. In general, it is rea-

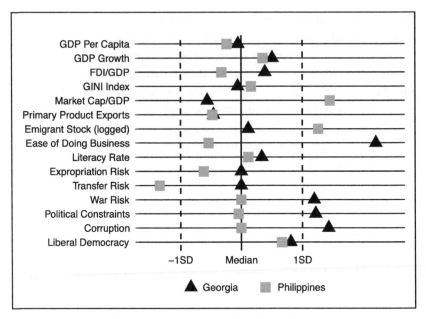

Fig. 3.1. *Georgia and the Philippines Compared to the Median Developing Country*

sonable to expect that the inferences drawn in the empirical chapters can be extended to developing countries that are broadly similar to Georgia and the Philippines. Thus to understand the scope of inference that is possible on the basis of this study, we must begin by comparing Georgia and the Philippines to other developing countries. I argue that, on the dimensions most relevant to this study, Georgia and the Philippines are actually quite typical of developing countries elsewhere in the world.

Figure 3.1 compares Georgia and the Philippines to other developing countries across a range of characteristics that are potentially relevant to the use of social ties in business and the size of the diaspora.[9] The vertical line in the center represents the median of all developing countries, while the dashed vertical lines represent one standard deviation below the median and one standard deviation above the median for all variables.

Georgia is typical of developing countries in that it presents a mix of challenges and opportunities for foreign investors that are similar to those in developing countries elsewhere. Georgia is a small country surrounded by volatile and sometimes hostile neighbors. It has only modest endowments of natural resources but is located on a major transport corridor for both energy (oil and gas) and goods between the Black Sea and Central Asia. While the amount of arable land is not vast, the climate allows cultivation of some high-value crops, including citrus and nuts. While Georgia cannot become wealthy on the strength of its natural endowments alone, with political stability and competent institutions it could certainly become so.

Following Mikheil Saakashvili's ascent to power in the "Rose Revolution" of 2003, Georgia embarked on a series of free-market reforms aimed at increasing foreign investment and integrating Georgia with the West both economically and politically. These reforms have born substantial fruit: Georgia rocketed up through the World Bank's Ease of Doing Business rankings and FDI surged from US $335 million in 2003 to a preconflict peak of US $1.7 billion in 2007. This brought FDI from well below average for developing countries to just above average as a share of GDP. Georgia's focused progress on moving up the Ease of Doing Business rankings has made it one of the top-rated developing countries in that area.

At the time of my survey in early 2010, however, Georgia remained a high-risk destination for foreign investment. Large protests in November 2007 underscored the fragility and unpredictability of the domestic political situation; a brief war between Russia and Georgia in August 2008 highlighted the international instability generated by Georgia's secessionist regions, which have remained outside of central government control since the early 1990s. Thus Georgia is average for developing countries in terms of expropriation risk, and riskier than average in terms of war risk and transfer risk (i.e., the risk that investors are unable to freely repatriate their earnings at the market exchange rate). Georgia is more corrupt than average, but its political system has in place a higher-than-average number of constraints on executive authority (i.e., political constraints), which investors tend to view favorably because it leads to policy stability. Thus Georgia's business climate is typical of developing countries overall—good in some areas, weak in others.

In terms of diaspora investment potential, Georgia is a bit above average for developing countries. Georgia has an emigrant population slightly above the developing-country median, and Georgia received 12% of GDP in remittances in 2013 compared to a developing-country average of 5.5%.[10] Georgia's diaspora is located primarily in Russia, though with substantial populations scattered throughout Europe and the United States. While many Georgian emigrants were displaced by the fighting in South Ossetia and Abkhazia, many more have left in search of economic opportunity.

The history of civil conflict in Georgia is relevant to the social and emotional theory of diaspora investment. Nielsen and Riddle (2010) theorize that nonpecuniary motivations may be more salient to diasporans whose homeland is a postconflict state. In Georgia, two separatist regions, Abkhazia and South Ossetia, waged wars of secession in the early 1990s and secured de facto territorial control. Fighting broke out between South Ossetia and the Georgian government in 2008, with Russian troops doing much of the fighting on behalf of the Ossetians. The war was brief, limited in scope, and minor in terms of its economic impacts, but it may have affected the relationship between segments of the Georgian diaspora and the Georgian government.

The Abkhaz and Ossetian diasporas (primarily residing in Russia) are very likely to oppose the Georgian government. Most of the Georgian diaspora, on the other hand, is comprised of ethnic Georgians and enjoys positive relationships with the government. Reflecting these good relations, the Georgian government established the Office of the State Minister of Diaspora in 2008 and has made substantial efforts to attract diaspora investment. For logistical reasons, this survey excluded firms in the contested regions of Abkhazia and South Ossetia, and all of the diaspora investors covered in the survey self-reported their ethnic identity as Georgian. Given these facts, existing theory suggests the 2008 war should have increased the positive relevance of social and emotional motivations for the diaspora investors captured in the survey.

This makes Georgia an apparently easy case in which to demonstrate a link between diasporans' social and emotional motivations and firm behavior. In particular, if diaspora-owned firms act with greater social responsibility than other foreign firms, Georgia is exactly the type of case in which such a difference should manifest itself. My failure to find such evidence in Georgia (see chapter 6) contradicts the general theory.

Like Georgia, the Philippines is quite typical of developing countries in terms of its level of economic and political development. Firms face a variety of political risks, but with a large domestic market and high levels of human capital, there are opportunities as well. One area in which the Philippines clearly stands out from other developing countries is in the size of its diaspora—the Philippines diaspora is one of the largest in the world. This is a useful characteristic in the context of this study because it means that the potential pool of diaspora owners and managers is large and thus, all else equal, we would expect the share of foreign firms that are diaspora affiliated to be larger in the Philippines than in other developing countries.

The Philippines is a democratically governed country—according to the Varieties of Democracy project it comes closer to the ideal of liberal democracy than the average developing country—but it has been plagued by severe political instability. This began in the 1980s when a popular uprising toppled the Marcos regime and has persisted through to the multiple coup attempts that characterized the Aquino years. This instability was interrupted only briefly during the Ramos presidency and resumed in force with another popular uprising, leading to the extra-constitutional removal of Estrada, as well as the corruption and elections-fixing scandals of the Arroyo administration.

In addition to regime instability, the Philippines has also been plagued with persistent civil conflict. The Mindanao region of the country has been the site of ongoing conflict for centuries, dating back to when the Spanish first arrived in the Philippines in the 16th century. Although Spain was able to exercise control over the rest of the country, Mindanao was never completely conquered, and conflict in the region has persisted, even after the arrival of the Americans at the end of the 20th century and the declaration of Philippine independence in 1946. The conflict is, in part, religious, with Mindanao's Muslim regional majority at odds with the rest of the predominantly Catholic country. However, the modern-day conflict also has roots in disputes over resources and the activities of logging and mining firms.

Over the past decade, the conflict has consistently produced several hundred casualties per year. However, because the fighting has been limited in geographic scope and located far from Manila, the effect on multinational firms has been limited. Despite the persistent violence, at the time of the survey the Credendo Group, a major political risk insurer, rated war risk in the Philippines as below average for developing countries.[11] The risk of violence occurring was high, but the risk of that violence affecting foreign firms outside of Mindanao was perceived to be low.

In addition to the political risks associated with regime instability, firms face challenges associated with low levels of bureaucratic function as well. For example, the Philippines is typical of developing countries in the difficulties of enforcing contracts through the domestic courts: according to the World Bank's Ease of Doing Business indicators, the Philippines ranks in the top quartile of developing countries regarding the cost of resolving a dispute through the courts, but in the bottom quartile for speed. It is approximately average for developing countries in terms of the level of corruption and strength of the rule of law, and it boasts above-average market capitalization.

Despite its typical level of economic and political development, the Philippines is less "foreign" as a destination for Western-based multinationals than many developing countries. The common description of colonial history in the Philippines is "300 years in the convent, fifty years in Hollywood."[12] While the 300 years in the convent refers to Spanish colonial rule, the fifty years in Hollywood refers to spending the first half of the 20th century under American rule before gaining independence in 1946. Close ties to the United States continued after independence—the last US military base in the country closed only in 1992 and the Philippines remains a close US ally. English is widely spoken and serves as the primary language of business; the universities in the country are well developed and modeled on the American system. The combination of American cultural influence and English makes the Philippines a relatively easy developing country for foreign investors to navigate, even if they are not diaspora affiliated.

I theorize that diaspora-affiliated firms are, in several ways, "less foreign" than other foreign firms. To the extent that the liability of foreignness is less severe in the Philippines than in other developing countries, this should reduce the degree of difference between diaspora-affiliated and nondiaspora-affiliated foreign firms. This makes the Philippines a relatively difficult case in which to observe the differences predicted by my theory of diasporans as transnational brokers. Thus the evidence I present in chapters 4, 5, and 6, which is consistent with my theory, is slightly more compelling than it would be if it came from a country in which the expected value of diaspora connections was higher.

The Value of Within-Country Comparison

While having data from only two cases is a limitation in terms of external validity (it would be ideal to have data from all developing countries), one offsetting benefit of this approach is the ability to conduct within-country comparisons between firms in each country. In contrast to a design that pools firms operating in many different developing countries into a single analysis, within-country analysis allows me to hold constant all the observable and unobservable factors that may vary across host countries.[13] Isolating the effects of the elements of firm type that are of interest (i.e., social networks and diaspora affiliation) still requires controlling for other firm characteristics such as firm size and sector, but the domain of possible omitted variables is restricted.

All or almost all developing countries are characterized by poorly functioning formal political institutions, and in all or almost all of these cases, social ties can be more useful in interacting with government officials. However, the type and severity of institutional shortcomings and the most effective means for using social ties to navigate around those shortcomings vary significantly across countries. It is therefore difficult to compare the use of social ties by a firm in one country to the use by a different firm in another country. If those two firms use networks differently, it may be because the firms are different, but it is just as likely because the political and social contexts are different. By comparing firms within a single country, I can hold the political and social environment constant and more easily isolate the effects of firm-level characteristics.

3.3. Survey Design

The overall structure of the surveys in Georgia and the Philippines is similar, but there are two key differences between the studies. First, differences in political culture and context between the two countries lead to differences in both sampling strategy and the type of sensitive questions it was possible to ask. Second, because the survey in the Philippines was conducted in 2014, five years after the survey in Georgia, I was able to expand the scope of the questions in the Philippines specifically to test aspects of my theory that were left untested in the Georgia case.

In Georgia, it was relatively easy to convince respondents to schedule a meeting with my team, which generated a high response rate (46%). Armed with a list of all the foreign firms registered to do business in the country and an enumerator team willing to travel across the country, I was able to survey a random sample of all recently registered firms operating in Georgia. This allows me to infer, with some minor caveats, that the firms in my sample are representative of the full population of foreign firms in Georgia.[14]

Unfortunately, while I was able to execute a random sampling strategy in Georgia, I was quite limited in what my enumerators could talk about. In particular, in the wake of the 2003 "Rose Revolution" and a related government crackdown on corruption, Georgian respondents were very sensitive to being asked questions in any way related to corruption. Thus I am unable to use data from Georgia to test hypotheses related to how firms resolve disputes, enforce contracts, interact with government officials, and influence policy.

In the Philippines, I found the reverse: getting firms to agree to interviews was extremely difficult, but fewer topics were off-limits. The response rate was so low when attempting to interview firms from a randomized sampling list that we had to abandon random sampling altogether in the Philippines. Instead we reverted to a snowball sampling strategy in which we first surveyed firms to which our team members had some form of pre-existing connection, and then we asked each respondent to provide referrals to additional firms that we might be able survey (e.g., Goodman 1961). While we were careful not to guide respondents to refer us to firms on the basis of diaspora affiliation or other characteristics that might confound future hypothesis tests, the nonrandom nature of the sample places limitations on the inferences that are possible (e.g., Erickson 1979). In appendix A, I discuss the Philippines sample in detail. There are some dimensions on which my nonrandom sample differs from what we would expect of a random sample, and thus some humility is necessary with respect to the scope of inference that is possible. Fortunately, there is no theoretical reason to expect these differences in the sample would produce the differences between diaspora-affiliated and nondiaspora-affiliated firms that I observe.

In contrast to the difficulty of securing interviews, once an enumerator was in the room in the Philippines, there were comparatively few limits on what she could ask. This freedom to discuss sensitive topics is likely driven primarily by political culture—corruption and the use of social ties in business and politics are simply less taboo topics in the Philippines.[15] For example, other survey work has shown that politicians in the Philippines are quite candid when it comes to seemingly sensitive topics, going so far as to complain about how expensive it has become to buy votes and rig elections.[16] In appendix A3.3 I describe the results of a modified list experiment in which we evaluate the sensitivity of questions related to firms' use of social ties to improve relationships with government officials.[17] We find that underreporting of these behaviors in the Philippines is low. Thus data from the Philippines allows for tests related to firms' specific uses of social ties, including their use of ties to manage relationships with government officials and influence policy. For full details on sampling, survey design, multiple imputation of missing values, and other issues related to research design, see appendix A.

3.4. Limitations of the Data

The data used in this book are cross-sectional. I survey each firm one time, and I compare the characteristics and behavior of diaspora-affiliated and nondiaspora-affiliated firms. In the following chapters I show that diaspora-affiliated firms are more connected and use social ties in business more than diaspora-affiliated firms. I interpret this as evidence consistent with my theory that diasporans provide valuable capabilities to the firms they own and manage. However, there are two other possible explanations for the findings I report. First, it is possible that my results are driven by selection effects or omitted variable bias—in other words, it is possible that diaspora-affiliated firms are systematically unlike nondiaspora-affiliated firms in a manner that affects both firms' social ties and their business strategy. Second, it is possible that my results are driven by reverse causality—in other words, it is possible that firms that use social ties in business are more likely to become diaspora affiliated, instead of the other way around.

To reduce the risk that my results are driven by selection effects or omitted variable bias, in the analysis I control for the characteristics of firms that are most likely to affect both diaspora affiliation and firms' social connectedness and business strategy. I control for firm size and age, for sector, and for the region in which the firm is based. I also control for whether the firm is 100% foreign-owned, majority foreign-owned, or minority foreign-owned, whether it is publicly traded, and whether it is located in a special enterprise zone. Thus while I cannot be absolutely certain that I have controlled for all possible omitted variables, I have controlled for those factors that are most likely to introduce bias, and my results still hold.

It is also possible that firms that need social ties to conduct their business are more likely to hire diaspora managers (or partner with diaspora co-owners). If this is the case, then firm strategy could lead to diaspora affiliation instead of the other way around. Fortunately, the risk posed by this particular source of reverse causation has limited implications for the interpretation of my results because the firms would only adopt this type of strategy if they believed my theory to be broadly correct. Becoming diaspora affiliated is only a reasonable response to the need for social ties in business if firms believe that diaspora affiliation provides them with valuable social-tie-based capabilities. In chapter 7, I suggest that firms should engage in exactly this type of behavior. My theory implies that many multinational firms could benefit from recruiting diaspora managers and co-owners to augment the firm's transnational brokerage capabilities, enhancing their ability to operate profitably in countries with low levels of institutional development.

The data collected for this book create, for the first time, the ability to directly compare diaspora-affiliated and nondiaspora-affiliated firms. However, the analysis in this book raises important new questions and considerably more data will be necessary to answer these new questions convincingly. One of the research questions that the data in this book cannot speak to is how firms become diaspora affiliated in the first place. At the individual level, it would be useful to know what types of diasporans are most likely to found firms that invest back in the homeland, and what types of diasporans are most likely to become managers of multinational firms. Answering these questions requires individual-level data on diasporans, including diasporans who do not own or work for multinational firms. Some data exists regarding diaspora entrepreneurship (e.g., Black and Castaldo 2009; Wahba and Zenou 2012), but there is less work on diaspora managers.

Also of interest is the question of when and why existing firms choose to become diaspora affiliated, and how diaspora owners or managers change the behavior of the firms they join. In addition to its effects on firm strategy, does the migration background of a firm's owners and managers shape where the firm invests? Prior work has shown that nationality diversity in a firm's top management team affects foreign entry strategies (e.g., Nielsen and Nielsen 2011), but better data is needed to get a clear picture of the effects of diaspora owners and managers on firm location choices, entry mode, and other aspects of firm strategy. The ideal data for these questions would be panel data on foreign firms that measures changes over time in diaspora affiliation, capabilities, strategy, profitability, and political influence.

Lastly, the strongest findings in the empirical chapters that follow show that diaspora-affiliated firms are better able than other firms to use social ties to manage government relations, and that they are more likely than other firms to attempt to influence government policy and succeed in doing so. These are exciting results, suggesting that diasporans don't just help firms navigate the political environment in the homeland, they help firms shape that environment. This raises urgent new questions about exactly what types of policy objectives diaspora-affiliated firms seek. Information on firms' political objectives and strategies is inherently sensitive, and thus challenging to collect. It is the sensitivity of this information that prevented me from asking more detailed questions in the surveys used in this book. However, some of the most interesting development implications of diaspora investment relate to the impact of these firms on the political development of the homeland, and those impacts are likely affected by the nature of their policy objectives. I hope that the theory and results presented here motivate new efforts to collect the data necessary to continue advancing our empirical knowledge in these areas.

3.5. How Results Are Presented

This book tries to balance methodological rigor with accessibility. To this end, each of the four empirical chapters (chapters 3–6) is paired with a technical appendix (appendixes A–D). The main text presents the results of hypothesis tests graphically and describes the analysis in terms accessible to a relatively nontechnical reader. The matching technical appendix for each chapter provides additional details on estimation techniques and robustness tests and provides full regression tables detailing the results. All sections of the appendix are numbered to correspond to the sections in the body of the book. For example, technical details related to the analysis in section 5.2 in the main text are provided in section 5.2 of appendix C.

3.6. Summary of the Empirical Strategy

Chapter 2 lays out my core theory and an alternative theory drawn from the literature. The key empirical task of the book is to determine whether each of these theories is borne out by the data. Are diaspora-affiliated firms actually better connected, do they use these connections more in business than other foreign firms, and does that generate political influence and other positive outcomes? At the same time, are diaspora-affiliated firms more socially responsible and do they contribute more to homeland development than their nondiaspora-affiliated peers?

To date, scholars have been unable to answer these questions because of a lack of firm-level data. If we want to understand the role of diasporans in shaping global capital flows and the behavior of multinational firms, we need data on the firms diasporans own and manage, and we need to be able to compare those firms directly to other foreign firms—namely to otherwise similar firms that are not owned or managed by diasporans.

The theory testing in this book is done at the firm level, using two new firm-level datasets collected specifically for this project—one from the Philippines and one from the country of Georgia. These datasets allow me to test a wide range of implications—I conduct 31 different tests related to transnational brokerage. This wide array of tests draws on data from two countries and employs multiple measures of key variables. This allows me to make the case that, while any individual test may be flawed, the consistency of the results across such a large and diverse collection of tests is extremely difficult to explain unless the underlying theory is broadly correct.

By identifying the capabilities and strategies of diaspora-affiliated firms, I gain policy insight as well as theoretical insight. The two theories I test each have distinct implications for the role of diaspora-induced FDI in homeland development and the role of diasporans in creating value for the firms they own and manage. Thus the same empirical strategy that allows for effective hypothesis testing also provides grist for data-driven policy and firm strategy. Chapter 7 draws out these implications for multinational firms and for governments in both wealthy and developing countries.

CHAPTER 4

Measuring Firms' Social Connectedness

My central theoretical claim is that diasporans provide value to the firms they own and manage by serving as transnational brokers, connecting foreign firms to business counterparts and government officials in the homeland. I contrast this claim with the predictions of an alternative theory drawn from the literature, which is based on diasporans' social and emotional motivations for homeland investment. However, my primary focus is on testing hypotheses derived from my own theory. This chapter tests several of these hypotheses at the firm level.

My theory has three central testable implications, each of which contrasts diaspora-affiliated firms with nondiaspora-affiliated foreign firms. I predict that diaspora-affiliated firms have more and stronger ties to business counterparts and political actors in the investment host country (i.e., the homeland); that diaspora-affiliated firms use social ties more frequently and in different ways; and that these social ties provide value to diaspora-affiliated firms. This chapter tests two of these implications. First, I evaluate the social connectedness of multinational firms in the Philippines to test whether diaspora-affiliated firms are indeed more socially connected than their nondiaspora-affiliated peers. Second, using data from both Georgia and the Philippines, I assess whether social ties are more important to the profitability of diaspora-affiliated firms than other foreign firms. In chapter 5 I test the third claim, assessing in detail a wide variety of specific uses of social ties, evaluating in each case whether diaspora-affiliated firms are more likely than other foreign firms to use social ties in that way.

There are several reasonable ways to conceptualize and measure the social connectedness of firms. One can assess the number of ties firms have to actors of various types, the strength of those ties, and firms' resulting positions within social networks. Therefore, rather than a single measure of social connectedness and a single hypothesis test, this chapter compares diaspora-affiliated and nondiaspora-affiliated foreign firms across a wide range of measures.

This use of multiple measures of a single core concept reflects the guiding empirical philosophy of the book. From a single theory, I derive a large number of distinct testable implications, setting up empirical tests across two different sources of data. Each test exposes a portion of the theory to falsification. If I consistently fail to falsify components of the theory, and as the number and diversity of tests conducted accumulate, I gain confidence that the overall theory is correct. It is rarely appropriate to have a great deal of confidence in the result of a single hypothesis test. Confidence is born of consistent results achieved across multiple diverse tests.

This chapter begins with a brief discussion of the data, including measurement of the key independent variable, which is *diaspora affiliated* (sec. 4.1). The first hypothesis tests assess ties between firms and four different types of actors: peer firms in the same sector; elected officials in local government; elected officials in national government; and bureaucratic officials (sec. 4.2). I assess the frequency of interaction between firms and each of these four types of actors, which provides an objective measure of tie strength, and also ask respondents to assess the strength of their ties to each type of actor on a 7-point Likert scale, generating a subjective measure of tie strength. In section 4.3, I assess what I refer to as direct political ties. These ties exist when current or former government officials own, manage, or serve on the board of directors of a firm. In section 4.4 I assess the importance of social ties to firm performance, and in section 4.5 I summarize and discuss the implications of my results. Additional technical details on the empirical analysis, including robustness tests and full regression tables that correspond to each of the figures in this chapter, are provided in appendix B.

To preview the findings of this chapter, I find strong evidence, across a range of measures, that diaspora-affiliated firms are more socially connected than other foreign firms and that they view social ties as more important for profitability. These results confirm key elements of my theory of diasporans as transnational brokers. Diasporans are able to parlay their individual-level social ties into valuable firm-level connections between the firms they own and manage and those firms' business and political counterparts in the homeland.

4.1. Data and Measurement

This chapter draws primarily on data from the Philippines, which provides the richest insight into the number and strength of firms' ties to business counterparts and political actors in the investment host country. As noted in chapter 3, the data in Georgia are more limited in this area because, in the post-Soviet context, asking firms about their social ties to politicians or even to other firms was quite sensitive, and many questions were struck from the survey during the pilot. In the Philippines, the same questions that had made respondents nervous in Georgia could be asked with little difficulty. Thus all assessments of the strength and number of firms' social connections are based on data from the Philippines. Measures of the importance of social ties to firm profitability are drawn from both surveys.

Measuring Diaspora Affiliation

To identify diaspora-affiliated firms, we rely on the responses of firm managers.[1] We first provide respondents with a definition of diaspora and then ask whether the firms' owners or managers fit this definition. In Georgia, we provide the following definition of diaspora:

> The Georgian diaspora includes all individuals who live outside of Georgia but who consider themselves to be Georgian. It includes people who were born in Georgia and emigrated to other countries. It also includes people who were born in other countries, but whose ancestors are from Georgia.

In the Philippines, there is a word in Tagalog, *balikbayan*, that translates roughly as "overseas Filipino." I use this term in the Philippines survey. However, as in the Georgian survey, the enumerators provided respondents with a direct definition: "We define balikbayan as any Filipino who has lived, worked, or studied overseas in the past."[2] Thus the survey definition of diasporans includes those whose emigration is temporary, including inpatriate managers and those educated at foreign universities. In both surveys, we ask respondents about both diasporans who are currently living abroad and those who have returned to live in the homeland (balikbayan).

As noted in the introduction, both of these empirical definitions are broader than the theoretical definition of diaspora. Both focus on whether an individual is living or has lived outside her homeland, not on whether or not she retains ties to the homeland. In the context of identifying diaspora-affiliated firms, this divergence may be of little practical significance. If an individual is serving as the owner or manager of a firm that operates in the homeland, it is hard to argue that the individual does not have at least some ties to the homeland. To the extent, however, that our survey identifies individuals as diasporans (and firms as diaspora affiliated) when their ties to the homeland are weak, this makes it less likely that I will observe the predicted differences between diaspora-affiliated and nondiaspora-affiliated foreign firms.[3] Individuals with weak or nonexistent ties to the homeland are unlikely to be able to serve as effective transnational brokers, and thus I expect the firms they own and manage to behave more like nondiaspora-affiliated foreign firms than diaspora-affiliated ones. In this chapter and in chapters 5 and 6, I find large differences between diaspora-affiliated firms and other foreign firms, even when applying this inclusive definition. If I was able to narrow the empirical definition of diaspora to capture only those individuals with strong ties to the homeland, I expect that the observed differences between diaspora-affiliated and nondiaspora-affiliated foreign firms would be even larger.

Diaspora Owned vs. Diaspora Affiliated

The central comparison in this book is between foreign firms that are diaspora affiliated and those that are not. Thus my independent variable of interest is a binary measure of diaspora affiliation. I operationalize this two different ways, based on data availability. In the Philippines data, where I have information on both diaspora management and diaspora ownership, I use the variable *diaspora affiliated*, which takes a value of one if at least one of the firm's owners or managers is a diasporan and zero otherwise. In the Georgia data, I only have information on diaspora ownership, not on diaspora management. Therefore when using the Georgia data I use the variable *diaspora owned*, which takes a value of one if at least one of the firm's owners is a diasporan and zero otherwise. To enhance comparability with the Georgia results, when using the Philippines data, I present the effects of *diaspora owned* alongside the effects of *diaspora affiliated*.

For both theoretical and pragmatic reasons, I do not investigate the independent effects of diaspora management in detail. Theoretically, investigation of the difference between diaspora-owned and diaspora-managed

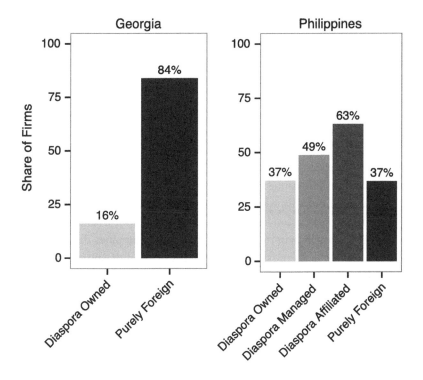

Fig. 4.1. *The Prevalence of Diaspora Affiliation*
Note: This figure is based on 154 randomly sampled foreign firms in Georgia
and 223 nonrandomly sampled foreign firms in the Philippines.

firms is distinct from, and thus a diversion away from, the questions of interest in this study, which relate to differences between foreign firms that are and are not diaspora affiliated. Pragmatically, diaspora ownership and diaspora management are highly collinear—almost two-thirds of diaspora-owned firms are also diaspora managed. Thus given the limited sample size in this survey data, it is not possible to estimate the independent effects of diaspora ownership and diaspora management with much precision. Thus while the following analysis does shed some light on the areas where diaspora management is likely most important, a detailed analysis of the relative merits of diaspora ownership and diaspora management falls outside the scope of this project.

Figure 4.1 displays the proportion of firms in the Georgia and Philippines samples that are diaspora owned, diaspora managed, and diaspora affiliated. In Georgia, 16% of the firms in the sample are foreign owned.

Given that the Georgia sample is a random sample of all foreign firms in the country, this 16% is a good estimate of the share of foreign firms in the country that are diaspora owned. Diaspora-owned firms are responsible for a substantial share of FDI into Georgia.

In the Philippines, more than one-third of firms are diaspora owned and almost two-thirds of firms are diaspora affiliated, which gives me (relatively) large numbers of both diaspora-affiliated and nondiaspora-affiliated foreign firms. This gives me considerable statistical power when comparing diaspora-affiliated and nondiaspora-affiliated foreign firms—statistical power that I am sometimes lacking in the Georgia sample, which is smaller to begin with and within which diaspora-owned firms are a distinct minority. One likely explanation for why the share of diaspora-owned firms in the Philippines is larger than in Georgia is that the Philippines diaspora is unusually large. Thus there is a larger pool of potential diaspora owners and managers to begin with.[4]

4.2. Strength of Ties

This section tests my prediction that, compared to other foreign firms, diaspora-affiliated firms have stronger social ties to actors in the homeland. I test this proposition across four different types of actor in the homeland and two different measures of tie strength.

When assessing the social connectedness of a firm, the most obvious starting point is with ties to peer firms. Most of the uses of social ties I theorize rely, either solely or in part, on ties between firms. This is true with regard to trust, contract enforcement, and access to information. Trust between business counterparts is fundamentally about social ties between firms. Stronger ties facilitate greater trust and more efficient transactions. Social enforcement of contracts is similar. If a firm violates a contract with one firm, that firm will ask all of its peers to refuse to do business with the violator. If the harmed firm's ties to its peers are strong and numerous, its peers will agree to withhold their business and the violator will be shut out of the market until it makes amends. If the harmed firm's ties are weak, its peers will not agree to withhold their business and collective enforcement will have no bite. Ties between firms have a role in information gathering as well—peers are not the only actors from whom firms seek information, but when it comes to market information in particular, they are a critical source.

Direct ties between firms and government officials are also critical. Developing countries are characterized by unstable policy environments and high levels of political risk. I expect that strong ties to government officials offer firms access to valuable private information about future policy decisions, thus allowing them to anticipate changes and move quickly to avoid risks and seize new opportunities. Perhaps more importantly, strong ties to government officials can provide a channel for firms to influence policy directly and shape the political environment in which they operate.

Lastly, I examine firms' ties to bureaucrats. It is the inefficiency and corruption of the bureaucracy that is central to many of the high costs of doing business in developing countries. In the World Bank's Ease of Doing Business indicators, the bureaucracy is the central player. Bureaucrats determine the speed and cost at which firms can achieve everything from registering a business to securing permits, importing and exporting goods, and paying taxes. However, the variation in these costs and delays across countries in the World Bank data tends to mask another important type of variation, namely variation across firms within each country. In any given country, not all firms pay the same fees or face the same delays. I expect that strong social ties with bureaucrats allow some firms to achieve a much greater "ease of doing business" than their peers, providing a large and sustained source of competitive advantage, particularly in the most poorly governed developing countries.

Two Measures of Tie Strength

I assess the social connectedness of firms by looking at both the number of actors they are connected to and how strong those connections are. I employ two distinct measures of tie strength, one that is narrow but objective, the other that is holistic but subjective. Thus the virtues of one measure balance out the shortcomings of the other. If my theoretical expectations are borne out across both measures, I gain greater confidence that the underlying theory is correct.

One narrow but objective way to assess the strength of a social tie between two parties is to measure the frequency with which those parties interact (e.g., Hammer 1984; Marsden and Campbell 1984; Marsden 1990). The intuition here is simple: we tend to have stronger relationships with people we interact with more often. Conversely, a holistic but subjective measure can be achieved by asking respondents directly to assess the strength of their ties to each group. Specifically, enumerators asked respondents, "How would you characterize the relationship your firm has with [type of actor], using the same scale of 1 being a very weak relationship and 7 a very strong relationship." This measure has the benefit of capturing multiple elements of tie strength—not just frequency of interaction but also level of trust, warmth, and so on. It captures the elements of strength most salient to the respondent.

The weakness of this holistic measure of tie strength is that it is subjective—what one respondent means by strength of tie may not be exactly what another respondent means. Fortunately, the objective nature of the frequency measure offsets the subjectivity of the holistic measure. While it is possible (though I believe unlikely) that respondents at diaspora-affiliated firms systematically differ from respondents at other foreign firms in the way they understand the concept of tie strength, it is much less likely that their understanding of terms related to frequency, like "once a month," varies in the same way. In contrast, the weakness of the tie strength measure is that it is overly narrow—it doesn't capture whether interactions are positive or negative, only how often then occur. Fortunately, while negative interactions might increase the frequency with which a firm reports interacting with someone, such negative interactions should **decrease** the subjective strength of the tie they report. Thus if I find that diaspora-affiliated firms score higher across both of these diverse measures of tie strength, I can be confident that this result is driven by a true relationship between diaspora affiliation and social connectedness, and not by any peculiarities in my measures.

Testing the Frequency Hypothesis

H4.1. The Frequency Hypothesis: *Compared to other foreign firms, diaspora-affiliated firms have more frequent interaction with:*
  A. *Local government officials*
  B. *National government officials*
  C. *Bureaucratic officials*
  D. *Other firms in their sector*

Testing the four components of the frequency hypothesis requires four distinct dependent variables, one for each type of actor. These are ordinal dependent variables with five possible values for frequency of interaction, ranging from "no relationship" to "weekly or more." For each type of actor, I expect that diaspora-affiliated firms report more frequent interaction than do other foreign firms. In the regression analysis, I use *diaspora affiliated* to predict frequency of interaction. A positive coefficient on *diaspora affiliated* indicates that, consistent with expectations, diaspora-affiliated firms interact more frequently with the group in question than do other foreign firms. I also present results from regressions in which *diaspora owned* is used in place of *diaspora affiliated*, rendering the results more directly comparable to those using the Georgia data.

I test the four frequency of interaction hypotheses using ordered logistic regressions.[5] In each regression, I control for the sector of the firm, the region of the firm's headquarters, firm size (in terms of revenues), the number of employees, the share of foreign ownership, whether the firm is publicly traded, and whether the firm operates inside a special economic zone (SEZ) in the Philippines. Collectively, these control variables help ensure that, when I compare diaspora-affiliated firms to nondiaspora-affiliated foreign firms, I am making an apples-to-apples comparison.

For example, it is possible that diaspora-affiliated firms are concentrated in certain sectors. If these sectors are ones in which social ties are particularly important, then I might find that, on average, diaspora-affiliated firms have stronger social ties than other foreign firms, even if there is no underlying causal relationship between diaspora affiliation and strength of social ties. The risk of this type of spurious relationship is called omitted variable bias. By controlling for a wide range of potential confounding variables, including a set of binary variables for different sectors, I reduce the risk that this type of bias accounts for my results. Details of the estimation procedure and full regression tables of the main results and robustness tests are provided in appendix B4.2.

Figure 4.2 presents estimates of the effect of diaspora affiliation on the strength of firms' social ties. The main hypothesis tests refer to the estimated effects of *diaspora affiliated*, which are given by the solid lines. The dot in the middle of the line gives the coefficient estimate from the regression—the estimated magnitude of the effect—while the line represents the 95% confidence interval. A coefficient greater than zero reflects a positive estimated relationship with tie strength, while a negative coefficient represents a negative relationship. This figure presents only the estimated effect of the variables of interest. For the effects of control variables, see the tables of regression results in appendix B4.2.

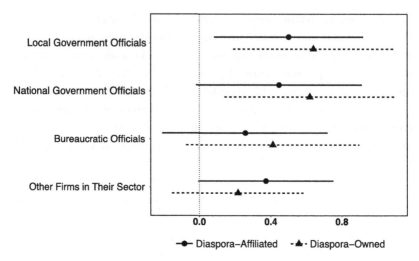

Fig. 4.2. *Frequency of Interaction with Elected Officials, Bureaucrats, and Peer Firms*
Note: Ordered logistic regressions with heteroscedasticity-robust standard errors. $N = 223$.

The simplest interpretation of confidence intervals is that, if the confidence interval is entirely to the right of zero, then I have estimated a statistically significant positive relationship. In these cases, I am able to reject the null hypothesis of no relationship and I have found support for my hypothesis of a positive relationship between diaspora affiliation and tie strength. To be more precise, if I were to replicate the study a large number of times, the confidence interval would contain the true (i.e., population) value of that coefficient 95% of the time.[6] But the general intuition is that when the confidence interval does not cross the zero line, I have reasonable confidence that the effect I have estimated is not driven by statistical noise.

Looking at the effects of diaspora affiliation in figure 4.2, the estimated effects are positive across all four types of actors, but the effect is only statistically significant ($p < 0.05$) with regard to ties to local governments. The effects on frequency of interaction with national government officials ($p = 0.062$) and other firms in this sector ($p = 0.056$) fall just short of this cutoff. Taken together these four hypothesis tests, while not conclusive, are consistent with my theory and lend support to the expectation that diaspora-affiliated firms have stronger social ties across a wide range of actors in the homeland.

The estimated effects of *diaspora owned* are very similar to those for *diaspora affiliated*. For *diaspora owned*, two of the results are statistically significant and two are not. Before moving too far into interpretation of these results, I will present the results from the other, Holistic and subjective, measure of tie strength.

Testing the Subjective Strength Hypothesis

> **H4.2. The Subjective Strength Hypothesis:** *Compared to other foreign firms, diaspora-affiliated firms have stronger ties to:*
> A. *Local government officials*
> B. *National government officials*
> C. *Bureaucratic officials*
> D. *Other firms in their sector*

As with the tests of the frequency hypothesis, there are four dependent variables associated with the strength hypothesis, one for each type of actor. These are ordinal variables with seven values ranging from "no relationship" to "extremely strong relationship." Figure 4.3 is similar in design to figure 4.2 and the control variables included in the regressions remain the same.

The results for the strength hypothesis line up closely with the tests of the frequency hypothesis, but are even stronger. Across all four types of actor, I estimate a positive relationship between *diaspora affiliated* and subjective tie strength. These results are statistically significant for all three types of political actor, namely local-level elected officials, national-level elected officials, and bureaucrats. The effect on ties to peer firms is not quite statistically significant ($p = 0.10$). These results complement the frequency results nicely, showing that the relationship between diaspora affiliation and social connectedness is not driven by some peculiarity of measurement. This is a relationship that holds across different measures of tie strength and across different types of actors. As predicted, diaspora-affiliated firms report stronger social ties to government officials and peer firms than do other foreign firms.

As with the frequency results, the effects of diaspora ownership are similar to the effects of diaspora affiliation with regard to all three types of political ties. Notably, however, the estimated effect of diaspora ownership on the strength of ties to peer firms is near zero. This suggests that, while diaspora ownership and management are likely both important in providing ties to government officials, managers' ties are probably more important when it comes to connecting firms to their peers.

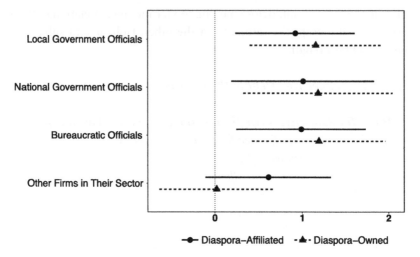

Fig. 4.3. *Diaspora Affiliation and the Subjective Strength of Ties to National Officials, Local Officials, Bureaucrats, and Peer Firms*
Note: Linear regressions with heteroscedasticity-robust standard errors.

Empirical Takeaway: Diaspora-affiliated firms report stronger social ties to both government officials and peer firms than do nondiaspora-affiliated foreign firms.

4.3. Direct Political Ties

The measures of political connectedness in the previous section are fundamentally about the strength and intimacy of relationships between firm personnel and government officials. However, a firm's political connectedness may be grounded in who firm personnel are, rather than simply whom they know. Some firms are owned by political elites or employ political elites directly as managers or members of the board of directors. I refer to this phenomenon—political elites who are also leaders of firms—as direct political ties between firms and the government.

The existing literature provides findings from several different contexts demonstrating that firms with direct ties outperform unconnected firms with regard to their ability to secure favors from the government, such as government loans at favorable interest rates. There is also evidence that firms with direct ties are more profitable. To pull two examples from this literature, Mian and Khwaja (2005) use data on Pakistani firms to show that firms with politicians on the board of directors enjoy preferential access to government banks—connected firms borrow 45% more and default 50% more often. Faccio, Masulis, and McConnell (2006) find that politically connected firms are more likely to receive government bailouts when they are in financial distress.[7] What is of particular interest to me is whether diaspora-affiliated firms are more likely to have this sort of direct tie than nondiaspora-affiliated firms.

Measuring Direct Political Ties

The Philippines data include separate measures of the positions held by a firm's owners or managers, and positions held by members of the board of directors. I examine positions held at all levels of government from the *Barangay*, or district/ward level, up through national level positions including congress members, senators, and cabinet members. Figure 4.4 depicts the different types of direct ties observed. The most common direct ties that firms have are direct ties to bureaucrats; ties to national-level elected officials are next most common. Few firms report ties to provincial or local-level officials, which likely reflects the fact that political power in the Philippines is relatively centralized, with most decision-making power residing with the national government.

Figure 4.4 shows that diaspora-affiliated firms are much more likely than other foreign firms to possess direct ties to government officials. Fully testing the direct ties hypothesis requires regression analysis with appropriate control variables in place. However, as shown in the following section, the results from the regression analysis match these simple descriptive statistics closely—diaspora-affiliated firms have more direct ties, even when other factors are controlled for.

Testing the Direct Political Ties Hypothesis

The Philippines data capture direct political ties at a high degree of disaggregation—looking at 14 distinct types of tie, some of which are rare.[8] The theory I wish to test, however, is quite straightforward: I predict that diaspora-affiliated firms have more direct political ties than nondiaspora-affiliated firms, and I expect this to be true across all types of direct political

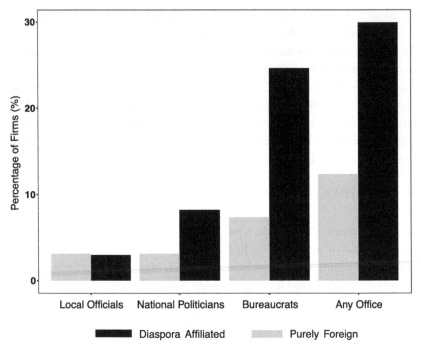

Fig. 4.4. *Frequency of Direct Political Ties*

ties. Thus the central test of my hypothesis comes from using diaspora affiliation to predict whether a given firm reports any direct political ties at
all. I then test for the same differences between diaspora-affiliated firms
across two subcategories of tie: national-level officials and bureaucrats. I
don't test a hypothesis specific to direct ties to local officials because these
ties are too rare to allow the appropriate regression models to converge (see
fig. 4.4).

> **H4.3. The Direct Ties Hypothesis:** *Compared to other foreign firms,*
> *diaspora-affiliated firms have more owners, managers, and board*
> *members serving as:*
>   A. *Government officials (any level)*
>   B. *National-level officials (congress, senate, and cabinet)*
>   C. *Bureaucratic officials*

The regressions used to test the direct ties hypothesis contain all the
same control variables used in the tests of H4.1 and H4.2. The only differ-

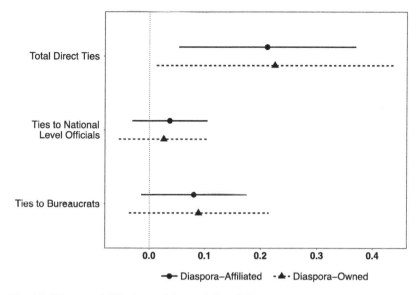

Fig. 4.5. *Diaspora Affiliation and Direct Political Ties*

ence in these models is that the dependent variable is binary instead of ordinal, and thus I use logistic regression instead of ordered logistic. Figure
4.5 displays the estimated effects of diaspora affiliation on each type of direct political tie. A full regression table is available in appendix B4.3.

Consistent with my theory, I estimate that diaspora-affiliated firms are
more likely than other foreign firms to report direct ties to national-level
government officials and to bureaucrats. However, this difference is only
statistically significant when I pool all types of ties together. Thus while the
observed differences match my theory across individual categories of ties,
the conclusion I can state with confidence is a general one: diaspora-
affiliated firms report more direct ties than do nondiaspora-affiliated foreign firms. The estimated effects of diaspora ownership are almost identical
to those for diaspora affiliation.

Empirical Takeaway: Diaspora-affiliated firms report more direct
ties to government officials than do nondiaspora-affiliated foreign
firms.

4.4. Importance to Firm Performance

Having established that diaspora-affiliated firms are more socially connected than other foreign firms, I move to ask whether those social ties are relevant to firm performance. Chapter 5 contains an array of tests looking at specific ways in which firms use social ties—the tests in this section are more holistic. Here I test the simple proposition that social ties are more important to the performance of diaspora-affiliated firms. While there are many different avenues through which social ties may affect firm performance, these holistic assessments capture the combined effect of all these mechanisms to provide an overall sense of importance.

> **H4.4. *The Importance Hypothesis:*** *Compared to other foreign firms, respondents at diaspora-affiliated firms view social ties as more important to firm performance. This should hold for:*
> A. *Owners' and managers' family ties*
> B. *Owners' and managers' friendship ties*
> C. *Owners' and managers' friendship and family ties combined*

I assess friendship ties separately from family ties because friendship ties alone offer a more challenging test of the theory. It is unlikely that nondiaspora owners or managers have family ties in the homeland, so the only family ties on which most nondiaspora-affiliated firms can draw are the family ties of their local managers. Thus it may be somewhat unsurprising that diaspora-affiliated firms are more likely to view these ties as important. However, it is much more likely that nondiaspora owners and managers have friends in the homeland. If I find that diaspora-owned firms (Georgia) and diaspora-affiliated firms (Philippines) assess social ties as being more germane to their business activities and profitability than do other foreign firms, this provides direct support for the core of my theory: diasporans exploit their unique social ties to provide value to the firms they own and manage.

The Georgia and Philippines surveys contain questions about the subjective importance of social ties that are similar but not identical. In the Philippines, respondents are asked how important social ties are to "your firm's business activities," while in Georgia the question is asked with regard to "increasing the profitability of your firm." In both cases possible responses ranged on a 7-point Likert scale from "not important at all" to "extremely important." In each dataset I also create a combined index measure of family and friendship importance to assess the overall importance of social ties.[9]

Figure 4.6 shows the relationship between diaspora ownership and the importance of social ties in the Georgia data, and the relationship between diaspora affiliation and social ties in the Philippines data. The regressions using the Philippines data contain the same control variables used in previous regressions, while the set of control variables used in the Georgia data is slightly different. In the Georgia analysis, I control for the number of employees; firm age; the share of foreign ownership; and whether the firm is located in the capital, Tbilisi, as well as vectors of dummy variables for sector and region.[10]

In both Georgia and the Philippines, we see that diaspora-affiliated firms consider social ties to be more important to their overall profitability than do other foreign firms. In the Georgia data the results are strong and statistically significant across all three dependent variables—friendship ties, family ties, and the two combined. Diaspora-owned firms deem their social ties to be more important for profitability than do other foreign firms. In the Philippines data we see similar results, but they are not as strong. The estimated effect of diaspora affiliation on the importance of ties is positive in all three tests, but not statistically significant. In the case of both ties to friends and combined ties, the estimated effects are just shy of statistical significance ($p = .068$ and $.0505$, respectively). The estimated effect of diaspora ownership in the Philippines is considerably weaker than the estimated effect of diaspora affiliation, suggesting that, in the Philippines, diaspora-managed firms are more likely than diaspora-owned firms to view their social ties as valuable. For full regression tables of these results, see appendix B4.4.

These results offer us the first opportunity to compare results from the Philippines and Georgia side-by-side, assessing firms' responses to two very similar questions. Recall that in Georgia, as in most developing countries, I expect that diasporans are able to provide a great deal of value via transnational brokerage because the liability of outsidership (i.e., the costs of being outside the right social networks) is high. In the Philippines, with business conducted in English and a fairly Westernized business culture, I expect this liability of outsidership to be somewhat lower, and hence the returns to effective transnational brokerage to be somewhat lower as well. Thus I expect to find support for my hypotheses in both countries, but the Philip-

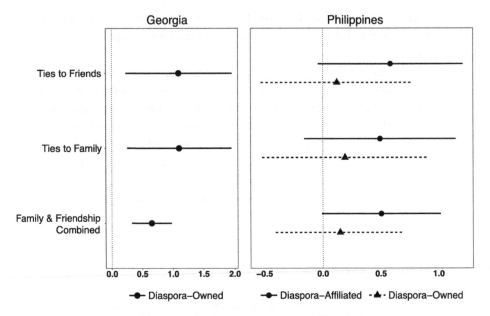

Fig. 4.6. *Diaspora Affiliation and Subjective Importance of Social Ties*

pines is the more challenging case for my theory. Consistent with this expectation, the results in the Georgia data are stronger than those in the Philippines. However, I estimate effects consistent with the importance hypothesis in both countries.

In contrast to the Philippines sample, which is nonrandom, the Georgia sample is drawn randomly, increasing my confidence that what is true of the Georgian sample is true of the entire population of foreign firms in Georgia. Thus the fact that the results from the Georgia sample are even more supportive of my theory than the results from the Philippines provides some additional evidence that sampling bias is an unlikely explanation for the Philippines results I present earlier in this chapter (and in chapter 5).

In a robustness check in tables B4.6 and B4.6a in the appendix, I control statistically for the identity of the respondent. In the Georgia data, I add a dummy for whether the respondent is an owner of the firm. In the Philippines data, I control for whether the respondent is a diasporan. In both cases, I still find that diaspora-owned and diaspora-affiliated firms report that social ties are more important for profitability. Indeed, with this additional control, the estimated effect of diaspora affiliation on combined importance becomes statistically significant in the Georgia data. These supplemental results make clear that the differences between diaspora-affiliated firms and nondiaspora-affiliated firms occur at the firm level—these results are not driven by the identity of the respondent within each firm. Social ties are more important to the profitability of diaspora-affiliated firms.

> **Empirical Takeaway:** Diaspora-affiliated firms view their owners'
> and managers' social ties as more important to firm performance
> than do nondiaspora-affiliated foreign firms.

4.5. Summary and Implications

This chapter begins the firm-level testing of my theory of diasporans as transnational brokers. I draw on two novel survey datasets from Georgia and the Philippines to compare diaspora-affiliated and nondiaspora-affiliated foreign firms in terms of the strength and nature of their social ties and the importance of those ties to firm performance. Across a wide range of tests, I find evidence that diaspora-affiliated firms are better connected than other foreign firms and benefit more from these connections. Table 4.1 summarizes these results.

Table 4.1. Summary of Results

Hypothesis	Strength of Supporting Evidence	Country	Details
Frequency of Interaction	Moderate	Philippines	Diaspora-affiliated firms report interacting more frequently with government officials and peers. All effects are in the expected direction with mixed statistical significance.
Subjective Strength of Ties	Strong	Philippines	Diaspora-affiliated firms report stronger ties to government officials and peers.
Direct Ties to Politicians	Strong	Philippines	Diaspora-affiliated firms report more direct ties to government officials.
Subjective Importance of Ties	Moderate	Georgia & Philippines	Diaspora-affiliated firms view their ties as more important in both countries, but the estimated effects in the Philippines are just shy of statistical significance.

These tests are among the first direct empirical comparisons between diaspora-affiliated and nondiaspora-affiliated foreign firms, and they provide an opportunity to test theory about how diasporans channel capital into their homelands and to begin to understand how diaspora investment differs from other types of FDI. This is a building-block chapter. It provides empirical evidence that diaspora-affiliated firms are more socially connected than other foreign firms and establishes a foundation for exploring how diaspora-affiliated firms use these social ties, which is the focus of the next chapter.

In evaluating the frequency, strength, and direct ties hypotheses, I assess one theoretical assertion—that diaspora-affiliated firms are more socially connected than other foreign firms—in seventeen tests. In all seventeen tests, I estimate a positive effect of diaspora affiliation on firms' social connectedness. In seven of the tests I can reject the null hypothesis of no difference ($p < .05$). In the other 10 tests, p-values range from 0.0505 to 0.286. The consistency of these results across different types of ties and different measures of connectedness increases my confidence that these findings reflect a true relationship between diaspora affiliation and social connectedness and are driven neither by flaws in any individual measure of connectedness nor by statistical noise. appendix B contains additional variations on these tests, including analyses that employ raw instead of imputed data. These appendix results are generally consistent with those in the main text and provide additional evidence that the differences I observe between diaspora-affiliated and other foreign firms are consistent and robust.[11] Collectively, these results provide strong support for my theory.

CHAPTER 5

How Do Diaspora-Affiliated Firms Use Social Networks?

This is the second of three empirical chapters that examine firm-level differences between diaspora-affiliated and nondiaspora-affiliated foreign firms. As with chapter 4, this chapter tests implications of my theory of diasporans as transnational brokers. Chapter 4 presents evidence that diaspora-affiliated firms possess stronger and more numerous social ties in the homeland and that they perceive their owners' and managers' social ties to be more important to profitability. This chapter takes the next step, examining exactly how diaspora-affiliated firms use social ties in business.

I expect that diasporans' ability to serve as transnational brokers allows diaspora-affiliated firms to enjoy a variety advantages based on their social networks. In particular, I predict that firms use social ties to: access information; avoid and resolve disputes; informally enforce contracts, including credit contracts; and influence both policymakers and bureaucrats. Because I expect (and find) that diaspora-affiliated firms are better connected than other foreign firms, I predict that they are more likely than their nondiaspora-affiliated peers to use social ties in each of these ways. This chapter presents a variety of tests that examine the extent to which firms use social ties for each of these tasks. My expectation is that, across the diverse range of firm behaviors that I examine, I will find that diaspora-affiliated firms systematically rely more heavily on social ties as they execute their business strategies.

The analysis in this chapter draws on data from both Georgia and the Philippines, though most of the hypothesis tests rely on data from the Philippines, where the various uses of social ties by firms are captured in more detail. To preview the results of the analysis, I find strong evidence that diaspora-affiliated firms use their social ties to improve government relations and influence policy, and that they enjoy large advantages over other foreign firms in these areas. However, in less explicitly political arenas, the advantage of diaspora-affiliated firms is reduced and I find firms of both types using social ties extensively. Diaspora-affiliated firms are substantially more likely to report using social ties to resolve disputes and rent or purchase real estate. However, I don't find clear differences between diaspora-affiliated and other foreign firms with regard to reliance on social ties to access information or their likelihood of offering credit to customers or receiving credit from suppliers.

5.1. Access to Information

The use of social ties to access information is central to my theory of diasporans as transnational brokers. First, lack of local public information is one of the major factors that prevent foreign firms from investing successfully in countries with low levels of institutional development (e.g., Khanna and Palepu 2013). Second, the ability of social ties to facilitate the flow of information is one of the best established and most studied uses of social ties, both in business and more generally (e.g., Granovetter 1973; Freeman 1977; Burt 1992, 2000; McEvily and Zaheer 1999). In an open-ended question about the effect of social ties on their firms, 42% of firms in Georgia and 19% of firms in the Philippines mentioned using social ties to access information. In short, we know firms use social ties in this way.[1]

However, the argument I make is not simply that access to information is an important means through which social ties deliver value to foreign firms in developing countries. I argue that access to information is an important area in which diaspora-affiliated firms have an advantage over other foreign firms. I argue that diaspora-affiliated firms are able to use their social ties to gather information in ways and to a degree that nondiaspora-affiliated foreign firms are not able to match, even though almost all of these nondiaspora-affiliated foreign firms employ local managers. Stated formally:

> **H5.1. The Information Hypothesis:** *Compared to other foreign firms, diaspora-affiliated firms are more likely to:*
> *A. Use social ties to gather information*
> *B. Rank social ties as their most important source of information*

To test the information hypothesis, enumerators provided each respondent with a list of eight possible sources of information, one of which is social ties (more specifically, "Friends/Family/Personal Networks"). Respondents were asked whether each of these eight sources is an important source of information for their firm, and then they were asked to select the most important source of information. In appendix C5.1, I present the results of regression analysis very similar to that used in chapter 4. However, because of the large number of sources of information being discussed, I opt to present simple bar plots comparing diaspora-affiliated and purely foreign firms. These comparisons lack the statistical controls employed in the regression analysis, but they offer a clean portrait of the relative importance of each source of information to each type of firm.

Figure 5.1 shows the percentage of respondents that considers each source of information to be important and the percentage that considers each to be the **most** important source. Looking at the most important sources of information, we see that, consistent with theory, social ties are extremely important. "Friends/family/ personal networks" takes the top spot, with industry organizations running a close second. However, the information hypothesis predicts that diaspora-affiliated firms are more likely to cite social ties, namely friends/family/personal networks, as an important source of information, and as their most important source of information. This is not borne out in the data—the rough equivalence between diaspora-affiliated and nondiaspora-affiliated firms in this regard is reflected in regression results as well as in the simple frequency comparisons in figure 5.1 (see appendix C5.1 for the regression results). It remains possible that diaspora-affiliated firms in the Philippines enjoy information-related advantages, particularly in terms of transferring information between foreign affiliates and headquarters, but the advantages that I expected to observe in terms of use of social ties to gather information do not seem to be strong.

To make sense of this null result, it is important to return to two different types of social ties—weak ties and strong ties. Granovetter's classic argument about the "strength of weak ties" is that even weak ties, such as ties to acquaintances, can serve as valuable sources of information because they connect individuals who are often dissimilar to one another (1973). Trust, on the other hand, is more exclusively a characteristic of strong ties. When I contrast the social ties of diasporans with the social ties of other foreign investors, it is in the area of strong ties that I expect diasporans to have the

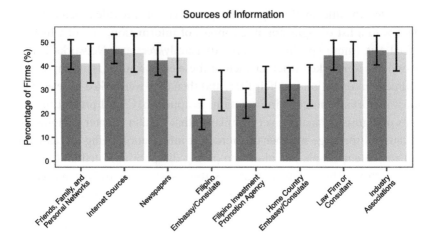

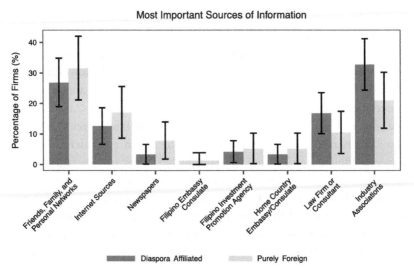

Fig. 5.1. *Sources of Information*

largest edge. In a few years of operating in the host country, we might expect the owners and managers of nondiaspora-affiliated foreign firms to develop networks of social acquaintances. What they lack are the stronger ties born of long history and repeated interaction, such as ties to family members and classmates that go back decades. Thus, nondiaspora-affiliated firms are likely to struggle in areas where strong ties are particularly valuable, like resolving disputes, yet it is perhaps not that surprising to find evidence that they use ties fairly effectively in areas where weak ties suffice, like gathering information. My results suggest that, while access to information is a valuable use to which foreign firms engage social ties, it also appears to be an area in which diaspora-affiliated firms are little differentiated from other foreign firms.

> **Empirical Takeaway:** Using social ties to access information is critical to foreign firms, but it is not only diaspora-affiliated firms that can do so successfully. Nondiaspora-affiliated foreign firms report using social ties in this way as well.

5.2. Dispute Resolution

Disputes between business counterparts are common. In rich industrialized countries with efficient civil judiciaries, such disputes can be litigated in the courts with swift, predictable, enforceable outcomes. This predictability, in turn, allows parties to resolve many disputes out of court—both sides can predict what will happen if the case goes before a judge, so the settlement is reached out of court. If the judicial system is weak, biased, or inefficient, there is no recourse to a predictable and enforceable outcome through the courts. In this context, disputes become more difficult and costly to resolve.

In chapter 2 (sec. 2.5), I describe the ways in which social ties can help firms establish trust with business counterparts, and how these ties can provide an alternative, informal means of dispute resolution. I expect that these alternative means of dispute resolution are an important way in which diasporans provide value to the firms they own and manage. Unlike information, which may be shared with at least some degree of effectiveness between acquaintances with relatively weak ties to one another, trust is strongly dependent on tie strength (e.g., Coleman 1988; Gulati 1995). Trust is essential to effective dispute resolution via social ties. Thus dispute resolution represents an area that is both of high importance to foreign firms in emerging markets and one in which there is strong theoretical reason to expect diaspora-affiliated firms to have a social-tie-based advantage over other foreign firms.

In particular, I expect that diaspora-affiliated firms are more likely to attempt to resolve disputes outside of the courts, while other foreign firms are more likely to rely solely on the courts. Among the noncourt-based options to which firms have access, I expect diaspora-affiliated firms to be particularly likely to turn to well-connected friends and family members for assistance.

H5.2. *The Dispute Resolution Hypothesis:* *Compared to other foreign firms, diaspora-affiliated firms are more likely to:*
  A. *Attempt resolution of disputes outside of court*
  B. *Use social ties to resolve disputes directly*

Testing the Dispute Resolution Hypothesis

To assess the use of noncourt and social-tie-based means of dispute resolution by firms, I ask a series of questions, beginning with whether the firm has had a dispute in the past two years.[2] Among those firms that have had a dispute, I gather information on whether they attempted to use the courts to resolve the dispute, and whether they attempted any of the out-of-court options listed in table 5.1. Many firms report attempting resolution through multiple mechanisms, often combining use of the courts with the use of one or more noncourt strategies.

Among the specific noncourt means I examine, the appeal to well-connected individuals is the option I use to test the dispute resolution hypothesis (particularly H5.2B). In figure 5.2 this category is abbreviated as "used social ties." However, it might be reasonable to expect that diaspora-affiliated firms are more likely than their nondiaspora-affiliated peers to attempt other noncourt means of enforcement as well. In chapter 4, I showed that diaspora-affiliated firms have stronger social ties than other foreign firms to a variety of different types of actors in the host country, including bureaucrats and elected officials. In general, the less formal the option that

Table 5.1. Methods of Dispute Resolution

Method of Resolution	Firms who used (%)
International or local arbitration	46%
Appeal to local government officials	19%
Appeal to home country embassy/consulate	14%
Appeal to well-connected individuals with whom your firm has close ties (such as friends or family members of a firm owner/manager)	39%
Work with a law firm	58%
Assistance from PEZA (special economic zone authority)	6%

is chosen, the larger role social ties might be expected to play.[3] Thus I expect that diaspora-affiliated firms are more likely to attempt to resolve disputes in a variety of less formal ways.

Figure 5.2 presents the results of my tests of the enforcement hypothesis. As with the figures in chapter 4, the dots represent the coefficient value and the horizontal lines represent 95% confidence intervals. If the confidence interval crosses the zero line, this indicates a result that is not statistically significant. For each dependent variable, I use one regression to estimate the effect of diaspora affiliation (solid line) and a second regression to estimate the effect of diaspora ownership (dashed line). A dot to the right of zero indicates a positive relationship between diaspora affiliation (ownership) and the dependent variable, and a dot to the left of zero indicates a negative relationship.

Hypothesis 5.2A predicts that diaspora-affiliated firms are more likely to attempt resolution outside of courts, while Hypothesis 5.2B predicts that they are more likely to use social ties directly as a means of contract enforcement. Figure 5.2 also presents results from regressions testing whether diaspora-affiliated firms are also more likely to go through the formal court system. The data in figure 5.2 provides information only regarding firms that have had a dispute in the past two years.

I find evidence in support of both elements of the enforcement hypothesis. Diaspora-affiliated firms are more likely to report attempting dispute resolution outside of the courts and more likely to report using social ties to do so. Both of these estimated differences are substantively large.[4] Holding other variables at their median value, the predicted probability that a firm reports attempting resolution outside of the courts rises from 30% to 98%. The probability that they report attempting to use social ties to resolve the dispute rises from 9% to 47%.[5] In both cases, the estimated effects of diaspora ownership are somewhat weaker, suggesting that diaspora managers may contribute meaningfully to firms' dispute resolution capabilities.

See appendix C5.2 for details of these results, as well as an evaluation of the other means of dispute resolution listed in table 5.1. These broader results show that diaspora-affiliated firms are also more likely to report using international or local arbitration. It is plausible that, because diaspora-affiliated firms value social ties more highly, they have a stronger preference for nonconfrontational means of dispute resolution, like arbitration, which are more likely to preserve the social bond between the firm and its counterpart in the dispute.

In addition to testing the enforcement hypothesis, figure 5.2 examines

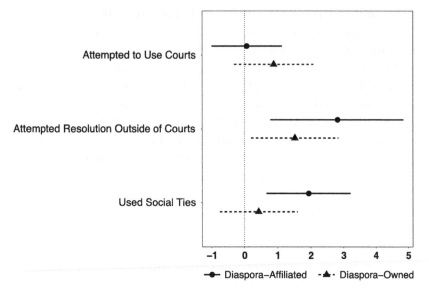

Fig. 5.2. *Diaspora Affiliation and Dispute Resolution*

whether diaspora-affiliated firms are more likely to report attempting to use the courts to resolve those disputes and finds little effect. This suggests that attempting outside enforcement is something that diaspora-affiliated firms do in addition to, rather than instead of, appealing to the courts. Indeed many firms report that they pursued multiple means of resolution.

> **Empirical Takeaway:** Diaspora-affiliated firms are more likely than other foreign firms to report seeking out-of-court resolution to business disputes, and they are more likely to report employing social ties directly as a tool for dispute resolution.

5.3. Extending and Receiving Credit

This section examines whether diaspora-affiliated firms are more likely than other foreign firms to offer credit to their customers or receive credit from their suppliers.[6] Offering credit, even in the short term, is an act of faith—faith that the borrower will repay, and do so on time. When this faith is weak, the supply of credit is low and its cost (i.e., the interest rate) is high.

In wealthy countries, lenders' faith in borrowers is supported by institutions that, on the front end, provide lenders with information about the credit-worthiness of potential borrowers and, on the back end, help creditors co-erce reluctant borrowers into repayment. At the individual level, consumer credit agencies like Experian, TransUnion, and Equifax in the United States assign numeric scores to consumers, which lenders use to decide whether to offer credit at all, as well as what interest rate they need to charge to cover their risk. For large corporations, credit information is provided by credit ratings agencies like Standard & Poor or Fitch, which also rate the credit worthiness of governments.

Credit rating agencies are "market intermediaries" that provide the in-formation necessary to keep the supply of credit high and the cost of it low. In the case of very large loans, lenders (often banks) can afford to conduct their own due diligence. If there is no market intermediary standing ready to rate a borrower's credit worthiness, the lender can make its own assess-ment. For small loans, this independent evaluation is too expensive to be profitable and the supply of small loans simply dries up, leaving many firms with limited access to credit.

On the back end, the enforcement of credit contracts is a fundamental function of the courts. The court system is the legal backstop that allows creditors, as well as additional market intermediaries like collection agen-cies, to repossess assets, force bankruptcy, and take other coercive steps to enforce credit contracts and collect debts. In the absence of an efficient and reliable judiciary, delinquent loans become difficult to collect, the supply of loans drops, and the cost of credit increases.

The type of credit markets that operate in the absence of judicial enforce-ment are perhaps best exemplified by the operation of a loan shark. Loan sharks offer loans under the table, namely they offer credit in the absence of a legally binding credit contract, often to borrowers who will use the funds in illegal ways or who otherwise want to avoid interacting with a bank. In the absence of judicial enforcement, the risk of nonpayment is high, so the inter-est rate is extremely high, often accruing weekly. Loan sharks enforce their informal credit contracts by employing extralegal forms of coercion—if you don't repay, they will literally break your kneecaps.

In the context of firm credit in countries with low levels of institutional development, credit contracts may be difficult or impossible to enforce through the courts, even if they are technically legally binding. If a lender tries hard enough and long enough, an enforceable judgment may eventually be reached through the courts. Particularly in the case of small loans, however, the cost of securing such a judgment may approach or surpass the value of the loan itself. Thus, like loan sharks, lenders in these markets must resort to informal means to secure repayment.

As described in chapter 2, social ties can work as substitutes for formal institutions on both the front end, substituting for credit ratings agencies by supplying information about borrowers' credit worthiness, and on the back end, providing an alternative means to enforce contracts. One of the crucial types of information that flows through social networks is information about the members of the network—for example, information about a firm's financial well-being, its repayment history on past loans, and other information necessary to evaluate credit worthiness. On the back end, the social enforcement of contracts offers a civilized alternative to breaking kneecaps. However, the fundamental logic remains the same. The lender offers a delinquent borrower a deal she can't refuse: repay the debt or be ostracized by the firms in the lender's social network.

These dynamics only work when both the lender and borrower are members of the same social network. If a lender is not well-connected, if the borrower is not well-connected, or if the lender's and borrower's networks do not overlap, the threat of social enforcement has no bite and the credit contract becomes unenforceable. Similarly, information about the borrower can only flow to the lender if the borrower and lender are connected to the same individuals.

There is some evidence in the existing literature that social ties are important for securing credit. Uzzi (1996) finds that, even in the United States where both the courts and credit rating agencies are of high quality, firms with social ties to managers at banks are more likely to be approved for loans and receive lower interest rates. McMillan and Woodruff (1999) find that network ties facilitate the offer of credit from suppliers to customers in Vietnam.

One of the ways in which I expect that diasporans provide value to the firms they own and manage is through facilitating their firms' participation in socially informed and socially enforced lending. I expect that, by connecting their firms to networks of suppliers, customers, and peer firms, diasporans allow the firms they own and manage to both offer credit to their customers and receive credit from their suppliers, giving their firms a competitive edge over competitors who cannot engage in relationship-based credit arrangements.

H5.3. The Credit Hypothesis: *Compared to other foreign firms, diaspora-affiliated firms are more likely to:*
   A. *Offer credit to their customers/clients*
   B. *Receive credit from their suppliers*

Testing the Credit Hypothesis

The questions that provide data for this hypothesis test are quite straightforward. "Does your firm ever offer credit to its customers or clients? Does your firm ever receive credit from its suppliers?" The expectation of the credit hypothesis is that, holding constant sector and firm size and other such firm characteristics, diaspora-affiliated firms are more likely than other foreign firms to report giving and receiving credit.

Figure 5.3 presents results from regressions that match those used to test the other hypotheses in this chapter. Full regression tables are available in appendix C5.3. What we see in figure 5.3 is a pair of null results. Diaspora-affiliated firms are possibly a bit less likely to report receiving credit from their suppliers and possibly a bit more likely to report extending credit to their customers, but the estimated differences are small and statistically insignificant. I fail to find support for the credit hypothesis. There is no evidence that this is an area where diaspora-affiliated firms enjoy an advantage over other foreign firms.

These null results are particularly puzzling in light of the findings presented in the previous section that show diaspora-affiliated firms are more likely to use social ties to resolve disputes. If diaspora-affiliated firms are using social ties to resolve disputes, we would expect them to also be using them to enforce credit contracts. Indeed I expect that disputes over repayment of credit constitute some of the disputes firms are referring to in their answers to the dispute resolution questions. If diaspora-affiliated firms are better able to enforce credit contracts, I would expect them to be more likely to extend credit to their customers.

The World Bank's Ease of Doing Business assessments provide some possible insight here. The Philippines courts score abysmally on the enforcement of contracts in general—they rank 124th in the world in this category—but they perform much better (ranked 50th) when it comes to resolving insolvency, which involves the breaking of credit contracts specifically.[7] So perhaps the Philippines is simply a place where firms can enforce credit contracts through the courts without relying on social enforce-

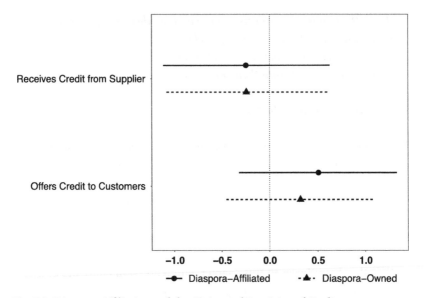

Fig. 5.3. *Diaspora Affiliation and the Giving and Receiving of Credit*

ment. Overall, 74% of the foreign firms in my Philippines sample report receiving credit from suppliers and 77% report offering credit to customers. Somehow these credit contracts are being enforced, and it does not seem that social enforcement is the primary means.

Another possible explanation is that social enforcement of contracts may only be common among smaller firms. In the literature on social enforcement, most of the existing firm-level empirical findings involve small domestic firms (e.g., McMillan and Woodruff 1999). Almost all of the firms in the Philippines sample are medium-to-large MNCs. One of the most urgent extensions of this research is to test the credit hypothesis in a country where resolving insolvency through the courts is more difficult, and in a sample that includes smaller firms.

> **Empirical Takeaway:** find no evidence that diaspora-affiliated firms are more likely than other foreign firms to offer credit to their clients/customers or receive credit from their suppliers.

5.4. Acquiring Real Estate

In the preceding sections, I tested whether diaspora-affiliated firms operating in countries with low levels of institutional development are more likely than other foreign firms to use social ties in three of the ways most discussed in the existing literature: accessing information, enforcing contracts, and giving/receiving credit. However, my theory of diasporans as transnational brokers suggests that social ties should provide value to diaspora-affiliated firms across a wide range of tasks and issue areas. Thus I can derive testable implications of my theory related to almost any business task, assuming that it meets two conditions: (1) all or almost all firms need to complete the same task, and (2) social ties are likely to be useful in efficiently and successfully completing the task at hand.

In Georgia, I examine the use of social ties to rent and purchase real estate. Almost all firms, regardless of sector, must rent or purchase at least some form of real estate—be it for offices, storefronts, warehouses, or other uses. The lack of formal building codes and a scarcity of modern, international-standard buildings in Georgia suggests that informal information about properties should be valuable in acquiring real estate in Georgia, in particular (e.g., Mghebrishvili 2012). Therefore if diaspora-affiliated firms make greater use of social networks than do other foreign firms, this is an area where that difference should be observable.

H5.4. The Real Estate Hypothesis: *Compared to other foreign firms, diaspora-affiliated firms are more likely use social ties to rent or purchase real estate.*

Testing the Real Estate Hypothesis

The test of the real estate hypothesis is the only one in this chapter conducted using the data from Georgia. Figure 5.4 compares diaspora-owned and nondiaspora-owned foreign firms—the Georgia data do not include information on diaspora management. The two questions used to test this hypothesis ask, "Has your firm ever rented or purchased real estate with the help of a family member [friend] of one of your firm's owners or managers?" My theoretical expectation is that, in both cases, diaspora-affiliated firms are more likely to report having done so.

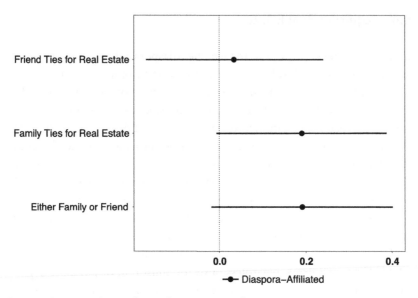

Fig. 5.4. *Diaspora Ownership and Acquiring Real Estate*

The regressions used to test the real estate hypothesis match those used to test the importance hypothesis in chapter 4, which also use data from Georgia. They are also similar to the regressions used to test hypotheses in earlier sections of this chapter, although the control variables are slightly different in the Georgia data because of the availability of different information in each dataset. One aspect of this hypothesis test is unique, however, in that I do not include firms that are actually in the real estate business because I expect that this question has quite a different meaning for such firms.

Consistent with the real estate hypothesis, I estimate that diaspora-owned firms are more likely than other foreign firms to report using their owners' or managers' friendship and family ties to acquire real estate. However, while these results are substantively large, they fall just short of statistical significance. Holding other variables at their median value, the probability that diaspora-owned firms use their owners' or managers' social ties (either family or friendship) to acquire real estate roughly doubles from 11% to 20%.[8] Looking only at the use of friendship ties, there is little difference between diaspora-owned and purely foreign firms. However, with respect to family ties and combined ties, the estimated difference between diaspora-owned and nondiaspora-owned foreign firms is positive and just short of statistical significance ($p = 0.061$ and $p = 0.077$, respectively). This result is consistent with my theory that diasporans' social ties are broadly useful across a range of business tasks, providing value through multiple diverse channels. However, given that the results fall short of statistical significance, I cannot firmly rule out the possibility that there is, in fact, no difference between diaspora-owned and nondiaspora-owned firms in this regard.

> **Empirical Takeaway**: Diaspora-owned firms are probably more likely than other foreign firms to report using family ties to help rent or purchase real estate.

5.5. Government Relations

From the perspective of foreign firms, a key consequence of operating in a country with low levels of institutional development is that they face a higher level of political risk. In institutionally underdeveloped countries, policy tends to be less stable, transparency is lower, and corruption is higher, all of which impose costs and risks. In chapter 4, I provide empirical evidence that diaspora-affiliated firms report more and stronger ties to bureaucrats and elected officials than do other foreign firms. In this chapter, I examine how those ties affect firms' strategies for interacting with government. My theory of diasporans as transnational brokers predicts that diaspora-affiliated firms are more likely to use their social ties to improve government relations and more likely to attempt and succeed at influencing policy.

Firms' ability to manage their relationships with government officials and to influence policy is critical to firm performance. These abilities are also important for understanding firms' impact on economic and political development in the homeland. If diaspora-affiliated firms achieve greater policy influence than other foreign firms, this has important implications for the relationship between diaspora investment and homeland development.

Handling Sensitive Questions about Government Relations

Questions about firms' interactions with government are inherently sensitive. As discussed in chapter 3, all of the questions about government relations had to be cut from the Georgia survey during the pilot because respondents found them too sensitive, fearing that the questions were aimed at assessing whether or not their firm was corrupt. Differences in political culture between Georgia and the Philippines made it much easier to ask about government relations in the Philippines, but we still took several steps to improve the validity of our measures in this area.

In examining firms' influence on government policy, the Philippines survey asks whether firms have attempted to influence policy in the past three years and whether they have succeeded in at least some of their objectives. To reduce sensitivity, my enumerators did not ask respondents exactly what sort of policy influence they were seeking. Some types of policy influence are more likely to be controversial than others, and firms may not want to disclose their exact policy objectives.[9]

To examine whether firms use social ties as a means for improving government relations, my enumerators asked which of four strategies firms used "to improve relations with government agencies and influence government policy." Three of the strategies were banal actions such as "Attend business forums and functions organized by the government." The strategy of interest was, "Reach out to government officials with whom your firm's owners or managers have personal relationships."

I was particularly worried, based on my experiences in Georgia, that because the question was potentially related to corruption, respondents would be reluctant to answer it. In the lead-up to the survey, my team conducted cognitive pretests, in which respondents took the survey as it would be conducted in the full rollout, but were then asked detailed follow-up questions about how they interpreted each question and whether they considered the questions sensitive (e.g., Forsyth and Lessler 1991). The pretest respondents indicated that the government-related questions were not sensitive.[10]

In light of the pretest results, we retained a number of direct questions regarding government relations in the Philippines survey, including the questions about direct ties to government evaluated in chapter 4. However, we also wanted to assess the sensitivity of these questions empirically. To that end, we selected what we perceived to be the most sensitive government-related question in the survey—whether firms used their social ties directly to improve government relations and influence policy—and conducted a modified list experiment to test whether respondents were more likely to report using social ties in this manner when their responses were shielded, compared to when they were asked directly (Corstange 2009). Shielded responses are those in which respondents were able to provide information about their strategies without actually admitting to using social ties.

In the list experiment, each respondent was randomly assigned to one of two groups. Respondents in the direct response group were asked directly whether they had used each strategy on the list. Respondents in the shielded group were read the list of all four strategies and then simply asked to indicate **how many** of the four strategies they had employed in the past year, rather than being asked about each strategy individually. If respondents are reluctant to admit to using social ties to influence policy and improve government relations, then, on average, respondents asked about each strategy individually should report using fewer total strategies than those that are asked simply for the overall number.

Firms in the shielded group reported using an average of 2.35 strategies, while firms that were asked directly reported an average of 2.28 strategies—nearly identical figures. This provides some empirical evidence that firms do not feel the need to hide their use of social ties in government interaction, increasing my confidence in the validity of the data with regard to this specific question, as well as with regard to the questions about firms' use of social ties and about government relations more broadly. For full details on this list experiment, see appendix A3.3.

The Use of Social Ties in Government Relations

My theory predicts that diaspora-affiliated firms are more likely than other foreign firms to use social ties as a means of improving government relations. Stated formally:

> **H5.5. The Government Relations Hypothesis:** *Compared to other foreign firms, diaspora-affiliated firms are more likely to use social ties as a means to improve government relations.*

The question on which this analysis is based is described in the previous section. In figure 5.5, I test whether diaspora affiliation increases the probability that a firm reports employing each of the four strategies. The government relations hypothesis predicts that diaspora-affiliated firms are more likely to employ a social-tie based strategy, in other words, "Reach out to government officials with whom your firm's owners or managers have personal relationships." There is no theoretical reason to expect differences be-

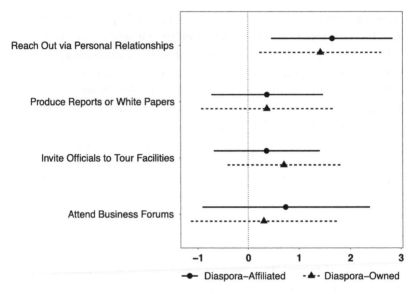

Fig. 5.5. *Diaspora Affiliation and Use of Social Ties to Interact with Government*

tween diaspora-affiliated firms and other foreign firms in their use of the three other strategies on the list, but I include those results for comparison.

Figure 5.5 shows that, consistent with the government relations hypothesis, diaspora-affiliated firms are more likely to report using social ties as a means of improving government relations. This is a strong result both substantively and statistically ($p = 0.007$). Holding other variables at their median value, the predicted probability that a firm reports using personal relationships in this way rises from 6% to 29%.[11] Across all four strategies I examine, I estimate that diaspora-affiliated firms are at least slightly more proactive than other foreign firms. However, the largest difference is the one I estimate with regard to the use of social ties. The estimated effects of diaspora ownership match the estimated effects of diaspora affiliation closely.

> **Empirical Takeaway:** Diaspora-affiliated firms are more likely than other foreign firms to report using social ties as a means of improving government relations.

Attempting and Achieving Policy Influence

Having shown that diaspora-affiliated firms report more and stronger ties to government officials (chapter 4) and that they are more likely to report using these ties to improve government relations (sec. 5.5), I am left with one final step to take to complete the causal chain. I now examine whether diaspora-affiliated firms are more likely than other foreign peers to attempt to influence policy, and whether they are more likely to succeed in doing so. Policy influence is a critical outcome of interest because it relates both to the ability of diaspora-affiliated firms to operate successfully in homelands with high levels of political risk and to the impact that we can expect diaspora-affiliated firms to have on the homeland. Are diaspora-affiliated firms more politically influential than other foreign firms, capable of affecting the political, as well as the economic, development of the homeland?

H5.6. *The Policy Influence Hypothesis:* *Compared to other foreign firms, diaspora-affiliated firms are more likely to attempt to influence policy and more likely to succeed in doing so.*

The analysis in this section is based on two parallel pairs of questions, one about local-level policy and the other about national-level policy. The first question in each pair asks, "In the past three years, has your firm taken any steps intended to affect government policy in the Philippines at the local [national] level?" Those firms that answer affirmatively are then asked, "In the past three years, have these attempts produced any of the results your firm was seeking?"

My theory of diasporans as transnational brokers suggests that, because they are more socially connected, diaspora-affiliated firms are better able to influence policy than their nondiaspora-affiliated peers. If one assumes that attempts to influence policy are costly, then one would predict that diaspora-affiliated firms are more likely than other foreign firms to attempt to influence policy. Firms are more likely to attempt policy influence if they expect to be successful.

The second question, did your firm succeed in influencing policy, is a bit trickier because I can only observe success or failure for those firms that actually make an attempt in the first place. Those firms that expect a low probability of success will most likely not attempt to influence policy. Mathematically speaking: if C is the cost of an attempt, B is the benefit to the firm of securing a policy change, and P is the probability of success (where $0 \leq P \leq 1$), then a firm will only attempt policy influence when $C < P*B$.

If the costs of attempting to influence policy are roughly similar between diaspora-affiliated and nondiaspora-affiliated foreign firms, then the probability of success among those firms who make an attempt is likely to be about the same. In other words, if we just use diaspora affiliation to predict firms' answers to the success question, it is not clear that we should expect diaspora-affiliated firms to answer "yes" more often.

I examine three different dependent variables in testing the policy influence hypothesis: *attempted to influence policy*, *success if attempted*, and *influenced policy*. The first variable captures whether a firm reports attempting to influence policy at either the local or national level. *Success if attempted* captures whether or not a firm reports succeeding in achieving at least some of its policy objectives, conditional on having made an attempt. Thus the test of this hypothesis has a smaller sample size—firms that did not report attempting to influence policy at either level are dropped from the sample. Lastly, *influenced policy* is coded the same as *success if tried* but is not conditional on an attempt being made—in other words, firms that report not attempting to influence policy are coded the same as those that report attempting and failing.

Figure 5.6 presents the results from this analysis. Full regression results and additional details are in appendix C5.5. Consistent with the policy influence hypothesis, I find evidence that diaspora-affiliated firms are indeed more likely to attempt to influence policy and more likely to succeed in doing so. These results are statistically significant and substantively large. Holding other variables at their median, diaspora-affiliated firms are almost twice as likely to report attempting to influence policy, and more than twice as likely to report achieving policy influence (i.e., trying and succeeding).[12]

Given the logic outlined earlier in this section, it is interesting to note that even within the subset of firms that report attempting policy influence—presumably only firms that expect they have some reasonable chance of achieving their objectives—diaspora-affiliated firms are still more likely to report succeeding. This suggests (though by no means shows conclusively) that diaspora-affiliated firms may not only be better at influencing policy but may also be better at knowing ex ante whether they can achieve influence or not. However, the overall takeaway is more straightforward: diaspora-affiliated firms are more likely to report attempting to influence policy and more likely to report success in doing so.

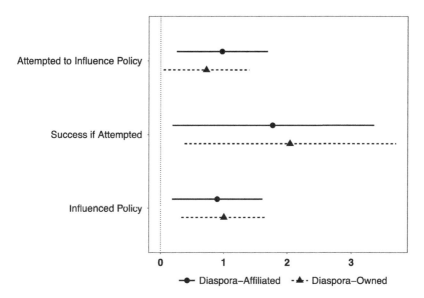

Fig. 5.6. *Diaspora Affiliation and Policy Influence*

Empirical Takeaway: Diaspora-affiliated firms are more likely than other foreign firms to report attempting to influence policy and to report success in achieving their policy objectives.

5.6. A Diaspora Downside?

In chapter 2 (sec. 2.6), I raise the possibility that diaspora-affiliated firms may face some liabilities associated with their diaspora owners and managers. One of these potential "diaspora downsides" is the risk that, while social ties can be assets, they can also be liabilities. In particular, it may be that socially connected diasporans (and socially connected firms) are constantly being approached for "favors," the granting of which may be more obligatory than optional. Such favors could undermine the success of diaspora-affiliated firms.

To explore this possibility, I examine responses to two similar open-ended questions that were asked in Georgia and the Philippines. In the Philippines, respondents were asked, "As a business expert, can you briefly describe how your owners' and managers' social relationships affect your firm?" In Georgia, the question was "Can you briefly describe the effects that your owners' and managers' friendships and/or family relationships have on the way your firm does business?" Note that neither question asks about "uses" of social networks, but rather both ask about effects, leaving open the possibility that some effects could be negative. In both surveys, I examined all the open-ended responses, looking for firms that mentioned any negative impact of social ties on their business.

In the Philippines, of 187 firms that offer some description of the effects of social ties on their firm, none mention anything negative. However, several mention a connection between social ties and charitable work undertaken by the firm, which may or may not entail net costs to firm profitability. In Georgia, of the 73 firms offering a description, only two mention anything negative. One respondent notes that many of the owners' relatives worked for the company and that this had "more negative effect than positive." A respondent at a second firm stated his firm explicitly avoided social relationships, albeit without indicating why.

I cannot be certain that social ties never impose costly obligations on firms, but it is striking that only two respondents surveyed find this type of obligation noteworthy enough to mention in their open-ended response.

Empirical Takeaway: I find little empirical evidence that owners' and managers' social ties impose a liability on their firms.

5.7. Conclusion

My theory of transnational brokers specifies a range of areas in which I expect that social ties provide a competitive edge to diaspora-affiliated firms. Because social ties are so valuable, particularly in the context of weakly institutionalized political systems, I expect that all types of foreign firms use them. However, because I expect that diaspora-affiliated firms are more socially connected than other foreign firms (see evidence in chapter 4), I also expect that they use social ties more and that they gain a comparative advantage from doing so. While almost all foreign firms employ local managers, a local manager with local ties and knowledge is still no substitute for a diasporan who can effectively bridge the gap between headquarters staff and valuable social networks in the homeland.

This chapter tests six hypotheses regarding specific differences in the use of social ties that I expect to observe between diaspora-affiliated and nondiaspora-affiliated foreign firms. Table 5.2 summarizes the results of these hypothesis tests.

In this chapter, I find evidence that social ties are critical to firm strategy in Georgia and the Philippines, that the effects of social ties are overwhelmingly positive rather than negative, and that diaspora-affiliated firms use and benefit from social ties more so than their nondiaspora-affiliated peers across a range of strategic domains. The nonrandom nature of the Philippines sample places some limits on the confidence with which I can infer that what is true of the sample is indeed true across the full population of multinational firms operating in the country (see sec. 3.3 in the main text and A3.3 in the appendix). Nonetheless, the observed differences between diaspora-affiliated firms and nondiaspora-affiliated foreign firms are striking.

In particular, diaspora-affiliated firms display advantages using social ties

Table 5.2. Summary of Results

Hypothesis	Strength of Supporting Evidence	Country	Details
Access to Information	Weak	Philippines	About 40% of diaspora-affiliated firms report using social ties to access information, but a similar share of nondiaspora-affiliated firms also report using ties in this way, yielding little difference between the two groups.
Dispute Resolution	Strong	Philippines	Diaspora-affiliated firms are more likely to report attempting out-of-court strategies for dispute resolution, and are more likely to report appealing to well-connected friends and family members in particular.
Offering and Receiving Credit	Not Supported	Philippines	Most diaspora-affiliated firms report exchanging credit with customers and suppliers, but so do most nondiaspora-affiliated firms, yielding little difference between the two groups.
Acquiring Real Estate	Moderate	Georgia	I estimate that diaspora-owned firms are roughly twice as likely to report using social ties to acquire real estate, but this difference, while substantively large, is just shy of statistical significance.
Government Relations	Strong	Philippines	Diaspora-affiliated firms are more likely to report using social ties to improve government relations.
Policy Influence	Strong	Philippines	Diaspora-affiliated firms are more likely to report attempting and achieving policy influence.

to resolve disputes and manage government relations, and they are more likely to report attempting to influence government policy and succeeding in doing so. In two areas—use of social ties to access information and the exchange of credit with business counterparts—I find little difference between diaspora-affiliated and nondiaspora affiliated firms. While most diaspora-affiliated firms engage in these behaviors, nondiaspora-affiliated firms do as well. Thus these are areas where diaspora-affiliated firms behave as my theory predicts, but where nondiaspora-affiliated firms also seem quite capable, leaving diaspora-affiliated firms with no clear advantage.

These results complement those in chapter 4, where I present evidence that diaspora-affiliated firms have more and stronger social ties than other foreign firms, and that these differences are most pronounced with regard to ties to bureaucrats and policymakers. Diaspora-affiliated firms certainly have and make use of ties to peer firms, just as they use social ties for such market activities as securing credit contracts and accessing market information. But the evidence in these two chapters shows that diasporans' advantages are likely concentrated in the political domains: their close ties to political actors and use of those ties to improve government relations and influence policy.

These are exciting results. They suggest that the causal link between migration and flows of foreign capital does not only arise from the spread of information, the efficient matching of buyers and sellers, and other direct functions of social ties in markets. It also arises from the political capabilities of diaspora-affiliated firms. Diasporans' role as transnational brokers goes beyond connecting foreign firms to domestic firms in the homeland; diasporans also serve to connect foreign firms to the homeland government. Transnational brokerage allows foreign firms to shape political environments, not just navigate them.

These political aspects of diaspora difference have big picture implications. When we evaluate the effect of diaspora investment on homeland development, we have to consider political development as well as economic development. Diaspora-affiliated firms are not just providers of capital but are powerful and connected actors in the politics, as well as the markets, of the homeland. Chapter 6 examines these twin aspects of the role of diaspora-affiliated firms in homeland development. Chapter 7 then articulates strategic implications for both multinational firms and developing-country governments.

CHAPTER 6

The Development Impact of Diaspora-Affiliated Firms

6.0. Paolo Ocampo

Paolo Ocampo[1] graduated from the University of the Philippines before emigrating to the United States to pursue a PhD in economics at the University of Illinois, specializing in natural resource and environmental economics. Four years into his studies, with a master's degree in hand but his dissertation incomplete, Mr. Ocampo returned to the Philippines to take a job working for a multinational oil company called Caltex. Mr. Ocampo later moved into a position in strategic asset management at Chevron Philippines, and eventually moved into corporate affairs. There he played a combined role as official company spokesperson and government liaison, managing relationships with the Department of Energy and both houses of Congress in the Philippines.

I profile Mr. Ocampo primarily to share his views on his role as a diaspora manager relative to Chevron's impact on development in the Philippines. However, Mr. Ocampo's story also speaks to the other issues central to this book—the power of social ties and cultural fluency in explaining the professional success of diaspora managers in multinational firms. It seems that ties formed in the United States were not pivotal for Mr. Ocampo's career. Instead Mr. Ocampo's time in the United States affected his professional life through other channels—language and cultural fluency. In his words:

> There is that advantage [to being a diasporan], especially if you are working for a multinational firm, because they do appreciate your multicultural experience, and that does make it easier for you to move around within the

organization, and . . . the management sees that you are able to, more able to adapt to different cultures, or to people from different cultures. . . .

[My friends from high school and college] are in various companies around Manila or they are in government, and so I maintain those relationships. Even fraternity relationships have been very important. . . . It has been useful for my profession, especially when I was in my corporate affairs role, because I had to reach out especially to government agencies and some of my friends from college were there. And of course for business also.

And then of course friendships I've made while working for Chevron must have been important and I developed them by being a member of one association or another. For example, I was a member of AmCham [The American Chamber of Commerce] and I was the Vice-President of Am-Cham Foundation so I built relationships. I was a member of the Petroleum Institute, so again, business. I was a member of the International Association of Business Communicators and the PRSP [Public Relations Society of the Philippines] so those relationships that you cultivate which are more personal and also professional.

When we asked Mr. Ocampo about Chevron's overall contribution to development in the Philippines, he was very enthusiastic. "We are proud that we have been part of the economic development of the Philippines by being able to distribute fuel across the country, to make it available. That's a critical element to growth, you know." He also believes that Chevron contributes more to development than do other firms in the sector—Chevron was an early mover in developing refining capacity in the Philippines and is making high-technology investments in both deepwater projects and power development of two geothermal fields.

With regard to social responsibility, he described in some detail a number of Chevron's corporate social responsibility (CSR) projects, but his overall assessment is that, compared to other firms in the sector, "I think we're about average. . . . There are certainly other foreign firms that I can see do a lot more than we do, but also firms that do less."

When asked about whether having a diaspora manager like himself affected the development contributions that Chevron made, Mr. Ocampo said, "To a certain extent, yes. I can remember that being a Filipino . . . one of my roles in the planning and strategic asset management role, I would fight for investment dollars to come to the Philippines. Because, you know, the company's investment capital is a finite resource and it has to be spread.

And so I would fight to get investment dollars into the Philippines, and so I think to a certain extent that was quite successful, that's why we were able to expand our market."

6.1. Assessing Impact on Development

Mr. Ocampo's story illustrates several elements of my theory of diasporans as transnational brokers. He has been able to leverage his social ties in the Philippines to create value for Chevron, and his time abroad helped him develop a high level of cultural fluency, which has enabled him to form strong relationships with headquarters personnel. However, Mr. Ocampo's story also contains threads related to the alternative mechanism I also introduce in chapter 2—diasporans' social and emotional motivations for engaging in the homeland. Mr. Ocampo is proud of his role in pushing Chevron to invest more resources in the Philippines, resources that he believes have been important to development in the Philippines. Thus his story provides a useful segue into an examination of both these motivations in particular, and the development impact of diaspora-affiliated firms more generally.

As noted in chapter 2, there is a lot of optimism in the policy community regarding the development potential of diaspora investment. In the past decade, the US Agency for International Development (USAID), the World Bank, and the United Nations, along with numerous NGOs, have poured millions of dollars into studying and promoting diaspora investment. These projects are predicated, at least in part, on the belief that diaspora direct investment in general, and diaspora-affiliated firms in particular, have a larger positive impact on development than does other FDI (e.g., Rodriguez-Montemayor 2012). However, this optimism is based on theory about diaspora investment that is almost entirely untested. One of the contributions of this project is to test the assumptions that have spurred many of these ongoing efforts to promote diaspora investment.

By evaluating the development impact of diaspora investment, this project informs a broader debate about the relationship between FDI and development in general. As noted in the introduction, poor countries are capital scarce, and FDI offers a potential lifeline, bringing in much-needed capital, along with knowledge and cutting-edge technology. But not all FDI contributes to development in this way. Some foreign firms hire and train large numbers of local employees, purchase inputs from local suppliers, and generate positive "spillovers" in terms of knowledge and technology diffusion out from the firm and into the host economy. Other foreign firms do none of these things. Instead they skirt local regulations, extract large tax incentives from the host government, damage the environment, and generally have a negative impact on economic, social, and political development in the homeland. Thus before governments and NGOs rush out to promote diaspora investment as the next great development tool, we need a sober, data-driven assessment of the relationship between diaspora investment and homeland development. Each of the theories I introduce in chapter 2 has a different implication for the effect of diaspora investment on homeland development. The purpose of this chapter is to test these implications.

Development Implications from Each Theory

My theory of diasporans as transnational brokers predicts that diaspora-affiliated firms are very similar to other foreign firms with regard to their impact on development. Indeed, under my theory, diasporans affect homeland development primarily by getting foreign firms to show up and helping them stay in business. They provide competitive advantages to the firms they own and manage, allowing these firms to invest successfully in developing countries they would otherwise be unable and unwilling to enter. This is not a trivial impact on development—developing countries are capital scarce and channeling foreign capital into these markets is critical. In a head-to-head comparison, I do not expect a diaspora-affiliated firm to behave in ways more beneficial to development than a nondiaspora-affiliated peer. However, I do expect diaspora-affiliated firms to be better able to operate successfully in challenging environments, and thus more willing to enter them in the first place.

In contrast, the alternative theory based on diasporans' social and emotional motivations for engaging with the homeland does imply a divergence in development-related behavior between diaspora-affiliated and nondiaspora-affiliated foreign firms. The expectation, discussed in some detail in chapter 2 (sec. 2.7), is that diasporans' engagement with the homeland is substantially motivated by their desire to improve economic conditions in the homeland and boost their own social standing in the diaspora community. These motivations are then expected to influence the behavior of diaspora-affiliated firms in general, and diaspora-owned firms in particular, inducing them to behave with greater social responsibility and in a manner designed to increase their positive impact on economic development in the homeland.

The results presented in chapters 4 and 5 support the core elements of my theory of diasporans as transnational brokers: diaspora-affiliated firms are more socially connected than other foreign firms and use social ties in business in ways and to a degree that other foreign firms do not. This chapter tests the central implications of the competing theory based on social and emotional motivations, namely whether diaspora-affiliated firms are more socially responsible than their nondiaspora-affiliated peers. I also evaluate several additional aspects of firm-level development impact, allowing for a more complete assessment of the role of diaspora-affiliated firms in homeland development.

> **Firm-Level Development Question:** Do diaspora-affiliated firms contribute more or less to development in the homeland than other foreign firms?

6.2. Diaspora Ownership and Social Responsibility

The most optimistic scenario for the relationship between diaspora investment and homeland development is one in which the social and emotional motivations of diasporans have a strong effect on the behavior of diaspora-affiliated firms. I begin the empirical analysis in this chapter by assessing a core empirical implication of this mechanism; I test whether diaspora-affiliated firms are more socially responsible than other foreign firms. I conduct these tests using survey data from Georgia, and thus the comparison is between diaspora-owned and nondiaspora-owned foreign firms—the Georgia data does not include information on diaspora management. These tests serve to evaluate both whether the social and emotional motivations theory operates as predicted and whether some of the more optimistic predictions regarding diasporans' impact on homeland development are warranted.[2]

Social responsibility is inherently difficult to measure, but fortunately there is a rich literature to draw on, both theoretically and empirically. Bowen (1953) defines social responsibility in business as "the obligations of businessmen to pursue those policies, to make those decisions, or to follow those lines of action which are desirable in terms of the objectives and values of our society."[3] Some scholars view firms' contributions to broader societal well-being as elements of long-run profit maximization (e.g., Porter and Kramer 2002), while others view firms' pursuit of socially desirable ends as extraneous to, or even in conflict with, the pursuit of profit (e.g., Freeman 1984; Donaldson and Preston 1995). This theoretical disagreement has motivated an extensive empirical literature that assesses the relationship between social responsibility and profitability.[4] Approaches to measurement include content analysis of firms' annual reports (Abbott and Monsen 1979), perceptions by outside observers (Cochran and Wood 1984; McGuire, Sundgren, and Schneeweis 1988), and survey-based measures (Aupperle, Carroll, and Hatfield 1985; Burton and Goldsby 2009).

Unfortunately, these existing measurement strategies are not well-suited to my purposes. First, both the annual reports approach and the perceptions measures are appropriate only to a narrow subset of firms: those that are large and publicly traded. Perceptions-based measures are only likely to be accurate for well-known firms,[5] and annual reports are made publicly available only by publicly traded firms. Thus one of the advantages of the survey-based measures I introduce here is that I have data across a range of firm sizes and include data on privately held firms.

The core empirical challenge in conducting this portion of the study is to construct a valid survey-based measure of social responsibility that reflects the type of social responsibility we would expect to observe if diasporans' social and emotional motivations are an important driver of firm behavior. Because I am testing not my own theory but rather a competing theory drawn from the literature, my objective here is to design a test that is as favorable as possible to the social and emotional motivations mechanism. Thus in addition to testing these hypotheses in Georgia, which should be a relatively easy case in which to find support for the social and emotional motivations theory (see sec. 3.2), I also strive to measure social responsibility in a way that captures precisely the types of socially responsible behavior that we would expect to observe in diaspora-owned firms if the social and emotional motivations mechanism is operating strongly.

Carroll (1979) divides firms' social responsibilities into four categories: economic, legal, ethical, and discretionary. I focus on discretionary behaviors, namely those behaviors that contribute to the well-being of society but are not legally required and the omission of which is not considered inherently unethical. This is the category of behavior in which a divergence between diaspora-affiliated and nondiaspora-affiliated foreign firms is most likely. I focus particularly on the treatment of employees, contributions to charity, and self-perceived contributions to economic development. I do not suggest that these behaviors capture the full range of means through which a firm can be socially responsible.[6] However, expectations regarding these behaviors are critical in shaping investment promotion and development policy, and theory predicts they should be observed at elevated levels in firms with socially and emotionally motivated owners.

Fair or generous treatment of employees is central to many definitions of CSR (see Hemphill 1997) and one that is central in theories of diasporans' social and emotional motivations (Riddle and Nielsen 2010). If diasporans wish to use their firms to benefit friends and family members in the homeland and raise their status in the diaspora community, providing high-quality employment opportunities is an attractive mechanism for doing so. Favorable employment conditions are also critical to the creation of sustainable livelihoods in the homeland, thereby providing a direct means for diaspora-affiliated firms to contribute to sustainable development (Fox 2004).

Treatment of employees, however, captures only a narrow subset of the ways in which diaspora-owned firms may engage in socially responsible behavior. Two other empirical areas I examine are much broader in the types of behavior and objectives they encompass. I examine both whether diaspora-owned firms are more likely than other foreign firms to contribute to charity and whether they self-report that they make above-average contributions to economic development in the homeland.

The self-report of contributions to economic development avoids circumscribing the means through which diaspora-owned firms might seek to contribute to economic development in the homeland, capturing any perceived success toward that end. Broader still, I examine whether firms contribute to any charitable organizations. The goals of such organizations are left entirely open, and may focus on economic development or other noneconomic objectives that firm owners may have. For almost any social objectives a diaspora investor might have, firm donations to charitable organizations represent a logical means (though certainly not the only means) through which those ends might be achieved. By choosing broad measures of this nature, I allow for the fact that firms' contributions to economic and social development of the host country may take place through avenues that are specific to both firms' individual capabilities and the unique needs of the communities in which they are operating.[7] If this social and emotional motivations mechanism operates strongly, I would expect to observe differences between diaspora-owned and nondiaspora-owned firms across at least some of the behaviors discussed above.

H6.1. *The Social Responsibility Hypothesis:* *Compared to other foreign firms, diaspora-owned firms are likely to engage in more socially responsible behavior, including:*
  A. *Paying higher wages, providing better working conditions, and prioritizing the hiring of locals (rather than expatriates)*
  B. *Being less likely to maximize profit at the expense of other objectives*
  C. *Being more environmentally friendly*
  D. *Being more likely to make charitable donations*

The tests of Hypothesis 6.1 proceeds in a manner identical to the tests conducted in chapters 4 and 5. This analysis draws exclusively on data from Georgia. The Georgia survey contains a battery of questions in which respondents are asked to assess the behavior of their firm in comparison to other firms in their sector. Table 6.1 provides the exact language of these statements. For all except the question about charitable contributions, respondents were asked to indicate their response to each statement on a 7-point Likert scale, from "strongly disagree" to "strongly agree."[8]

Table 6.1. Assessing Social Responsibility

Variable	Survey Question/Statement
Higher Salaries	This firm offers higher salaries than other firms in this sector
Quality of Life	Compared to employees at other firms in this sector, employees at this firm are able to provide a higher quality of life for their families
Professional Development	Compared to employees at other firms in this sector, employees at this firm have many opportunities for professional development
Profit Focused	This firm always invests its resources where they can generate the most profit
Minimize Labor Costs	This firm keeps its total labor costs as low as possible
Prioritize Local Hiring	This firm gives priority to hiring local staff over foreign staff
Green	Compared to other firms in this sector, this firm is a "green" firm with a low environmental impact
Donations	Does your firm make any donations to charitable causes?

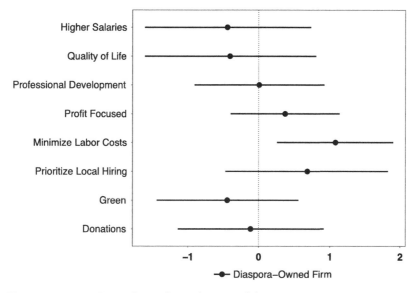

Fig. 6.1. *Diaspora Ownership and Social Responsibility*

Figure 6.1 presents the results from these hypothesis tests.[9] As in the figures in chapters 4 and 5, each dot represents the coefficient on the independent variable of interest, which in this case is a dummy variable for diaspora ownership. Thus a dot to the right of zero indicates a positive relationship between diaspora ownership and the dependent variable, and a dot to the left of zero indicates a negative relationship. The horizontal lines represent the 95% confidence interval around these coefficients. If the confidence interval crosses the zero line, this indicates a result that is not statistically significant. For full regression tables and discussion, see appendix D6.2.

The results in figure 6.1 are not consistent with the social responsibility hypothesis. Across eight different indicators of social responsibility, I find no evidence that diaspora-owned firms are more socially responsible than other foreign firms. Most of the coefficients are near zero. I do see some evidence (albeit not quite statistically significant) that diaspora-owned firms are more likely to prioritize the hiring of local staff, which is potentially consistent with a socially or emotionally motivated desire to create employment opportunities in the homeland. However, I also see that diaspora-owned firms are more likely to report that they keep labor costs as low as possible. This suggests that the most reasonable interpretation of the local employment result is not actually so uplifting—the priority given to hiring local staff is likely serving more often as part of a strategy for minimizing labor expenditures rather than as part of a strategy to maximize a given firm's positive impact on development.

Making inferences on the basis of a null result is always challenging, but here I have the benefit of having conducted several related tests on the same sample of firms. In chapter 4 (sec. 4.4), I used this exact same set of firms to confirm a quite substantial difference between diaspora-owned and nondiaspora-owned firms with regard to the importance of social ties to firm profitability. Thus it is not the case that this sample is too small, or the statistical tests too weak, to identify differences between diaspora-owned and nondiaspora-owned foreign firms in general. Also many of the statistically insignificant differences estimated indicate that diaspora-owned firms are (slightly) less socially responsible than their nondiaspora-owned peers—most notably, diaspora-owned firms are slightly *less* likely to report giving to charity. More statistical power here would not alter the conclusion. There is no indication that diaspora-owned firms are more socially responsible than other foreign peers, and in fact they may actually be less socially responsible.

> **Empirical Takeaway:** I find no evidence that diaspora-owned firms are more socially responsible than other foreign firms.

Implications of a Lack of Social Responsibility

So how damning is this finding of no difference between diaspora-owned and nondiaspora-owned firms? Does this indicate that social and emotional motivations are unimportant for understanding diasporans' engagement in the homeland? Are the organizations hard at work promoting diaspora investment as a development tool wasting their money? Not necessarily.

The existing literature on diasporans' social and emotional motivations has established clearly that these motivations are relevant for explaining several important dimensions of diasporans' homeland engagement, including diaspora philanthropy (e.g., Brinkerhoff 2004, 2009; Nyberg-Sørensen 2007; Schulte 2008; Bandelj 2008). What my findings indicate is that, at least in the case of Georgia, few diasporans are using

their firms as a vehicle to act out these motivations through socially responsible firm behavior.

This leaves several possible explanations for the findings in figure 6.1.
Most plausibly, diasporans' desire to aid the homeland may be directed primarily through channels other than socially responsible firm behavior—
channels such as personal philanthropy, remittances, and potentially also
their engagement in homeland politics. Diaspora-affiliated firms seem to
function as most firms do, namely as vehicles for producing an economic
return on investment. Because diasporans' ability to serve as transnational
brokers directly affects firms' bottom line, it directly and substantially affects their behavior. Diasporans' social and emotional motivations are less
relevant to firms' bottom line and thus less relevant to firm behavior.

Perhaps it should have been intuitive from the outset that social and
emotional motivations are not a strong determinant of behavior in most
diaspora-affiliated firms. Socially and emotionally motivated diasporans
enjoy a range of avenues for homeland engagement, many of which provide
more direct means of enhancing social outcomes than does direct investment. If diasporans wish to increase the income of their extended family, it
may be more efficient to send money home (i.e., remittances) than to try to
start a successful business that offers high-quality employment opportunities to some family members. If diasporans want to raise their standing in
the local community, it might make more sense to engage directly in philanthropy rather than trying to encourage a multinational firm that they
own or manage to behave in a more socially responsible manner. I do not
conclude that social and emotional motivations are unimportant for explaining diasporans' homeland engagement in general, but I show that
these motivations are not strong predictors of the behavior of diaspora-
owned firms in Georgia.

6.3. Positive Spillovers

Social responsibility encompasses the deliberate or intentional ways in
which firms can increase their positive impacts on homeland development.
However, it is not only firms with deliberate social responsibility strategies
that can have a positive impact on development in the investment host
country. The literature on FDI discusses at length the prospects for positive
"spillovers" from multinational firms into the host economy and the various

ways in which the profit-seeking activities of firms can lead, often inadvertently, to increases in the productivity of domestic workers and domestic firms, and to increases in economic growth well beyond the economic activity of the firm itself. This literature has identified a range of channels through which these spillovers can occur, as well as the types of firms and elements of firm behavior that determine which foreign firms produce the largest positive spillovers. Thus in order to test whether diaspora-affiliated firms have a larger and more positive impact on homeland economic development, it is necessary to examine the wider range of firm characteristics. We must evaluate whether diaspora-affiliated firms are more likely than other foreign firms to behave in ways that are associated with large positive spillovers in the homeland economy.

This section examines four aspects of firm strategy related to pro-growth spillovers: labor intensity, export earnings, reinvested earnings, and Greenfield investment (i.e., entry into the host country by starting a new firm from scratch, as opposed to acquiring or merging with an existing enterprise). I selected these aspects of firm behavior because they are prominent in the literature on FDI and development, and because they arose frequently in my conversations with government officials in Georgia and the Philippines and with development professionals in the NGO community.[10]

The analysis in this section serves a policy relevance purpose rather than a direct theory testing purpose. Neither of the two theories I test in this book has clear and direct implications regarding these particular spillovers. If the social and emotional motivations of diasporans are important in shaping the behavior of diaspora-affiliated firms, we might expect diaspora-affiliated firms to outperform other foreign firms in all four of the areas discussed in this section, but the clearest implications for this mechanism are about social responsibility and *deliberate* actions taken to maximize development impact, which I have already tested. The areas I examine in this section are development-relevant but more likely to reflect fundamental firm strategy than choices made with development impact in mind.

Similarly, while my theory of diasporans as transnational brokers offers some guidance with regard to the types of strategies that diaspora-affiliated firms should be most likely to adopt, the predictions in these particular areas are not clear.

So why conduct these tests? While they don't tell us a great deal about the mechanisms through which diaspora affiliation shapes firm behavior, these tests are critical in helping to formulate sound policy recommendations for developing-country governments and the organizations that seek to assist them in this particular issue area. Understanding the nature of the positive spillovers associated with diaspora-affiliated firms allows for a more informed assessment of the benefits associated with promoting this type of investment.

Greenfield Investment

When we think about the positive effects of FDI on development, often the beneficial investment we have in mind is a Greenfield investment—a new business venture, erected from scratch by a multinational firm: the shiny new factory, the bustling back-office processing center, the state-of-the-art port. While investment via cross-border acquisition simply transfers a firm from one owner to another, Greenfield investments add a new firm to the economy, increasing the capital stock and contributing directly to economic growth (Mencinger 2003; Wang and Wong 2009; Harms and Meon 2011).

Mergers and acquisitions (M&A) are generally viewed as less favorable for development (e.g., Agosin and Mayer 2000). Indeed when domestic firms are acquired by foreigners, this acquisition is often cause for concern among some host country constituencies who fear that, among other things, acquired firms may transition to more capital-intensive strategies or replace domestic workers with foreigners, leading to layoffs (Norbäck and Persson 2007; Lee, Biglaiser, and Staats 2014; Pandya 2014: 41). In its 2000 World Investment Report, the United Nations Commission on Trade and Development (UNCTAD) expressed concern that "FDI entry through the takeover of domestic firms is less beneficial, if not positively harmful, for economic development than entry by setting up new facilities." This conclusion from the United Nations overstates the current academic consensus, but the weight of the evidence suggests that, in most cases, Greenfield investment is more growth-promoting than entry via cross-border M&A. Thus one of the questions on the mind of government officials and development practitioners is, "How do we attract more Greenfield investment projects?"

Whether one does this by attracting more diaspora-affiliated firms is not clear from my theory. The transnational brokerage mechanism implies that diaspora-affiliated firms should have advantages both in identifying favorable local acquisitions targets and managing relationships with local joint-venture partners, giving diaspora-affiliated firms an edge in cross-border M&A. However, Greenfield investments are generally considered to require more local information than M&A (Herrman and Datta 2006) and local joint-venture partners are sometimes theorized to play many of the crucial roles managing host-country risk that I theorize diasporans can play effectively.[11] Thus it is unclear in which entry mode, Greenfield or M&A, I should expect diasporans' capabilities to be most valuable.

Reinvested Earnings

When multinational firms operate profitability, they have the option of taking these profits and plowing them back into their business in the host country and expanding or improving their operations; or they can repatriate these profits to either pay out to the owners or invest elsewhere. From the perspective of the host country, the reinvestment of earnings in the local economy is strongly preferred, as it grows both the business and the economy of the host country.

Among the four areas addressed in this section, this is the area in which I have the strongest reason to expect that diaspora-affiliated firms behave in a more pro-development manner. I expect that diaspora-affiliated firms have competitive advantages that are specific to the homeland. Thus given the option to reinvest earnings in the homeland or to use these earnings to fund investment in other markets, I would expect diaspora-affiliated firms to be more likely to pursue the former strategy.

Data on reinvested earnings are only available from the Philippines survey, where I ask each firm, "Over the past three years, approximately what portion of your firm's earnings was reinvested in the Philippines?" As with many questions, I give ordinal answer choices to make the question less sensitive. In other words, I don't ask for an exact number but give a series of buckets, in this case: none or almost none; less than half; more than half; all or almost all. This ordinal measure captures the difference between export-focused and nonexport-focused firms, but with a low degree of granularity.

Export Earnings

Export earnings are valuable to developing countries as both a driver of growth and a protection against destabilizing crises. On the growth side, China, South Korea, and other developing-country success stories of the past several decades have followed strategies of export-led growth, which emphasize specialization, openness to trade, and the development of globally competitive sectors. On the crisis side, one of the most common types of financial crisis that strikes developing countries is a balance of payments crisis. Balance-of-payments crises emerge when a country persistently imports more than it exports, and thus developing-country governments are perpetually eager to boost exports and avoid running persistent current account deficits. To the extent that foreign firms generate export revenue, they enhance both growth and stability in the host economy.

Here the implication of my theory of diasporans as transnational brokers is somewhat more pessimistic about the development impact of diaspora-affiliated firms. My theory implies that diaspora-affiliated firms have significant advantages related to access to private information about local market conditions—information that might be particularly useful to firms that serve the domestic market. If these information advantages are large, it implies that diaspora-affiliated firms are more likely to serve the domestic market and slightly less likely to export. The survey measure of export earnings is also ordinal, assessing the share of a firm's revenue that is generated from overseas sales of goods and services.

Employment Intensity

The previous section (6.2) discusses firms' treatment of employees in the context of social responsibility. Here I look simply at whether diaspora-affiliated firms are more labor-intensive than other foreign firms. A significant concern of any government is job creation and keeping unemployment low.[12] All else equal, firms that employ more workers are likely to have a larger and more positive effect on the economy. Theoretically, if the social and emotional motivations mechanism is dominant, one would expect diaspora-affiliated firms to be more labor-intensive for the same reasons one would expect them to treat their employees better. The transnational brokerage mechanism has no clear implication here.

The most straightforward measure of employment intensity is simply the number of employees in a firm, divided by total firm revenue. In the Philippine survey I have data on both revenue and the number of employees, but unfortunately these data are ordinal rather than continuous. Thus my empirical strategy uses diaspora affiliation to predict the (ordinal) number of employees while controlling for (ordinal) revenues. In other words, holding constant the approximate size of the firm, how does diaspora affiliation affect the approximate number of employees? This provides a test that is reasonable but not particularly precise.

Results for Greenfield, Reinvested Earnings, Exports, and Labor Intensity

Table 6.2 summarizes the expectations that my theory provides. Figure 6.2 tests the effect of diaspora affiliation on each of these four variables.

The regressions that underlie figure 6.2 draw on data from both Georgia and the Philippines for Greenfield investment and data from the Philippines alone for export earnings, reinvested earnings, and labor intensity. The data on Greenfield investment are binary and analyzed via logistic regression, whereas the data on reinvested earnings, exports, and employees is ordinal and analyzed via ordered logistic regression. In other aspects, the regressions in figure 6.2 match those in figure 6.1. For full regression tables and discussion, see appendix D6.3.

The general story in this figure is that, across all four dimensions, diaspora-affiliated firms report behaviors that are slightly more development-inducing than those reported by other foreign firms, but all of these differences are small and none are statistically significant. The strongest theoretical expectation in this section is that diaspora-affiliated firms are expected to be more likely to reinvest earnings—this is a prediction associated with both the transnational brokerage mechanism and the social and emotional motivations mechanism—and it is here that we see some of

Table 6.2. Theoretical Expectations Regarding Greenfield, Reinvestment, Exports, and Labor Intensity

Variable	Mechanism	Predicted Effect of Diaspora Affiliation
Greenfield	Transnational brokerage	Unclear
	Social and emotional motivations	Unclear
Reinvested Earnings	Transnational brokerage	Positive
	Social and emotional motivations	Positive
Export Earnings	Transnational brokerage	Negative
	Social and emotional motivations	Unclear
Employment Intensity	Transnational brokerage	Unclear
	Social and emotional motivations	Positive

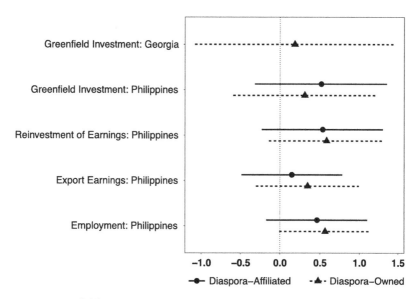

Fig. 6.2. *Greenfield Investment, Reinvested Earnings, Export Earnings, and Employment Intensity*

the strongest results. In some of the alternative specifications shown in appendix D6.3—including the fully controlled regression run on the raw (not imputed) data, this result is actually significant ($p < .05$). The employment effect also approaches statistical significance. However, cumulatively these results do not justify a strong claim that diaspora-affiliated firms reinvest earnings at a higher rate than do other foreign firms.

> **Empirical Takeaway:** I find only weak evidence that diaspora-affiliated firms have, on average, a more positive impact on development than other foreign firms.

6.4. Sensitivity to Conflict

The ravages of war are a nontrivial part of the economic struggles of many institutionally underdeveloped countries. One of the most important development-related hopes that have been attached to diaspora investment is that diaspora investors may be less deterred by war and political violence than other foreign investors. Both my theory of diasporans as transnational brokers and the alternative mechanism of social and emotional motivations give some reason to expect that diaspora-affiliated firms may indeed be less deterred by conflict than other foreign firms.

With regard to transnational brokerage, if diasporans are able to connect their firms to valuable social networks in the homeland, these social networks may be able to provide local private information that is particularly useful in times of conflict, when firms must constantly monitor battlefield events and adapt strategy according to the scope, severity, and location of the fighting. Financial markets often freeze during war, making it essential that firms be positioned to provide short-term credit to customers and access short-term credit from suppliers. The informal enforcement of credit contracts in this context is a potential function of social ties. Recall that, while I find no evidence that diaspora-affiliated firms are more likely than other foreign firms to extend credit to customers or receive credit from suppliers, one possible explanation for this nonfinding is that enforcement of credit obligations through the courts in the Philippines is possible for most firms. In the context of ongoing violence, there is reason to expect that the role of social ties in the giving and receiving of credit may be greater, and the advantage of diaspora-affiliated firms more pronounced.

However, a willingness to invest in the face of political risk is also a possible implication of social and emotional motivation. One of the few existing data points we have regarding social and emotional motivations involves war risk in particular. In their study of Palestinian-Americans in the 1990s, Gillespie, Sayre, and Riddle (2001) find that diasporans' self-reported interest in investing in Palestine declined very little as the economy deteriorated and the respondent-perceived level of political risk increased between 1994 and 1998. The authors also find that altruism is a strong predictor of diasporans' interest in homeland investment. It is plausible that this altruistic motivation may make diasporans more willing to tolerate risks that deter other investors.

Empirically, the Georgia data provide me an excellent opportunity not only to assess whether diaspora-affiliated firms are less affected by war risk than are other foreign firms but also to analyze the cause(s) of this difference.[13] The Georgia survey was conducted in the spring of 2010, less than two years after Georgia was involved in a small, weeklong war with Russia. I capitalized on this proximity to a recent conflict to assess how firms viewed the risk of conflict renewal, which at the time was considered quite likely. The survey included questions about how likely investors perceived a future conflict to be, how that risk of renewed violence affected their current business plans, and how a return to violence would affect their profitability if it occurred.

The answers to these questions offer insights into several key aspects of firms' relationship to war risk. Both the transnational brokerage mechanism and the social and emotional motivations mechanism imply that diaspora-affiliated firms should be less sensitive to war risk, giving rise to the first of two war-related hypotheses.

H6.2. The War Risk Hypothesis: *The risk of violent conflict has a weaker impact on the business strategy of diaspora-owned firms than other foreign firms.*

This hypothesis raises two additional questions. First, if diasporans are indeed less sensitive to war risk, is this just about risk perception? In other words, are diaspora-affiliated firms less likely to report that the conflict affects their plans simply because they perceive the renewal of conflict to be less likely? This is something I evaluate empirically in the following section. Diaspora-affiliated firms indeed assess the risk of war recurrence as slightly less likely, and so I control for these expectations in assessing the war risk hypothesis.

Second, and more importantly, if the war risk hypothesis is correct, which mechanism is at work? Is this about firms' strategic capabilities to manage risk, as my theory of transnational brokers predicts? Or does the lack of sensitivity to war risk reflect firms' willingness to accept a lower risk-adjusted rate of return if necessary to contribute to development in the homeland?

To parse between these two mechanisms, I evaluate whether diaspora-affiliated firms differ from other foreign firms with regard to the expected effects of war on firm profitability. The transnational brokerage mechanism implies that diaspora-affiliated firms are more capable of mitigating war risk, and thus they should be less likely than other foreign firms to anticipate a negative impact on firm profitability. However, if I find that diaspora-owned firms expect the same effects on profitability as other foreign firms but are still less likely to adjust their investment plans, then the most plausible explanation would be that diaspora-owned firms are simply more risk acceptant, which would be consistent with a dominant role for social and emotional motivations.

To state the implication of my theory of transnational brokers as a second formal hypothesis:

H6.3. The War Impact Hypothesis: *Diaspora-owned foreign firms are less likely than other foreign firms to anticipate that violent conflict would decrease their firm's profitability.*

A Brief Synopsis of the Georgia-Russia Conflict

Since the early 1990s, two unrecognized states, Abkhazia and South Ossetia, have existed on territory claimed by Georgia. Both of these territories sit along the Georgian border with Russia, and both have been able to survive thanks to Russian support, both military and economic.[14] In 2004, the Georgian government began intermittent efforts to close trade with the separatist region, and in August 2008, following escalating provocations from the Ossetian side, Georgia attempted to reclaim the territory by military force. The Georgian offensive was initially successful, but then Russian troops arrived in support of the Ossetians and quickly crushed the would-be reconquest, driving Georgian troops back out of the disputed territory. Russian troops continued a short distance into Georgian territory and then withdrew two weeks later.

The 2008 Georgia-Russia war was short in duration, limited in geographic scope, and caused approximately 600 deaths—not trivial, but not a catastrophe.[15] The 2010 survey includes an open-ended question that asks respondents to describe the effects of the war on their firms' profitability and investment plans. Almost universally, respondents commented on the negative impacts of the conflict on the economy overall. Most common were complaints about a decreased willingness of foreigners to invest and a drop in consumer confidence and domestic spending. Firms dependent on trade with Russia were hit particularly hard.

Conflict Sensitivity Results

The analysis in this section draws on three measures: First, *Conflict Likelihood*, a Likert-scale assessment of the likelihood of conflict recurrence; second, *Business Strategy Effect*, a Likert-scale assessment of how strongly the **risk** of future violent conflict affects each firm's business strategy;[16] third, *Predicted Profit Impact*, a binary measure of whether a return to violent conflict would negatively affect each firm's profitability. The assessment of

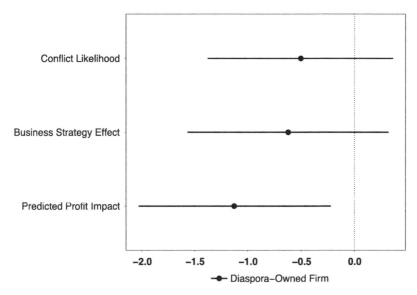

Fig. 6.3. *Conflict Likelihood, Business Strategy Effect, and Predicted Profit Impact*

conflict likelihood is worded as follows: "When your firm is making strategic plans, does your firm think that a return to violent conflict in South Ossetia or Abkhazia in the next three years is likely or unlikely?" The aim is to capture the strategic assessment of the firm as a whole, and not simply the personal opinion of the respondent. Figure 6.3 presents results from a set of regressions that closely match those in previous sections.

Consistent with my expectations, I estimate that diaspora-owned firms both report a weaker effect of war risk on their business strategy and are less likely to anticipate that a return to conflict would negatively impact their profitability. Diaspora-owned firms are simply less concerned about a return to violence than their nondiaspora-owned peers. Of these two effects, only the difference with regard to expected impact on profitability is statistically significant.

This difference in the level of concern raises the question of whether this can simply be attributed to differences in the perceived probability of conflict recurrence. It is possible that diaspora-affiliated firms report a lower impact of conflict risk on their business plans simply because they assess the risk to be lower, not because they are less sensitive to risk. Is the difference I observe just an artifact of optimism about the level of risk?

The data suggest this is not the case: diaspora-owned firms rate the risk of a return to conflict as lower than do other foreign firms, but only by a very small amount. Indeed if I rerun the two hypothesis tests controlling for the perceived likelihood of conflict recurrence, the results are robust—diaspora-owned firms are still systematically less concerned.

One small note on the predicted profit impact: there were three respondents who reported that a return to conflict would actually increase their firm's profitability. My results are not sensitive to dropping these "profiteer" firms from the sample. For full regression tables and additional technical details, see appendix D6.4.

> **Empirical Takeaway:** In Georgia, diaspora-owned firms are less likely than other foreign firms to expect a negative profit impact from war.

6.5. Conclusion

Looking back at the empirical results presented earlier in the book, chapters 4 and 5 confirm key elements of the transnational brokerage mechanism, demonstrating that diaspora-affiliated firms are both more socially connected than other foreign firms and use and benefit from social ties more than do other foreign firms. This chapter tests a key implication of this motivation mechanism—that diaspora-owned firms are more socially responsible than other foreign firms—and finds no evidence to support it. I find some limited evidence that diaspora-affiliated firms may reinvest a higher share of their earnings, but generally I find little difference between diaspora-affiliated and nondiaspora affiliated foreign firms in terms of their impact on development.

I find some (limited) evidence that diaspora-owned firms report weaker impacts of war risk on their business strategy than other foreign firms. This finding is consistent with either a transnational brokerage mechanism—diaspora-owned firms may be more capable of mitigating war risk—or a social and emotional motivations mechanism—diasporans may be less sensitive to war risk because their investment is not solely motivated by pursuit of a favorable risk-adjusted rate of return on their investment. However, I find stronger evidence that diaspora-affiliated firms are less likely to expect that a return to war in Georgia would damage their profitability—this is consistent with the transnational brokerage mechanism. These results do not indicate that social and emotional motivations are irrelevant, but they are consistent with a capabilities-based story in which diaspora-affiliated firms adjust their business plans less in response to conflict risk because they expect that, even if conflict breaks out, they can continue to operate profitably.

While the most important finding in this chapter is the failure to find support for the social and emotional motivations theory, the conflict sensitivity results have important implications for my theory of diasporans as transnational brokers. Like chapters 4 and 5, the analysis in this chapter takes a testable implication of my theory of diasporans as transnational brokers, places that implication at risk of falsification, and fails to falsify it. In addition to being more socially connected and making better use of social ties, I now have evidence that diaspora-affiliated firms also perceive themselves as more likely to be able to sustain profitability in the face of violent conflict in the investment host country. The evidence in favor of the importance of transnational brokerage continues to accumulate.

These findings also have important implications for the big picture relationship between migration and development. The evidence presented in this chapter indicates that diaspora-affiliated firms are no better for homeland development than other foreign firms. They may reinvest a higher share of their earnings, which is positive, but they are no more socially responsible and do not perceive themselves as better for development than do other foreign firms. Conditional on being able to get a foreign firm to invest in the first place, a host country appears to be just as well off if the investing firm is not diaspora-owned. There is no added benefit to attracting diaspora-affiliated firms.

However, to conclude that diaspora-affiliated firms have no greater development impact than other foreign firms would be to ignore the development implications of the transnational brokerage mechanism. Diasporans provide important capabilities to the firms they own and manage and there is good theoretical reason to expect that these capabilities are most valuable in the types of poorly governed homelands where most multinationals fear to tread. This implies, though it does not prove, that diaspora-affiliated firms are more willing than other foreign firms to enter capital starved homelands that otherwise would struggle to attract much needed investment. The most important development contribution of diaspora-affiliated firms is simply showing up.

CHAPTER 7

Conclusion

Implications for Governments and Multinational Firms

Growth in FDI and migration is currently reshaping the global economy, and the growth of these two flows is more closely intertwined than is commonly understood. In particular, migrants and their descendants play a pivotal role in the ability of multinational firms to overcome the difficulties of operating in foreign markets in general, and to manage the challenges associated with institutionally underdeveloped countries in particular. Increasingly, migration is driving FDI. While past scholarship has identified migrants as critical to the overseas investment decisions of multinational firms (e.g., Weidenbaum and Hughes 1994; Saxenian 2006; Riddle and Nielsen 2010) and to global flows of FDI (Kugler and Rapoport 2007; Leblang 2010; Javorcik 2011; Burchardi, Chaney, and Hassan 2016), we are still trying to understand the exact role diasporans play in helping multinational firms invest and thrive in their homelands. This book provides a clear answer: diasporans provide value to the firms they own and manage by serving as transnational brokers and connecting them to valuable social networks in the homeland.

Because diasporans play a critical role in facilitating cross-border investment, some of the most fundamental policy decisions that will shape the future of the global economy are decisions regarding who will be allowed to migrate and to where. Wealthy countries are weighing the potential long-run economic benefits of inward migration against perceived cultural threats and increased labor market competition for native born workers.[1] Migration is also being considered as a substitute for foreign aid.[2] With support from their countries of settlement, diasporans can be a significant positive force in developing and stabilizing the homelands from which they emigrate.[3] As citizens and leaders in wealthy countries weigh these tradeoffs, they deserve a more complete accounting of the economic benefits that migrants can generate for their countries of settlement. Diasporans bolster the capabilities of the firms they own and manage, allowing these firms to do business successfully in politically challenging homelands. When diaspora-affiliated firms thrive, it benefits both the country of settlement and the homeland.

For the first time, we have systematic data and a detailed picture of exactly what diaspora-affiliated firms look like and how they differ from their nondiaspora-affiliated peers. This evidence complements existing knowledge about the development impacts of remittances and makes clear the power of diasporans to positively transform the economies they depart. In light of this evidence, arguments that migration from developing countries should be limited to prevent "brain drain" are no longer empirically supported in most cases. The long-term economic value diasporans provide to their homelands is simply too large. This knowledge can guide developing-country governments as they deploy scarce resources to recruit inward investment, as they seek political will for difficult institutional reforms, and as they attempt to leverage their diaspora populations as a positive force for economic and political development.

7.1. The Firm-Level Findings

Diasporans serve as transnational brokers, providing value to the firms they own and manage by connecting them to valuable social networks in the homeland. The strength of the empirical evidence for this claim rests on the cumulative consistency of the results across a wide variety of tests. In chapters 4, 5, and 6, I test for differences between diaspora-affiliated and nondiaspora-affiliated foreign firms in terms of their capabilities, strategies, and performance. There may be flaws in any single hypothesis tests, and not all results are statistically significant on their own. However, when assessed together the pattern of results becomes very difficult to explain unless the underlying theory is largely correct.

Table 7.1 summarizes the results of 31 tests of my theory of diasporans as transnational brokers. Across these 31 tests, 29 results are in the expected direction, 13 are statistically significant ($p < 0.05$), and eight more have p-values less than 0.1. The p-value for each test indicates the probability that I

Table 7.1. Tests of Transnational Brokerage

Hypothesis	Sub-Hypothesis	Direction Correct?	*p*-value
H4.1: The Frequency Hypothesis	Local Government Officials	**Yes**	**0.020**
	National Government Officials	Yes	0.062[†]
	Bureaucratic Officials	Yes	0.276
	Peer Firms	Yes	0.056[†]
H4.2: The Subjective Strength Hypothesis	Local Government Officials	**Yes**	**0.009**^{**}
	National Government Officials	**Yes**	**0.017**
	Bureaucratic Officials	**Yes**	**0.010**^{**}
	Peer Firms	Yes	0.097
H4.3: The Direct Ties Hypothesis	Government Officials (any level)	**Yes**	**0.010**^{**}
	National Level Officials (Congress, Senate, and Cabinet)	Yes	0.286
	Bureaucratic Officials	Yes	0.098[†]
H4.4: The Importance Hypothesis	Owners' and managers' family ties (Georgia)	Yes	0.067[†]
	Owners' and managers' friendship ties (Georgia)	**Yes**	**0.032**
	Owners' and managers' friendship and family ties combined (Georgia)	**Yes**	**0.003**^{**}
	Owners' and managers' family ties (Philippines)	Yes	0.140
	Owners' and managers' friendship ties (Philippines)	Yes	0.068[†]
	Owners' and managers' friendship and family ties combined (Philippines)	Yes	0.056[†]
H5.1: The Information Hypothesis	Use social ties to gather information	Yes	0.107
	Rank social ties as their most important source of information	No	0.428
H5.2: The Dispute Resolution Hypothesis	Attempt resolution of disputes outside of court	**Yes**	**0.007**
	Use social ties to resolve disputes directly	**Yes**	**0.003**
H5.3: The Credit Hypothesis	Offer credit to their customers/clients	Yes	0.228
	Receive credit from their suppliers	No	0.579
H5.4: The Real Estate Hypothesis	Friend ties for real estate	Yes	0.745
	Family ties for real estate	Yes	0.061[†]
	Either family or friend	Yes	0.077[†]
H5.5: The Government Relations Hypothesis	Reach out via personal relationships	**Yes**	**0.007**^{**}
H.5.6: The Policy Influence Hypothesis	Attempted to influence policy	**Yes**	**0.008**^{**}
	Influenced policy	**Yes**	**0.014**
H6.2: The War Risk Hypothesis	Business Strategy Effect	Yes	0.198
H6.3: The War Impact Hypothesis	Predicted Profit Impact	**Yes**	**0.014**

Note: The regression analysis for the **H5.1** information hypotheses can be found in appendix C.
[†]$p < 0.1$, $p < 0.05$, ^{**}$p < 0.01$; *p*-values in bold (< 0.05) are statistically significant.

would still estimate a difference this large if my theory was incorrect and there was, in fact, no difference between diaspora-affiliated and nondiaspora-affiliated foreign firms.

In chapter 4 I show that diaspora-affiliated firms report having more and stronger social ties than other foreign firms, both in terms of ties to peer firms and ties to government officials at all levels. I also show in both Georgia and the Philippines that diaspora-affiliated firms view social ties as more important to firm performance than do other foreign firms. In chapter 5 I show that diaspora-affiliated firms also report using social ties more extensively. I assess five areas in which I expect social ties to be useful for successfully conducting business: accessing information, resolving disputes, extending and receiving credit, acquiring real estate, and interacting with government officials and influencing policy.

I find strong support with regard to dispute resolution, real estate acquisition, and interacting with government officials and influencing policy. The evidence with regard to accessing information and extending and receiving credit is more mixed. In both cases, diaspora-affiliated firms behave as expected, but most nondiaspora-affiliated firms also give credit to and receive credit from business counterparts and use social ties to access information. Thus it seems diaspora-affiliated firms have little advantage in these areas. I therefore focus on the two most policy-relevant areas in which it is clear that diaspora-affiliated firms have an advantage: resolving disputes with other firms and interacting with and influencing the homeland government. In both chapters 4 and 5 it is notable that the advantages of diaspora-affiliated firms are most pronounced in the areas that are most political—namely in the strength and extent of their ties to government officials and in their ability to use social ties to resolve disputes and influence policy.

In chapter 6, I use data from Georgia to assess whether diaspora-affiliated firms are less likely than other foreign firms to adjust their investment plans in response to the risk of violent conflict, and whether they are less likely to report that a return to violent conflict would negatively impact their profitability. I find evidence that diaspora-affiliated firms are more confident that they can operate profitably in the face of violent conflict. If diaspora-affiliated firms' optimism about their ability to maintain profitability during wartime is justified, it implies that they may be more likely than other foreign firms to continue operating when the risk of violence increases.

Empirical Takeaway: Diaspora-affiliated firms are more socially connected than nondiaspora-affiliated foreign firms, they use social ties more in business, and they benefit from doing so.

Diasporans and Development

In chapter 6 I also test an alternative theory of diaspora investment based on diasporans' social and emotional motivations for engaging with the homeland. This theory is important to evaluate empirically because it underlies some of the more optimistic views in the policy community regarding the development impact of diaspora investment (e.g., Foreign Service Institute 2010; Debass and Ardovino 2009). As noted in chapter 2, governments and NGOs often justify their efforts to promote diaspora investment on the expectations that diaspora investment is somehow more effective at catalyzing development than other types of FDI. In chapter 6 I test the expectation that diaspora-owned firms are more socially responsible than other foreign firms. If this is true, then the development impact of diaspora investment would be expected to be very large indeed. As summarized in table 7.2, I find no support for this expectation.

Also in chapter 6 I assess whether, outside of social responsibility, diaspora-affiliated firms behave in ways that might produce larger pro-development spillovers in the homeland. I find only very weak evidence that they might—diaspora-affiliated and nondiaspora-affiliated foreign firms are quite similar in this regard. Thus the empirical results lead me to the conclusion, which I will expand substantially in the following section, that diaspora-affiliated firms impact development primarily through their

Table 7.2. Tests of Social and Emotional Motivation

Hypothesis	Sub-Hypothesis	Direction Correct?	p-value
H6.1: The Social Responsibility Hypothesis	Higher Salaries	No	0.438
	Quality of Life	No	0.514
	Professional Development	Yes	0.984
	Profit Focused	Yes	0.372
	Minimize Labor Costs	**No**	**0.010**[**]
	Prioritize Local Hiring	Yes	0.244
	Green	Yes	0.389
	Donations	No	0.830

[†] $p < 0.1$, [*] $p < 0.05$, [**] $p < 0.01$. p-values in bold (< 0.05) are statistically significant.

ability to thrive under political conditions that confound and deter other multinational firms. Within these adverse settings, just the ability of foreign firms to succeed in doing business is an important step toward economic development.

7.2. Implications for Developing-Country Governments

From the perspective of someone optimistic about the development potential of diaspora investment, my failure to find any evidence that diaspora-affiliated firms are more socially responsible than their nondiaspora-affiliated peers, and my failure to find that they behave in ways likely to produce unusually large positive spillovers, is disappointing. However, consistent with my theory I find that diaspora-affiliated firms are more capable than other foreign firms. The development implications of these capabilities should not be undervalued.

One of the most fundamental economic problems facing developing countries is a scarcity of capital. This is particularly true for countries with low levels of institutional development, where political risk deters inward investment by firms that might otherwise find market conditions appealing. Diaspora-affiliated firms can have a large impact on development just by behaving like normal, albeit highly capable, profit-seeking firms. What developing countries need are capital, technology, and expertise—foreign firms bring these things even when they come only with the intention of making money.

If diaspora owners and managers help foreign firms thrive in the homeland, and I provide evidence that they do, then diasporans are driving economic development in an important way. Diaspora-affiliated firms buy inputs, employ workers, and sell goods and services, and all of these things contribute to growth and development. Diaspora-affiliated firms contribute to development in the homeland by thriving where most other foreign firms cannot. Particularly in capital-scarce countries with low levels of institutional development, foreign firms that can simply do business can be a godsend.

The policy implications of this argument relate most directly to how developing-country governments deploy scarce resources to recruit FDI. Such governments often expend substantial resources to promote investment, both in terms of efforts to educate potential investors about opportunities and in terms of financial incentives, like tax breaks (e.g., Blomström and Kokko 2003; Harding and Javorcik 2011; Jensen, Malesky, and Walsh 2015). Many developing countries already have in place at least limited programs aimed at increasing economic engagement from their diasporas (IOM 2005; Riddle and Nielsen 2010). My theory suggests that targeting investment promotion efforts at the diaspora is efficient because the social-tie-based capabilities of diaspora-affiliated firms are homeland-specific. A member of the Filipino diaspora conveys advantages on the firm he/she manages that are specific to the Philippines, and which provide much less value to the firm if it invests in Malaysia or Thailand instead. Thus when the Philippines government seeks to recruit investment from diaspora-affiliated firms, they do so with a built-in advantage over other countries competing for the same investment.

Many developing countries have already taken the step of integrating investment promotion efforts into more general outreach to the diaspora, and some have specific diaspora investment promotion agencies (e.g., Riddle, Brinkerhoff, and Nielsen 2008).[4] My findings suggest that this is sound practice and should be expanded. My theory implies that, dollar for dollar, money spent promoting diaspora investment is likely to generate more investment than money spent educating and offering incentives to broader populations of potential investors whose capabilities are not country-specific.

My theory does not suggest, however, that just any diasporan can return to the homeland, launch a firm, and enjoy business success. Diasporans' abilities to serve as transnational brokers depend on the social networks they possess and the business relevance of the communities those ties connect. Existing research provides some guidance as to which diasporans are most able to found new firms and spearhead new investments.[5] Not surprisingly, Black and Castaldo (2009) find that diasporans who gain work experience and accumulate savings while abroad are those most likely to found new firms upon their return to the homeland.[6] Black and Castaldo also find that membership in a diaspora organization increases entrepreneurship; many of these organizations have the express purpose of facilitating homeland investment and philanthropy (e.g., Orozco and Lapointe 2004). When governments seek to recruit diaspora investment, these organizations offer a valuable starting point; wealthy diasporans and those with overseas work experience also stand out as potentially fruitful targets.

Policy Takeaway: Developing countries should target investment promotion efforts at diasporans and diaspora-affiliated firms.

Taking Politics Seriously

The most important difference in capabilities and strategy that I identify between diaspora-affiliated and nondiaspora-affiliated foreign firms involves the use of social ties to interact with government officials and influencing policy. This deserves particular attention in the context of the impact on development because concern about the political power of foreign firms has long been an important theme among critics of FDI in developing countries (e.g., Leonard 1980; Hymer 1982). The interests of foreign firms may conflict with the interests of the domestic public, and it is potentially problematic if foreign firms are able to achieve political outcomes that privilege their interests over the preferences of local citizens. However, the core interests of foreign firms in promoting a more favorable investment climate may also mean that they pursue policy objectives consistent with fostering long-run economic growth. In this respect, the interests of foreign firms and the domestic public may be closely aligned.

The development implications of politically influential diaspora-affiliated firms thus depend on the policy preferences of those firms.[7] In a best-case scenario, the most salient political preferences of diaspora-affiliated firms are for things like strong rule of law, stable policy outcomes, and civil peace, which also benefit the domestic public. To the extent that the political influence of diaspora-affiliated firms furthers these goals, it is likely good for development. In a worst-case scenario, diaspora affiliated firms derive a substantial portion of their competitive advantage from their ability to manage the political risks associated with low levels of institutional development. Because a high level of political risk deters entry by potential competitors, diaspora-affiliated firms may actually prefer that political risk remains high.[8] This could lead diaspora-affiliated firms to use their political influence in ways that actually undermine institutional development.

The truth likely lies somewhere in between. I expect that, for almost all foreign firms, the benefits of lowered political risk outweigh the costs from increased competition, leading even very capable diaspora-affiliated firms to prefer lower political risk. However, I also expect that diasporans use their political influence to secure favorable treatment from government officials, which sometimes benefits the firm at the expense of local citizens in the homeland.

The development takeaway regarding political influence thus runs toward the middle ground. Politically powerful diaspora-affiliated firms represent a powerful constituency in favor of reforms that strengthen the quality of the investment climate. However, particularly in homelands with endemic corruption, these are also firms well-situated to exploit institutional weaknesses for profit. Understanding exactly how the political preferences of diaspora-affiliated firms differ from the political preferences of nondiaspora-affiliated foreign firms is necessary before we can draw out these implications with greater precision.[9]

Empirical research on the political activities of firms is inherently very difficult, particularly when firms are seeking policy outcomes that may be publicly unpopular. Firms have little to gain and much to lose by discussing their political objectives with researchers. This is why the surveys conducted for this project studiously avoided asking firms about the nature of their political objectives. However, given that I have now identified diaspora-affiliated firms as a type of firm with unusual capabilities for influencing policy, a necessary next step in this research agenda is to find a way to examine the policy outcomes that these firms seek.

7.3. Implications for Governments in Wealthy Countries

The volume of diaspora investment globally is shaped in part by the investment promotion policies of developing-country governments and the pace of institutional reform in these countries. These flows are shaped much more profoundly, however, by the past immigration policies of wealthy nations, which determine how many individuals from developing countries will become diasporans. As noted in the introduction, within poor countries 40% of adults would emigrate permanently if they could (Esipova, Ray, and Pugliese 2011). The binding constraints on migration are the policies of wealthy migrant-receiving countries.[10]

My findings add to a large and growing body of evidence that the negative effects of brain drain are substantially offset, and often overwhelmed, by the long-term economic benefits of a large and educated diaspora (e.g., Mountford 1997; Kapur 2004; Agunias 2006; UNDP 2009; Beine, Docquier, and Rapoport 2001, 2011; Djajic and Vinogradova 2015). This view is not universal, of course. De Haas (2012) even suggests that optimism in this area may be beginning to retreat. I hope the evidence in this book helps retain this optimism, as I believe it is justified.

Migration into wealthy nations is restricted for many reasons, but among the most salient is a desire in migrant-receiving countries to protect native-born workers from competition—specifically a desire to protect wages and employment (Zimmerman 1995; Scheve and Slaughter 2001; Borjas 2013). Thus an important contribution of this book is to point clearly to transnational brokerage by diasporans as an important economic benefit that accrues to wealthy countries when they allow inward migration. When diasporans facilitate successful investment from their country of settlement into their homeland, economic benefits accrue to both countries. Firms that invest successfully overseas may increase employment in the head-quarters country, create additional tax revenue from their increased profits, and, more broadly, contribute to economic growth in the headquarters country. These benefits should weigh in the calculus of migrant-receiving countries when they consider the economic tradeoffs related to increased inward migration.

Perhaps more importantly, though, I provide a direct counterargument to concerns about the negative effects of brain drain on poor countries. While it is not only wealthy and politically connected diasporans who can serve as transnational brokers, this is an elite-focused theory. I expect that wealthier and better-connected migrants are more likely to provide value as transnational brokers. That is, many of the same individuals that have the most to offer the homeland economy if they do not emigrate also have the greatest likelihood of serving as transnational brokers if they do. As noted in the introduction, rigorous empirical work examining the remittance be-havior of African-born doctors in Canada and the United States shows that even if we only consider wage remittances, the financial benefits of high-skilled emigration are positive for developing countries (Clemens and Pet-tersson 2008; Clemens 2011). When we include the role of high-skilled mi-grants as potential transnational brokers, the case becomes even more clear cut and the potential benefits much greater.

Brain-drain-based arguments for limiting high-skilled migration from poor countries to wealthy ones are by now arguments with little or no de-fensible empirical basis. For most developing countries, the long-run eco-nomic benefits of a large diaspora far exceed the short run economic costs of outward emigration by the highly educated. The huge IT sector that has transformed the domestic skilled-labor market in India only emerged be-cause so many highly skilled engineers emigrated to Silicon Valley. This emigration was a large short-term loss to the Indian economy, but when these migrants returned to India carrying newfound expertise and bringing

American capital in tow, they launched a domestic IT industry that would likely never have been born had those engineers not emigrated in the first place (Saxenian 2006; Kapur 2012).

In the wake of frequent, albeit relatively minor, terrorist attacks in Europe and the United States in 2016 and 2017, the migration debate in the United States and Europe has understandably been dominated by security concerns (e.g., Nixon 2016; Walker 2016). However, the economic case for increased skilled migration remains sound. Given their dependence on high-skilled labor, technology companies such as Google and Microsoft have been persistent advocates of raising or abolishing the annual cap on the number of H1-B visas that are issued by the United States each year (e.g., Schouten and Gomez 2013). The findings in this book lend additional weight to arguments for such a policy change. More wealthy, skilled, and well-connected migrants entering America today means more transnational brokers creating value for American firms tomorrow.

Policy Takeaway: Wealthy countries should relax immigration restrictions, particularly with regard to immigration by wealthy and educated individuals.

7.4. Implications for Multinational Firms

The business community has long recognized the value of social ties in business, particularly in developing countries. For foreign firms that are not diaspora-owned, many seek to gain access to local social networks by hiring local or diaspora managers. This strategy appears to be very widespread. Almost no foreign firms attempt to do business in the Philippines without either diaspora affiliation or a local manager.[11] Foreign firms know that they need local connections. What has not been established empirically before, and what my findings make clear, is that diaspora-affiliated firms have large advantages over firms with local managers and no diaspora connections. The social ties of diasporans are not only valuable, they are difficult to substitute for. A firm cannot simply replace a diaspora manager with a local manager without losing much of the value that the diaspora manager creates. This finding is new, and it has important implications for firm strategy.

What is unique and irreplaceable about diasporans is that they have social ties not only in the homeland but also in their country of settlement.

They serve as a rare connection between their network of relatives, child-hood friends, and classmates in the homeland and their network of neigh-bors, colleagues, and friends in the country of settlement. They are frequently fluent in multiple languages and, more importantly, fluent in multiple cul-tures, giving them an advantage over nonmigrants in forming new social ties, adding to their advantage over time. It is the strong ties to headquarters personnel that diasporans frequently have and local managers often lack. As discussed in chapter 2, a local broker you can't trust is a local broker you can't use. Much more so than local managers, diasporans are brokers that head-quarters personnel can trust and communicate with efficiently.

By establishing diasporans and their capabilities for transnational bro-kerage as potentially valuable firm assets, this book invites multinational firms to do several things. First, firms need to assess their diaspora-based capabilities relative to their competitors. What diasporans do they currently employ, and how well are they making use of the transnational brokerage capabilities those diasporans possess? Second, firms should develop strate-gies to enhance their diaspora-based capabilities—hiring, promoting, and even creating more diaspora managers. Lastly, firms need to use knowledge of their current diaspora-based capabilities to guide strategic decisions, es-pecially location choices for new investments.

The self-evaluation piece is not trivial. Diasporans are, on average, bet-ter positioned to serve as transnational brokers than nondiasporans. How-ever, not all migrants retain strong enough ties to the homeland to even be considered diasporans, let alone to serve effectively as transnational bro-kers. Evaluating an individual's potential as a transnational broker requires more than knowing her ethnicity or migration history—it requires an as-sessment of her ties both to the relevant political and economic elites in the homeland and to individuals in the firm headquarters. Once potential dias-pora brokers are identified, making effective use of those individuals' ties remains no small feat (e.g., Schotter and Beamish 2011). Research shows, for example, that autonomy in their role within the firm enhances individu-als' ability to establish and manage high-trust relationships with counter-parts outside the firm (Perrone, Zaheer, and McEvily 2003). Thus an impor-tant part of self-evaluation involves assessing how well a firm is making use of the diaspora capabilities already at its disposal.

For firms whose transnational brokerage capabilities are lacking relative to their peers, or relative to their strategic needs, hiring and promoting di-aspora managers offers a potential fix, as does the creation of diaspora managers from current employees. Diaspora managers are created by a practice referred to as "inpatriate" management, in which multinational firms take local managers and transfer them to work in the headquarters country. In doing so, multinational firms induce migration and create diasporans. After some period of time spent working in the headquarters country, inpatriate managers often return to positions working in their homeland, having transformed themselves from local managers into diaspora managers (e.g., Harvey, Speier, and Novicevic 2000; Reiche 2011). They retain the same homeland ties that they had as local managers, but now also possess greater fluency in the culture of the headquarters country and stronger social ties to headquarters personnel, greatly increasing their value to the firm. Inpatriate management can be difficult and expensive. However, the findings in this book provide hard evidence that the payoffs are frequently substantial, particularly in countries with low levels of institutional development.

Pushing these insights a little further, a firm's understanding of its capabilities for transnational brokerage should shape its strategic decision-making, particularly its location choices. Most capabilities from which multinational firms derive their competitive advantage are globally relevant. Proprietary technology, managerial expertise, and economies of scale benefit multinational firms wherever they do business. Diaspora-based capabilities for transnational brokerage are location-specific. Imagine a multinational firm based in Monterey Park, California, which is home to a sizable population of Taiwanese immigrants. If that firm employs a large number of Taiwanese-American managers, and if those managers have ties to the relevant economic and political elites in Taiwan, this offers the firm a substantial advantage in investing successfully in Taiwan. While not entirely irrelevant, these advantages will not serve the firm as well in South Korea or the Philippines. Thus those firms who evaluate their leadership teams and discover particular diaspora-based capabilities should consider the long-term location-related strategies that allow them to capitalize on those capabilities most effectively.

Management Takeaway: Multinational firms with affiliates in countries with low levels of institutional development should invest in recruiting diaspora managers and creating diaspora managers via inpatriate management programs. Firms should also shape their location decisions around the diaspora capabilities they already possess.

7.5. Next Steps in This Research Agenda

The empirical advances in this book were made possible, first and foremost, by new data. To take the next steps in this research agenda, more and better data remains the critical missing piece. The results in this book raise questions as well as answering them, and there is need for more detailed data in a range of areas: how firms become diaspora affiliated; how diaspora affiliation affects firm behavior over time; and exactly what policy objectives diaspora-affiliated firms seek.

More data is also necessary to probe the robustness and the scope of the findings presented here. The empirical analysis draws on data from two countries, Georgia and the Philippines, both of which are typical of the universe of countries to which my theory of transnational brokers applies—countries with weakly institutionalized political systems. While there are many benefits from making empirical comparisons between firms operating within the same country, there are limits on the inferences that are possible on the basis of data from just two countries. The analysis in this book allows for at least cautious inference to countries that are, broadly speaking, similar to Georgia and the Philippines.

My hope is that future research will produce data covering a wider range of countries, including wealthy industrialized countries with strong formal political institutions. While I expect that diasporans' social ties are most valuable when formal political institutions are weak, social ties play an important role in business in even the most strongly institutionalized contexts. It may be that diaspora affiliation provides firms with important competitive advantages in these contexts as well. There is also an urgent need for data that tracks firms over time, allowing us to observe how and why firms become diaspora affiliated, and how becoming diaspora affiliated (or shedding diaspora affiliation) changes their behavior. This book takes a large step forward in our empirical knowledge of diaspora investment, and I hope more steps will be taken soon.

7.6. Conclusion

The central contribution of this work is to present and test theory about the mechanisms through which diasporans provide value to the firms they own and manage. My empirical results have three primary implications: (1)

developing-country governments should target their investment promotion at diasporans and diaspora-affiliated firms, whose advantages are country-specific; (2) wealthy country governments should consider the economic benefits of transnational brokerage when evaluating immigration policy, and should consider relaxing restrictions on immigration by wealthy and educated individuals in particular; (3) multinational firms should invest in recruiting diaspora managers or transforming local managers into diaspora managers via inpatriate management programs.

This is an optimistic set of implications. They focus on ways that the unique capabilities of diasporans can be enhanced and unleashed. While I argue that existing hopes regarding the social responsibility of diaspora-owned firms are largely unsupported empirically, the development potential of diaspora investment is nonetheless enormous and growing. Outward migration is caused, in part, by poor economic performance and institutional failures in the homeland, but the same migrants driven out by development failures are themselves valuable assets in the forging of future development success.

The surge of migrants out of North Africa and the Middle East in 2015–2017 has generated substantial fear and consternation in Europe, and even in the United States where few have actually arrived. However, this book suggests that these migrants don't just represent short-term disruption, they also represent long-run economic potential. In the future I expect that many of these migrants will serve as transnational brokers, connecting European firms into social networks in their homelands and providing those firms with important advantages in navigating the challenges inherent to rebuilding a country after years of violence. These diasporans will provide value both to the countries in which they are now settling and to the fragile homelands from which they have departed.

APPENDIX A: SUPPLEMENTARY MATERIALS FOR CHAPTER 3

Research Design and New Firm-Level Data

A3.3. Survey Methodology

The two theories being tested in this book make predictions regarding topics that are extremely sensitive to firms, and that are likely only known to high-ranking individuals within each firm—how firms and governments interact, how they use social ties in business, and how socially responsible they are. This introduces two key methodological challenges. The first involves gaining access to a respondent at each firm with an in-depth knowledge of firm strategy, such as an owner or manager,[1] and the second is to elicit accurate and complete information from those individuals about these sensitive topics.

Face-to-Face Enumeration

In both Georgia and the Philippines, I worked with multilingual enumerators and prepared translated versions of the survey instrument. In Georgia, respondents were given a choice of taking the survey in Georgian, Russian, or English. In the Philippines, respondents were given a choice between English and Tagalog. Both survey instruments were taken through multiple rounds of reverse translation, for example, translated from English to Tagalog by one translator, and then translated back into English by a different translator, to ensure equivalence between versions (e.g., Harkness and Schoua-Glusberg 1998).

An important advantage of in-person enumeration was that we were able to ensure that the intended respondent was indeed the one who answered the questions. In mail or e-mail-based surveys, questionnaires are sometimes completed by subordinates rather than firm managers.

Sampling Strategy

The Georgia data are particularly valuable because my team was able to survey a random sample of the foreign-owned firms operating in Georgia. The power of a random sample is that one can infer that whatever is true in the sample is, within a margin of error, true of the entire population from which the sample was drawn—in this case, the full universe of recently registered foreign firms operating in Georgia.

The sampling frame was derived from two sources. First, we surveyed all the firms from a list of foreign-owned firms provided by the Georgian Ministry of Finance. The list included all foreign firms that met the following criteria: (1) a for-profit enterprise; (2) at least 10% foreign ownership; (3) registered as active and paying taxes as of June 1, 2009; and (4) obtained its first registration in Georgia after the year 2000. We supplemented the tax list with a random sample of 300 of the 450 firms that responded to the Ministry of Finance's Balance of Payments survey in 2009. These firms also met criteria 1–3, but some were initially registered prior to 2000.[2]

In total, we attempted to contact 1,024 firms in Georgia. Only 484 could be contacted and, of these, only 362 met the criteria above. Among the firms that could not be contacted, many were firms that had closed but had not been removed from the tax rolls. For others, the contact information was simply out of date.[3] Of the 362 firms that were successfully contacted and which met the criteria for inclusion in the study, full interviews were conducted with 154, yielding a 44% response rate. At thirteen firms, enumerators failed to interview a manager but were able to collect some basic information about the firm; 195 firms refused to participate. For additional details on the sample, including a comparison of respondents and nonrespondents by home country, see Graham (2014).[4]

In the Philippines, my collaborator Cesi Cruz and I initially hoped to create a similar random sample, but these efforts were stymied by an extremely low survey response rate in the pilot. In Georgia, being an American researcher made me sufficiently novel to get respondents to talk to my team; in the Philippines, respondents were less impressed. Making matters worse, a rumor was in circulation that a couple of years previously, an individual posing as a Japanese researcher used a survey as cover for corporate espionage against a number of Filipino firms. We never found any concrete evidence that such espionage occurred, but the rumor was widely believed, making it more difficult for our team to establish credibility with potential respondents.

Changing course, Professor Cruz and I joined forces with additional local scholars,[5] hired additional staff, and began the labor-intensive work of recruiting a snowball sample of foreign firms (e.g., Goodman 1961). We began by tapping the social networks of all of our team members: two of our collaborators were business school professors in the Philippines, and one of our enumerators was the daughter of a former finance minister, all of which helped tremendously. We reached out to business organizations, including the Philippines Chamber of Commerce and Industry, the Management Association of the Philippines, and many others.[6] And at the end of each survey, we asked respondents to suggest managers at other foreign firms they believed might be willing to talk to us. Firms were eligible for inclusion in the sample if they were (1) at least partially foreign owned; (2) not state owned; and (3) not micro-enterprises.

While not our first choice, this snowball sampling strategy had an offsetting benefit. Because our team approached each potential respondent through a social tie, our enumerators entered each interview with a higher baseline level of trust than we would have enjoyed otherwise. When contacting a firm, we were able to say, "X suggested that you might be willing to talk with us." Respondents knew that one of their friends or colleagues, often someone who had been through the interview process already, was willing to put a piece of their reputation on the line to recommend us.

Respondents in the Philippines were very open in their responses, and this allowed us to gather detailed information about firms' use of social ties in business. Many of these questions had to be struck from the survey in Georgia because they were too sensitive, but they proved not to be a problem in the Philippines. Some of this can likely be attributed to cultural differences—Georgia is a postcommunist country in which discussions of issues potentially related to corruption are much more fraught. But I believe much of the difference is also attributable to difference in sampling strategy—a higher baseline level of trust goes a long way.

The final Philippines sample was about 40% larger than the Georgian sample, but unlike the random sample surveyed in Georgia, the average foreign firm in the Philippines sample may not be representative of the average foreign firm operating in the Philippines overall. To assess how similar the Philippines sample is to the overall population of foreign firms in the Philippines, the following section compares the sample of firms surveyed in the Philippines to a list of the largest foreign firms in the country, which was obtained from the Philippines Securities and Exchange Commission (SEC), and to the distribution of economic activity across sectors in the Philippines economy overall.

Philippines Sample Comparison

The list of firms secured from the Philippines SEC covers the 1,224 largest foreign firms in the Philippines and includes information on each firm's home country, sector, and its profitability.[7] This allows me to compare our sample with the largest foreign firms in the Philippines across multiple dimensions. While I expect the firms in our sample to be, on average, smaller than the firms on the SEC list, if our sample is representative, it should be similar to the SEC firms in terms of sector, home region, and profitability. I also compare the sectorial distribution of firms in the Philippines sample to the sectorial distribution of economic activity in the Philippines economy overall.[8]

Figure A3.3 shows the proportion of firms in each sector for two groups of firms: those in the Philippines sample and those on the SEC list of large MNCs. It also shows the share of economic activity in the Philippines economy that occurs in each sector.[9] Figure A3.4 compares the distribution of firms by home region between the Philippines sample and the SEC list. Figure A3.5 compares the proportion of firms in the Philippines sample that reported earning a profit in 2013 to the proportion of firms from the SEC list that reported earning a profit in 2010.[10] Taken together, these three figures show that, in general, the sample of firms drawn in the Philippines survey is similar to the population of firms in the Philippines overall.

Figure A3.3 shows that in most sectors the share of firms from our sample in a given sector is either similar to the SEC list or it falls between the SEC list's figure and the overall economy figure. Nonetheless, we control for sector in all of the analyses conducted in the book.

Figure A3.4 shows that the proportion of firms drawn from Europe and from countries outside the United States, Europe, and Asia are similar. However, the number of firms headquartered in Asia differs significantly. Looking at the underlying data, 28% of the firms in the SEC sample are

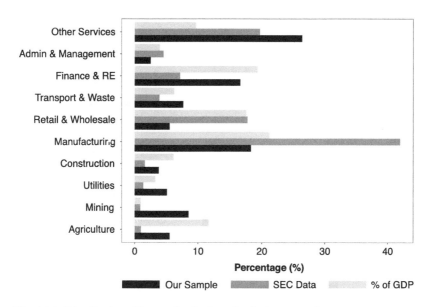

Fig. A3.3. *Distribution of Sectors for the Sample, the SEC List of Large Foreign Firms, and the Philippines Economy Overall.*

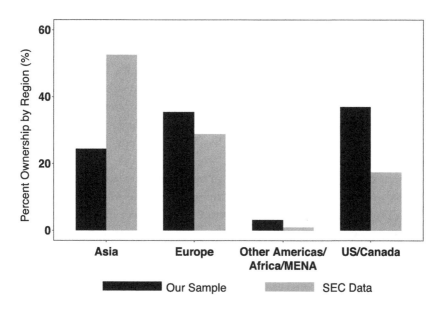

Fig. A3.4. *Share of Sample by Region*

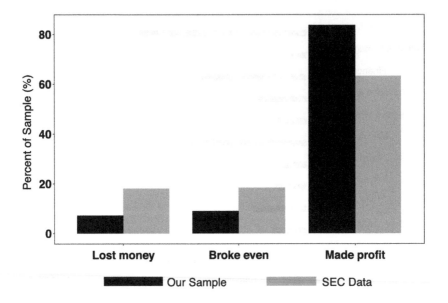

Fig. A3.5. *Share of Firms Earning a Profit*

based in Japan, but only 5% of firms in our sample are Japanese. This may be connected to the incident I mentioned early, where someone posing as a Japanese researcher conducted corporate espionage in the Philippines. This incident may have had a particularly chilling effect on the willingness of Japanese firms to cooperate with this study. I control for home region in my analysis, but to the extent that Japanese firms are different from other foreign firms with regard to the role of diasporans, it is possible that this underrepresentation biases my results.

Figure A3.5 shows that the firms in our sample are similar to the SEC sample with respect to profitability, though slightly more likely to report being profitable. This difference, while small, may reflect an underlying difference in the two pools of firms, or it may reflect that firms are more likely to report profitability to academic enumerators than to the Philippines government, to which firms must pay taxes on those profits.

One of the factors that cannot be observed from the SEC list is the social connectedness of firms, and this is an area where I expect our sample to be different than the population of multinationals in the Philippines overall. I expect our sample is skewed toward firms that are more socially connected than other foreign firms. Because we were relying on social ties to identify potential respondents, if a firm was not socially connected our team never found it (e.g., Erickson 1979). Thus for both diaspora-affiliated and nondiaspora-affiliated foreign firms, I expect the firms in our sample are better connected than the average foreign firm in the Philippines. Fortunately, I have no reason to expect that this bias is likely to be more present in our sample of diaspora-affiliated firms than in our sample of nondiaspora-affiliated foreign firms. Thus this difference is important but unlikely to actually bias my hypothesis tests.

Given a nonrandom sample, it is not possible to make strong inference that what is true in our sample of firms is necessarily true of the full population of medium and large foreign firms in the Philippines. However, what these analyses confirm is that the firms in the Philippines sample are well-distributed across sectors and represent a range of home countries and regions, and the sample includes both profitable and struggling enterprises. Critically for theory testing purposes, there is no reason to suspect that this sample of firms is a particularly favorable one in which to find support for my theory.

My ability to assess the reliability of the Philippines results is enhanced by the fact that the Philippines data are complemented by a random sample of firms from the Georgia case. In the empirical chapters I present support for my theory drawn from both cases. The fact that the support I find for my theory in the Philippines is matched by similar support in analysis using the Georgia data provides additional reason to believe that sample bias is an unlikely explanation for the Philippines results. Indeed in figure 4.6, where I am able to use both the Philippines data and the Georgia data to test the same hypothesis, the support I find for my theory is stronger in the Georgia data, which is based on a random sample. Taken together, the evidence in this section suggests that sample bias is an unlikely explanation for the results I report in the main text.

Sensitive Topics and Social Desirability Bias

As noted above, the theories I test in this book involve information that firms are reluctant to share. Managers tend to be cautious when discussing their business operations because even simple information like a firm's annual revenues and profitability can be of use to competitors (e.g., Bloom and Van Reenen 2010). These concerns are even greater with regard to detailed information about firm strategy, requests for the names of other firms to whom they have ties, questions about the use of social networks in business, and questions about how the firm interacts with government officials.

The obvious first step in addressing these issues is to ensure the anonymity of respondents (a web page and e-mail address at an American university helps with credibility here), and to pretest and pilot the survey instruments extensively. Cognitive pretesting of the survey instrument in Georgia revealed that many topics had to be avoided entirely to avoid making respondents uncomfortable. For this reason, the Georgia data provides only limited information on firms' social connectedness. In the Philippines, our pretesting suggested that respondents were remarkably willing to talk openly about their social ties and about behaviors that bordered on corruption. However, in the main survey, we still wanted to test whether respondents were systematically underreporting the use of social ties in certain sensitive capacities. To quantify underreporting, we conducted a modified list experiment, using the *listit* technique introduced by Corstange (2009).[11]

We first select what we considered to be the most sensitive question on the survey, which asked respondents whether their firm used their owners' and managers' social relationships with government officials as a means for improving government relations for the firm. The question provided respondents with a list of four different "things that businesses can do to improve relations with government agencies and influence government policy." The list included three strategies deemed to be noncontroversial and one potentially sensitive strategy involving the use of social ties. The four items were:

1. Other than required inspections, invite officials to visit/inspect your business to highlight your contribution to the local economy and community
2. Attend business forums and functions organized by the government
3. Reach out to government officials with whom your firm's owners or managers have personal relationships
4. Produce white papers or reports to submit to government agencies

To conduct the list experiment, we randomly assigned each respondent to one of two groups. Respondents in the direct response group were asked to indicate which of the four strategies their firm had employed in the past year—in other words, they were asked about each strategy individually. Re-

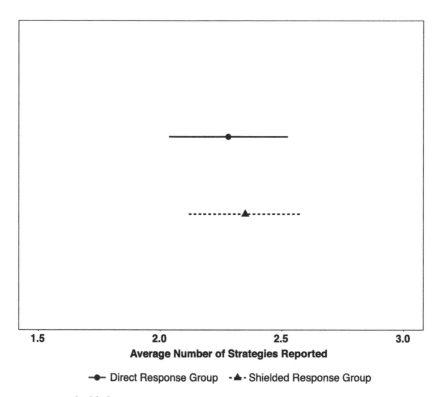

1.5   2.0   2.5   3.0
Average Number of Strategies Reported

─●─ Direct Response Group   ·▲· Shielded Response Group

Fig. A3.6. *Shielded vs. Direct Response Comparison*

spondents in the shielded response group were asked *how many* of the strategies their firm had employed in the past year. Thus in the shielded response group it was possible for firms to accurately answer the question without revealing whether or not their firm had used their owners' or managers' social ties to influence government officials.

If respondents are reluctant to admit to using social ties to influence government officials, this would cause the average number of strategies reported by respondents in the direct response group to be lower than the average number reported by respondents in the shielded response group. If respondents are willing to discuss controversial uses of social ties openly, we should see an equal number of strategies reported by each group. The average number of strategies reported by respondents in each group are presented in figure A3.6.[12]

The mean number of items mentioned by respondents whose responses were shielded was 2.35, while the mean number of items reported in the group that was asked about each item individually was 2.28—a decrease of 3%. This suggests that it is rare for firms in the Philippines to underreport socially undesirable behavior, even when asked about it directly. This increases my confidence that social desirability bias—namely respondents' desire to give the "correct" answer and look good to enumerators—is not driving results in the survey overall.

A3.4. Multiple Imputation and Descriptive Statistics

Almost all survey data includes at least some level of item nonresponse, a type of missing data that occurs when a respondent declines to answer a particular question on the survey. In both the Georgia and Philippines data, I employ multiple imputation to address item nonresponse. When conducting hypothesis tests later in the book, I treat the analysis conducted on the imputed data as the "primary" specification for each hypothesis test, and then conduct robustness tests using the raw, or unimputed, data.

The methodological literature is unambiguous that multiple imputation is a best practice when dealing with item nonresponse. Compared with the alternative of analyzing only those cases for which all data are present, known as list-wise deletion or complete case analysis, multiple imputation reduces bias and avoids a reduction in sample-size, allowing full use of all the information collected in the survey (e.g., King et al. 2001).[13] List-wise deletion is appropriate if less than 5% of cases contain a missing value on any variable and the data are missing completely at random (MCAR), namely if the probability that a particular value will be missing does not depend on observed or unobserved values (Graham 2009). However, in practice these conditions are rarely met. With both the Georgian and the Philippines data, I employ the multiple imputation by chained equations (Raghunathan et al. 2001; Van Buren 2007; Royston 2004, 2009).[14]

For each missing value in the dataset, multiple imputation uses observed values of other variables to predict the missing value. This process is repeated multiple times, creating several "complete" datasets. Because multiple imputation creates several estimates for each missing value, these values reflect the uncertainty of the imputations and result in more accurate standard errors. If the observed data are a good predictor of the missing values, the imputations will be more consistent across each imputation, resulting in smaller standard errors (Greenland and Finkle 1995). I impute only the independent variables used in the analyses and not the dependent variables.

Table A3.1a provides descriptive statistics on the imputed data for the Philippines, comparing the raw values to the imputed values for each variable and noting the percentage of the values that are imputed. Table A3.1b presents the same information from the Georgia imputation.

Table A3.1a. Descriptive Statistics Table on the Imputed Data: The Philippines

	Original Obs	Imputed Obs	Original Missing	Original Mean	Imputed Mean	Original Min	Imputed Min	Original Max	Imputed Max	Original SD	Imputed SD
Diaspora Affiliated*	211	223	0	0.61	0.62	0	0	1	1	0.49	0.48
Diaspora Owned	211	223	12	0.39	0.39	0	0	1	1	0.49	0.49
Diaspora Managed	221	223	2	0.49	0.49	0	0	1	1	0.50	0.50
Firm Age (logged)	221	223	2	2.80	2.80	0	0	5.10	5	1.04	1.03
Size (Revenue)	182	223	41	3.52	3.43	1	1	5	5	1.59	1.60
Number of Employees	222	223	1	3.32	3.32	1	1	5	5	1.35	1.34
Foreign Ownership Share	210	223	13	3.87	3.85	2	2	5	5	1.18	1.19
Publicly Traded	221	223	2	0.48	0.48	0	0	1	1	0.50	0.50
Special Enterprise Zone	221	223	2	0.33	0.34	0	0	1	1	0.47	0.47
Ethnicity of Owners: Chinese	214	223	9	0.07	0.07	0	0	1	1	0.26	0.25
Diaspora Respondent	214	223	9	0.06	0.06	0	0	1	1	0.24	0.24
Local Manager	218	223	5	0.93	0.93	0	0	1	1	0.26	0.26
Diaspora CEO	218	223	5	0.08	0.10	0	0	1	1	0.27	0.30
Sector-Agriculture	223	N/A	5	0.05	N/A	0	N/A	1	N/A	0.23	N/A
Sector-Mining	223	N/A	0	0.08	N/A	0	N/A	1	N/A	0.27	N/A
Sector-Utilities	223	N/A	0	0.05	N/A	0	N/A	1	N/A	0.22	N/A
Sector-Construction	223	N/A	0	0.04	N/A	0	N/A	1	N/A	0.20	N/A
Sector-Manufacturing	223	N/A	0	0.19	N/A	0	N/A	1	N/A	0.39	N/A
Sector-Retail/Wholesale	223	N/A	0	0.06	N/A	0	N/A	1	N/A	0.24	N/A
Sector-Transport& Waste	223	N/A	0	0.07	N/A	0	N/A	1	N/A	0.25	N/A
Sector-Finance/Real Estate	223	N/A	0	0.16	N/A	0	N/A	1	N/A	0.37	N/A
Sector-IT/Tech Science	223	N/A	0	0.17	N/A	0	N/A	1	N/A	0.38	N/A
Sector-Restaurants/Hotels	223	N/A	0	0.06	N/A	0	N/A	1	N/A	0.23	N/A
Sector-Admin & Management	223	N/A	0	0.02	N/A	0	N/A	1	N/A	0.15	N/A
Sector-Arts/Edu/Health	223	N/A	0	0.04	N/A	0	N/A	1	N/A	0.20	N/A
Region-Americas	223	N/A	0	0.22	N/A	0	N/A	1	N/A	0.41	N/A
Region-Europe & MENA	223	N/A	0	0.21	N/A	0	N/A	1	N/A	0.41	N/A
Region-Asia/Pacific	223	N/A	0	0.21	N/A	0	N/A	1	N/A	0.41	N/A
Region- The Philippines	223	N/A	0	0.37	N/A	0	N/A	1	N/A	0.48	N/A

* Because *diaspora affiliated* takes a value of one if either *diaspora owned* or *diaspora managed* is one, this variable is not imputed independently. Instead it is created as a "passive" variable after the imputation is complete, based on the values that are imputed for *diaspora owned* and *diaspora managed*.

Table A3.1b. Descriptive Statistics Table on the Imputed Data: Georgia

Variable	Original Obs	Imputed Obs	Original Missing	Original Mean	Imputed Mean	Original Min	Imputed Min	Original Max	Imputed Max	Original SD	Imputed SD
Diaspora Owned	151	161	10	0.20	0.20	0	0	1	1	0.40	0.40
Respondent = Owner	157	161	4	0.24	0.24	0	0	1	1	0.43	0.43
Employees (logged)	144	161	17	2.81	2.86	0	−1	7.24	7	1.70	1.72
Firm Age (logged)	160	161	1	1.76	1.76	0	0	3.71	4	0.60	0.60
Share of Foreign Ownership	157	161	4	4.48	4.48	2	2	5	5	0.76	0.76
Location=Tbilisi	161	N/A	0	0.79	N/A	0	N/A	1	N/A	0.41	N/A
Region-Middle East	161	N/A	0	0.17	N/A	0	N/A	1	N/A	0.38	N/A
Region-FSU[a]	161	N/A	0	0.17	N/A	0	N/A	1	N/A	0.38	N/A
Region-West	161	N/A	0	0.43	N/A	0	N/A	1	N/A	0.50	N/A
Primary Sector	156	161	5	0.07	0.08	0	0	1	1	0.26	0.26
Secondary Sector	156	161	5	0.30	0.30	0	0	1	1	0.46	0.46
Tertiary Sector	156	161	5	0.49	0.49	0	0	1	1	0.50	0.50

[a]Twenty-eight firms are based in the Middle East and 28 are based in the Former Soviet Union (FSU), leading these two rows to be identical.

Fortunately, due to careful piloting of the survey instrument in advance, item nonresponse in both the Georgia and the Philippines was quite low, meaning that relatively little data needed to be imputed. In Georgia, the independent variable of interest, *diaspora owned*, is 6% missing and firm demographic characteristics used as controls are between 2% and 11% missing. In the Philippines, the independent variables of interest, *diaspora affiliated, diaspora managed*, and *diaspora owned*, are 5%, 1%, and 5% missing, respectively. The firm demographic characteristics used as controls are between 1% to 19% missing.

I imputed missing values for all independent variables used in the analysis, except those for which no values were missing. However, I did not impute missing values for dependent variables. Thus the sample size in the analyses in chapters 4–6 varies depending on the number of missing values for the dependent variables. In some analyses, the dependent variables are only collected for a subset of firms. For example, the questions regarding what strategies firms used to resolve disputes were only asked of those firms

Table A3.2a. Descriptive Statistics Table on the Dependent Variable: Chapter 4

Variable	Mean	Std. Dev.	Min	Max	N
Ch.4 Frequency of Interaction Hypothesis					
Local Govt Officials	1.08	1.41	0.00	4.00	298
Nat'l Govt Officials	1.05	1.45	0.00	4.00	298
Bureaucrats	1.42	1.58	0.00	4.00	297
Peer Firms	2.49	1.25	0.00	4.00	300
Ch.4 Subjective Strength of Ties Hypothesis					
Local Govt Officials	1.93	2.50	0.00	7.00	298
Nat'l Govt Officials	2.01	2.65	0.00	7.00	300
Bureaucrats	2.42	2.64	0.00	7.00	296
Peer Firms	4.41	2.25	0.00	7.00	299
Ch.4 Direct Political Ties Hypothesis					
Total Direct Ties	0.39	0.74	0.00	3.00	302
Ties to Nat'l Officials	0.08	0.27	0.00	1.00	291
Ties to Bureaucrats	0.19	0.39	0.00	1.00	291
Ch.4 Subjective Importance of Social Ties: The Philippines					
Family	3.93	2.26	1.00	7.00	294
Friends	4.05	2.16	1.00	7.00	294
Combined	−0.002	1.82	−2.70	2.72	293
Ch.4 Subjective Importance of Social Ties: Georgia					
Family	2.59	1.94	1.00	7.00	147
Friends	4.15	2.18	1.00	7.00	148
Combined	0.00	0.77	−1.03	1.77	134

Table A3.2b. Descriptive Statistics Table on the Dependent Variable: Chapter 5

Variable	Mean	Std. Dev.	Min	Max	N
Ch.5 Source of Information					
Social Ties	0.80	0.40	0.00	1.00	298
Internet	0.88	0.32	0.00	1.00	298
Newspapers	0.76	0.43	0.00	1.00	298
Philippine Embassy/Consulate	0.28	0.45	0.00	1.00	279
Philippine Investment Promotion Agency	0.33	0.47	0.00	1.00	295
Home Country Embassy/Consulate	0.45	0.50	0.00	1.00	272
Law Firm or Consultant	0.77	0.42	0.00	1.00	297
Industry Associations	0.85	0.36	0.00	1.00	298
Ch.5 Most Important Source of Information					
Friends, Family and Personal Networks	0.31	0.46	0.00	1.00	271
Law Firm or Consultant	0.14	0.34	0.00	1.00	271
Industry Association	0.28	0.45	0.00	1.00	271
Ch.5 Dispute Resolution Hypothesis					
Dispute in the Past 2 Years	0.46	0.50	0.00	1.00	302
Attempted to Use Courts	0.50	0.50	0.00	1.00	138
Attempted Resolution Outside of Courts	0.73	0.45	0.00	1.00	135
Used Social Ties	0.39	0.49	0.00	1.00	135
Ch.5 Methods of Dispute Resolution					
Int'l or Local Arbitration	0.45	0.50	0.00	1.00	135
Local Govt	0.21	0.41	0.00	1.00	135
Home Country Embassy/Consulate	0.13	0.34	0.00	1.00	134
Appeal to Well-Connected Individuals	0.39	0.49	0.00	1.00	135
Work with Law Firm	0.56	0.50	0.00	1.00	135
Assistance from PEZA	0.06	0.24	0.00	1.00	133
Ch.5 Giving and Receiving of Credit Hypothesis					
Receives Credit from Supplier	0.79	0.41	0.00	1.00	291
Offers Credit to Customers	0.74	0.44	0.00	1.00	293
Ch.5 Interact with Government Hypothesis					
Reach out via Personal Relationships	0.51	0.50	0.00	1.00	149
Invite Officials to Tour Facilities	0.55	0.50	0.00	1.00	150
Attend Business Forum	0.80	0.40	0.00	1.00	150
Produce Reports or White Papers	0.45	0.50	0.00	1.00	149
Ch.5 Policy Influence Hypothesis					
Attempted to Influence Policy	1.00	0.86	0.00	2.00	294
Success if Attempted	1.43	0.83	0.00	2.00	105
Influenced Policy	0.67	0.84	0.00	2.00	281
Ch.5 Acquiring Real Estate Hypothesis					
Family Ties	0.12	0.32	0.00	1.00	144
Friend Ties	0.25	0.44	0.00	1.00	143
Either Family or Friend	0.32	0.47	0.00	1.00	146

Table A3.2c. Descriptive Statistics Table on the Dependent Variable: Chapter 6

Variable	Mean	Std. Dev.	Min	Max	N
Ch.6 Social Responsibility Hypothesis					
Higher Salaries	4.77	1.32	1.00	7.00	126
Quality of Life	4.77	1.20	1.00	7.00	124
Professional Development	5.44	1.38	1.00	7.00	129
Profit-Focused	5.42	1.30	1.00	7.00	126
Minimize Labor Costs	4.01	1.66	1.00	7.00	138
Prioritize Local Hiring	6.30	1.08	3.00	7.00	139
Green	6.25	1.22	1.00	7.00	127
Donations	0.59	0.49	0.00	1.00	145
Ch.6 Positive Spillover Effects					
Greenfield Investment (Georgia)	0.76	0.43	0.00	1.00	154
Greenfield Investment (The Philippines)	0.87	0.34	0.00	1.00	300
Reinvestment of Earnings (The Philippines)	3.44	0.93	1.00	4.00	263
Export Earnings (The Philippines)	1.96	1.16	1.00	4.00	283
Employment (The Philippines)	3.27	1.32	1.00	5.00	299
Ch.6 Sensitivity to Conflict Hypothesis					
Conflict Likelihood	3.72	1.64	1.00	7.00	137
Business Strategy	4.98	1.28	2.00	7.00	146
Profit Impact	0.65	0.48	0.00	1.00	144

who had experienced a dispute in the past two years. Tables A3.2a, A3.2b, and A3.2c provide descriptive statistics for the dependent variables used in chapters 4, 5, and 6, respectively.

In addition to the descriptive statistics provided on each variable across the full sample of firms, figures A3.7 and A3.8 show how diaspora-affiliated firms compare to other foreign firms across each of the firm characteristics used as control variables in the main analysis. Figure A3.7 describes the data for Georgia and A3.8 describes the data for the Philippines. The solid vertical line in the middle of each plot represents the mean value for the entire sample. The dashed vertical lines represent values that are one standard deviation above and below the mean. In both countries and across all variables, the mean of diaspora-affiliated firms and the mean of nondiaspora-affiliated foreign firms falls within one standard deviation of the mean. This indicates that diaspora-affiliated firms are quite similar in their basic characteristics—namely their age, size, share of foreign ownership, and so on. What is truly different about diaspora-affiliated firms is their access to social ties and their use of those ties.

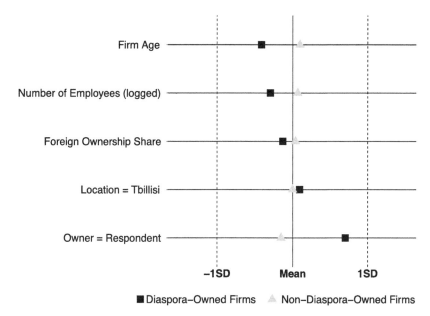

Fig. A3.7. *Comparing Diaspora-Owned and NonDiaspora-Owned Foreign Firms in Georgia*

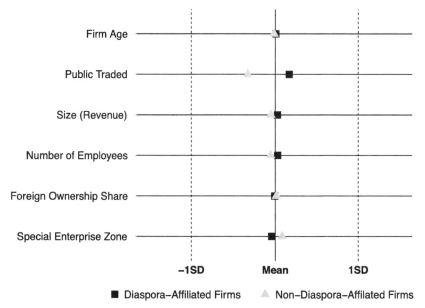

Fig. A3.8. *Comparing Diaspora-Affiliated and NonDiaspora-Affiliated Foreign Firms in the Philippines*

APPENDIX B: SUPPLEMENTARY MATERIALS FOR CHAPTER 4

Measuring Firms' Social Connectedness

This appendix provides additional technical details, including full regression tables, for the empirical results presented in chapter 4. As is also the case in chapters 5 and 6, the figures in the main text present the estimated effect of the independent variables of interest, *diaspora affiliated* and *diaspora owned*. These coefficients are drawn from regressions that control for a wide range of firm attributes, and one of the key purposes of providing full regression tables for each analysis is to examine the effects of these control variables. The set of control variables is distinct between Georgia and the Philippines, but within each dataset, the same controls are used throughout the book. Descriptive statistics for all variables are provided in appendix A. The analysis in chapter 4 relies primarily on data from the Philippines, but the assessment of the importance hypothesis (H4.4) is conducted on data from both Georgia and the Philippines.

In addition to providing regression tables that match the figures in the main text, this appendix also discusses the results from identical regressions run on the raw, unimputed data. These results match those in the imputed data quite closely, showing that my results are not driven by any idiosyncrasies of the imputation process. The section numbering in this appendix matches that in the chapter; not all sections of the chapter require additional details here in the appendix. This appendix begins with details regarding the measurement of diaspora affiliation and then proceeds to present regression tables for each of the four hypotheses tested in chapter 4.

B4.1. Measuring Diaspora Affiliation

To identify diaspora-owned firms in the Georgia survey, enumerators first read the following text to each respondent:

> *I'm going to refer to the "Georgian diaspora" in some of the following questions. The Georgian diaspora includes all individuals who live outside of Georgia but who consider themselves to be Georgian. It includes people who were born in Georgia and emigrated to other countries. It also includes people who were born in other countries, but whose ancestors are from Georgia. If a Georgian owner of the firm was living abroad when he decided to start this firm in Georgia, we count this as diaspora investment even if the owner moved back to Georgia.*

Respondents were then asked, "Are any of the owners of your firm members of the Georgian diaspora?" The answers to this question generate a binary measure of diaspora ownership.

In the Philippines, there is a word in Tagalog, *balikbayan*, which refers to Filipinos who have emigrated and then returned. In this survey, our enumerators asked both of the following questions. First, "Are any of the owners of your firm Filipinos who live abroad?" Then, "We define balikbayan as any Filipino who has lived, worked, or studied overseas in the past. Are any of the owners of your firm balikbayan?" I identify firms as diaspora owned if they are at least partially owned by either a Filipino living abroad or a balikbayan. Our enumerators also asked whether any of the firm's managers are balikbayan or Filipinos living abroad, creating a binary measure of diaspora managed. Firms that are either diaspora owned or diaspora managed are considered diaspora affiliated.

Note that in both Georgia and the Philippines the survey questions measuring diaspora identity capture anyone who is living or has lived outside the homeland but is still identifiable as a member of the national community of the homeland, namely is identified by their colleagues as Georgian or Filipino. This is a close, but not a perfect, match to the conceptual definition of diaspora given by Sheffer (1986: 3), which defines diasporans as people "residing and acting in host countries but maintaining strong sentimental and material links with their countries of origin—their homelands."[1]

B4.2. Testing the Frequency Hypothesis

Table B4.2 presents the regression results that underlie figure 4.2 in the text. These results show that diaspora-affiliated firms interact more frequently with peer firms and government officials than do other foreign firms. The coefficients on *diaspora affiliated* and *diaspora owned* in this table correspond to the coefficients presented in figure 4.2, and the standard errors on those coefficients are reflected in the confidence intervals displayed in the figure.

Few of the control variables used in this analysis have statistically significant effects. Older firms interact less frequently with their peers than do more recently established firms, perhaps because more recently established firms are still more active in finding and screening potential customers and suppliers. Firms with more employees interact less frequently with bureau-

Table B4.2. Frequency of Interaction with Elected Officials, Bureaucrats, and Peer Firms

	(1)	(2)	(3)	(4)	(5)	(6)	(7)	(8)
	Local Elected Officials		Nat'l Elected Officials		Bureaucrats		Peer Firms	
Diaspora Affiliated	0.501*		0.447$^\tau$		0.258		0.373$^\tau$	
	(0.214)		(0.238)		(0.236)		(0.194)	
Diaspora Owned		0.641**		0.621*		0.412$^\tau$		0.216
		(0.231)		(0.245)		(0.248)		(0.188)
Firm Age	−0.124	−0.105	−0.046	−0.028	0.040	0.050	−0.190*	−0.180*
	(0.125)	(0.125)	(0.124)	(0.125)	(0.114)	(0.114)	(0.088)	(0.089)
Publicly Traded	0.257	0.256	0.067	0.069	0.237	0.237	0.081	0.111
	(0.236)	(0.240)	(0.248)	(0.246)	(0.257)	(0.259)	(0.180)	(0.180)
Size (Revenue)	0.090	0.124	0.071	0.098	0.144	0.160	0.032	0.041
	(0.107)	(0.113)	(0.105)	(0.105)	(0.116)	(0.117)	(0.083)	(0.085)
Number of Employees	−0.090	−0.109	−0.025	−0.039	−0.255*	−0.266*	−0.052	−0.046
	(0.112)	(0.115)	(0.119)	(0.119)	(0.126)	(0.129)	(0.091)	(0.093)
100% Foreign Owned	0.106	0.055	−0.193	−0.250	0.482	0.434	−0.110	−0.104
	(0.312)	(0.320)	(0.293)	(0.303)	(0.360)	(0.364)	(0.253)	(0.258)
Majority Foreign Owned	−0.277	−0.299	−0.474$^\tau$	−0.499$^\tau$	−0.133	−0.153	−0.459$^\tau$	−0.445$^\tau$
	(0.250)	(0.251)	(0.272)	(0.265)	(0.284)	(0.282)	(0.233)	(0.235)
Special Enterprise Zone	−0.197	−0.107	0.142	0.238	0.385	0.450$^\tau$	−0.226	−0.204
	(0.233)	(0.234)	(0.243)	(0.244)	(0.273)	(0.270)	(0.201)	(0.205)
Sector Dummies	Yes	Yes	Yes	Yes	Yes	Yes	Yes	Yes
Region Dummies	Yes	Yes	Yes	Yes	Yes	Yes	Yes	Yes
Constant	1.826**	1.722**	1.845**	1.722**	2.298**	2.202**	3.335**	3.392**
	(0.599)	(0.589)	(0.603)	(0.590)	(0.670)	(0.663)	(0.403)	(0.396)
Observations	219	219	219	219	219	219	221	221

Note: The dependent variables are ordinal measures of frequency of interaction. Standard errors in parentheses. Linear regressions with robust standard errors.
$^\tau p < 0.10$, $^* p < 0.05$, $^{**} p < .01$

crats. However, this effect is conditional on controlling for a second measure of firm size, based on firm revenues, which has a negative estimated effect. These two measures of firm size are highly colinear (Spearman's rho = 0.70), making their independent effects difficult to interpret.

I also evaluate a set of regressions identical to those presented in table B4.2 but drawing on the raw, unimputed data. In these regressions, missing values for various control variables cause the sample size to fall to between 158 and 164 firms, depending on the dependent variable. With this smaller sample size, the precision of the coefficient estimates is reduced. I do not present a table of these results, but the estimated effect on frequency of interaction with local government officials falls just below the threshold for statistical significance, and the strength of the other estimated effects is reduced as well ($p = 0.07$ for local government officials; $p = 0.21$ for national government officials; and $p = 0.15$ for peer firms).

B4.3. Testing the Subjective Strength Hypothesis

Table B4.3 presents the results related to figure 4.3 in the main text. These results show that diaspora-affiliated firms have stronger ties to both peer firms and government officials, and the effects of diaspora affiliation on ties to all three types of government officials are statistically significant. I also estimate that diaspora-affiliated firms have stronger ties to peer firms, but this effect falls just short of statistical significance ($p = 0.097$). None of the control variables have statistically significant effects, though I estimate that publicly traded firms are more likely to have strong ties to all three types of government officials. Publicly traded firms may have stronger incentives to seek ties with government officials if these firms are subject to more extensive regulation.

As with the frequency of interaction results, the estimated effect of diaspora affiliation on strength of ties is slightly weaker in the raw, unimputed data. The results for local elected officials remains statistically significant, but the estimated effects on ties to national elected officials and bureaucrats both fall from statistical significance ($p = 0.74$ and $p = 0.17$, respectively). All of the estimated effects of diaspora affiliation on tie strength remain positive.

Table B4.3. Diaspora Affiliation and the Subjective Strength of Ties to National Officials, Local Officials, Bureaucrats, and Peer Firms

	(1)	(2)	(3)	(4)	(5)	(6)	(7)	(8)
	Local Elected Officials		Nat'l Elected Officials		Bureaucrats		Peer Firms	
Diaspora Affiliated	0.920**		1.009*		0.989**		0.611$^\tau$	
	(0.350)		(0.420)		(0.380)		(0.366)	
Diaspora Owned		1.155**		1.182**		1.192**		0.020
		(0.387)		(0.439)		(0.393)		(0.333)
Firm Age	−0.004	0.026	−0.117	−0.085	−0.069	−0.036	−0.075	−0.057
	(0.206)	(0.207)	(0.219)	(0.220)	(0.214)	(0.215)	(0.166)	(0.169)
Publicly Traded	0.448	0.454	0.493	0.510	0.582	0.599	−0.136	−0.065
	(0.424)	(0.431)	(0.456)	(0.453)	(0.443)	(0.445)	(0.324)	(0.326)
Size (Revenue)	0.077	0.122	−0.003	0.046	0.024	0.073	0.026	0.028
	(0.183)	(0.192)	(0.202)	(0.205)	(0.200)	(0.202)	(0.158)	(0.161)
Number of Employees	0.041	0.016	0.058	0.036	−0.105	−0.127	0.077	0.105
	(0.199)	(0.201)	(0.224)	(0.226)	(0.216)	(0.218)	(0.172)	(0.176)
100% Foreign Owned	0.006	−0.091	−0.196	−0.288	0.436	0.327	0.468	0.537
	(0.576)	(0.592)	(0.598)	(0.621)	(0.561)	(0.573)	(0.529)	(0.530)
Majority Foreign Owned	−0.495	−0.541	−0.780	−0.812	−0.505	−0.538	−0.538	−0.462
	(0.436)	(0.436)	(0.503)	(0.492)	(0.486)	(0.471)	(0.401)	(0.405)
Special Enterprise Zone	−0.158	0.016	0.173	0.351	0.317	0.505	−0.137	−0.157
	(0.395)	(0.396)	(0.433)	(0.437)	(0.444)	(0.445)	(0.377)	(0.385)
Sector Dummies	Yes	Yes	Yes	Yes	Yes	Yes	Yes	Yes
Region Dummies	Yes	Yes	Yes	Yes	Yes	Yes	Yes	Yes
Constant	2.193*	2.051*	3.944**	3.813**	2.798**	2.645**	4.274**	4.508**
	(0.965)	(0.975)	(1.063)	(1.046)	(0.963)	(0.998)	(0.869)	(0.844)
Observations	219	219	221	221	219	219	220	220

Note: The dependent variables measure subjective tie strength on a 7-point Likert scale. Standard errors in parentheses Linear regressions with robust standard errors.
$^\tau p < 0.10$, $^* p < 0.05$, $^{**} p < 0.01$

B4.4. Measuring Direct Political Ties

Firms' direct political ties are measured with the following question: "Have any of your firm's owners or managers held any of the following offices in the Philippines? Please include yourself in this count if applicable." The enumerator then reads off each of the offices from the following list, eliciting a separate response for each office.

A. Barangay captain, barangay council or other barangay-level position
B. Mayor
C. Municipal council or other municipal-level position
D. Governor
E. Provincial council or other provincial-level position

F. Official of the bureaucracy

G. Congressman, senator, or cabinet member

Respondents were then asked if their firm had a board of directors and, if it did, the question was repeated with regard to board members.

B4.5. Testing the Direct Political Ties Hypothesis

Table B4.5 matches figure 4.5 in the text. Consistent with the direct ties hypothesis, I find that diaspora-affiliated firms are more likely to have current or former government officials working directly at their firm, for example, serving as owners, managers, or board members. This effect is only statistically significant when all types of ties are pooled together—each type

Table B4.5. Diaspora Affiliation and Direct Political Ties

	(1)	(2)	(3)	(4)	(5)	(6)
	Total Direct Ties		Ties to Nat'l Level Officials		Ties to Bureaucrats	
Diaspora Affiliated	0.212**		0.037		0.080$^\tau$	
	(0.081)		(0.034)		(0.048)	
Diaspora Owned		0.225*		0.026		0.089
		(0.108)		(0.041)		(0.064)
Firm Age	0.016	0.023	−0.016	−0.016	−0.011	−0.009
	(0.046)	(0.046)	(0.021)	(0.021)	(0.032)	(0.032)
Publicly Traded	−0.143	−0.138	0.002	0.005	−0.015	−0.013
	(0.123)	(0.124)	(0.047)	(0.047)	(0.067)	(0.068)
Size (Revenue)	0.089$^\tau$	0.098*	0.043$^\tau$	0.044$^\tau$	0.017	0.021
	(0.046)	(0.048)	(0.023)	(0.024)	(0.030)	(0.031)
Number of Employees	0.025	0.022	−0.021	−0.021	0.044	0.043
	(0.051)	(0.052)	(0.025)	(0.025)	(0.031)	(0.031)
100% Foreign Owned	−0.005	−0.022	0.018	0.017	0.036	0.029
	(0.144)	(0.148)	(0.061)	(0.063)	(0.087)	(0.089)
Majority Foreign Owned	0.040	0.036	−0.005	−0.004	0.054	0.052
	(0.124)	(0.126)	(0.050)	(0.051)	(0.073)	(0.074)
Special Enterprise Zone	−0.063	−0.029	−0.021	−0.018	−0.059	−0.046
	(0.107)	(0.103)	(0.042)	(0.041)	(0.064)	(0.063)
Sector Dummies	Yes	Yes	Yes	Yes	Yes	Yes
Region Dummies	Yes	Yes	Yes	Yes	Yes	Yes
Constant	0.168	0.150	0.143	0.146	0.097	0.089
	(0.282)	(0.274)	(0.153)	(0.149)	(0.131)	(0.133)
Observations	223	223	214	214	214	214

Note: Standard errors in parentheses; linear regressions with robust standard errors.
$^\tau p < 0.10,$ * $p < 0.05,$ ** $p < 0.01$

of tie individually is quite rare, making precise estimation difficult. Only one of the control variables has statistically significant effects—I estimate that firms with larger annual revenues are more likely to have direct ties. This makes sense if these larger firms are better able to afford steps like hiring politicians onto their board of directors. As noted in the main text, I do not estimate the effect of diaspora affiliation on ties to local government officials because these ties are too rare and the appropriate regression models do not converge.

When the same analysis is conducted on the raw data, the estimated effect of diaspora affiliation on direct ties is stronger across all three dependent variables. The effect on total ties remains statistically significant and the effect on ties to bureaucrats becomes statistically significant ($p < .05$).

B4.6. Testing the Importance Hypothesis

While the three hypotheses regarding the number and strength of firms' social ties are tested using only data from the Philippines, the importance hypothesis is tested using data from both Georgia and the Philippines. Figure 4.6 in the main text displays the results for both countries side-by-side. Each survey asks similar questions about the importance of social ties to profitability, but they include different sets of questions that are used to measure control variables. Therefore I display the regression results related to figure 4.6 in two separate tables. Table B4.6 presents the results from the Philippines and table B4.6a presents results from Georgia.

Because respondents' assessments of the relationship between social ties and firm profitability are both complex and subjective, in this analysis I want to take particular care to ensure that the differences I observe between diaspora-affiliated and nondiaspora-affiliated foreign firms are driven by actual differences in firm capabilities, and not by differences in who the exact respondent is at each firm. Therefore in the models in the right-hand half of both table B4.6 and table B4.6a, I add an additional control variable regarding whether the respondent is also the owner of the firm.

Looking at the control variables in table B4.6, we see that, in the Philippines, older firms, firms with more employees, firms with a higher share of foreign ownership, and firms located in special enterprise zones are less likely to view social ties as important to profitability. In table B4.6a, we see that in Georgia firms based in Tbilisi are more likely to view social ties as important.

Table B4.6. Diaspora Affiliation and Subjective Importance of Social Ties: Philippines

	(1)	(2)	(3)	(4)	(5)	(6)	(7)	(8)	(9)	(10)	(11)	(12)
	Ties to Family		Ties to Friends		Combined Ties		Ties to Family		Ties to Friends		Combined Ties	
Diaspora Affiliated	0.494 (0.333)		0.584ᵀ (0.319)		0.505ᵀ (0.262)		0.384 (0.337)		0.621ᵀ (0.322)		0.474ᵀ (0.267)	
Diaspora Owned		0.192 (0.363)		0.122 (0.332)		0.149 (0.282)		0.145 (0.360)		0.131 (0.330)		0.133 (0.283)
Firm Age	-0.218 (0.187)	-0.206 (0.186)	-0.285ᵀ (0.166)	-0.271 (0.166)	-0.231 (0.149)	-0.219 (0.147)	-0.232 (0.186)	-0.225 (0.185)	-0.279ᵀ (0.167)	-0.268 (0.166)	-0.235 (0.148)	-0.225 (0.147)
Publicly Traded	0.338 (0.363)	0.373 (0.368)	0.024 (0.344)	0.075 (0.352)	0.162 (0.277)	0.202 (0.284)	0.319 (0.359)	0.343 (0.364)	0.029 (0.343)	0.079 (0.353)	0.156 (0.278)	0.190 (0.286)
Size (Revenue)	0.027 (0.185)	0.032 (0.188)	0.080 (0.162)	0.082 (0.165)	0.051 (0.142)	0.054 (0.145)	0.036 (0.189)	0.040 (0.191)	0.078 (0.162)	0.081 (0.165)	0.054 (0.143)	0.058 (0.146)
Number of Employees	-0.261 (0.203)	-0.244 (0.204)	-0.421* (0.186)	-0.396* (0.188)	-0.304ᵀ (0.158)	-0.285* (0.159)	-0.251 (0.207)	-0.237 (0.209)	-0.426* (0.186)	-0.399* (0.188)	-0.302ᵀ (0.159)	-0.284ᵀ (0.161)
100% Foreign Owned	0.247 (0.577)	0.258 (0.594)	-0.012 (0.488)	0.022 (0.512)	0.110 (0.444)	0.130 (0.465)	0.161 (0.575)	0.162 (0.589)	0.013 (0.495)	0.034 (0.519)	0.084 (0.449)	0.094 (0.468)
Majority Foreign Owned	-0.300 (0.408)	-0.267 (0.410)	0.383 (0.395)	0.435 (0.403)	0.056 (0.319)	0.095 (0.325)	-0.369 (0.411)	-0.350 (0.415)	0.403 (0.389)	0.445 (0.399)	0.035 (0.321)	0.063 (0.328)
Special Enterprise Zone	-0.639ᵀ (0.384)	-0.622 (0.391)	-0.379 (0.354)	-0.381 (0.366)	-0.453 (0.304)	-0.446 (0.313)	-0.649ᵀ (0.384)	-0.638 (0.390)	-0.374 (0.355)	-0.378 (0.368)	-0.455 (0.305)	-0.451 (0.313)
Diaspora Respondent							1.248ᵀ (0.741)	1.364ᵀ (0.723)	-0.404 (0.720)	-0.204 (0.711)	0.360 (0.584)	0.508 (0.572)
Constant	4.497** (0.839)	4.624** (0.842)	4.097** (0.850)	4.301** (0.840)	0.238 (0.673)	0.393 (0.670)	4.577** (0.837)	4.681** (0.834)	4.074** (0.852)	4.295** (0.841)	0.262 (0.674)	0.415 (0.669)
Sector Dummies	Yes	Yes	Yes	Yes	Yes	Yes	Yes	Yes	Yes	Yes	Yes	Yes
Region Dummies	Yes	Yes	Yes	Yes	Yes	Yes	Yes	Yes	Yes	Yes	Yes	Yes
Observations	216	216	215	215	215	215	216	216	215	215	215	215

Note: Standard errors in parentheses; linear regressions with robust standard errors.
ᵀ $p < 0.10$, * $p < 0.05$, ** $p < 0.01$

The inclusion of the additional control for respondent identity affects the results only slightly. In the Philippines data, the coefficients are mostly stable; the estimated effect of diaspora affiliation on the importance of ties to friends becomes slightly stronger ($p = 0.055$), while the effect on the combined importance of ties becomes slightly weaker ($p = 0.077$). In the Georgia data, the additional control reduces the estimated effects of diaspora ownership slightly, but enough to cause the effect on family ties to fall just below the threshold for statistical significance. The overall stability of these estimates when controlling for the identity of the respondent shows that these results are not contingent on the identity of the respondent and indeed reflect the characteristics of the firm itself.

When I rerun the regressions from tables B4.6 and B4.6a using the raw data, the estimated effect of diaspora ownership strengthens in the Georgia data, with all three results remaining significant ($p = 0.04$ for family ties; $p = 0.015$ for ties with friends; and $p < 0.001$ for family and friendship ties combined). However, the Philippines results are somewhat weaker in the

Table B4.6a. Diaspora Affiliation and Subjective Importance of Social Ties: Georgia

	(1) Family	(2) Friends	(3) Combined	(4) Family	(5) Friends	(6) Combined
Diaspora-Owned Firm	0.942$^\tau$	1.094*	0.556**	0.849$^\tau$	0.874$^\tau$	0.462*
	(0.509)	(0.504)	(0.183)	(0.509)	(0.499)	(0.184)
Firm Age (logged)	−0.238	0.108	−0.071	−0.240	0.081	−0.086
	(0.250)	(0.337)	(0.110)	(0.254)	(0.327)	(0.107)
Employees (logged)	−0.008	−0.098	−0.032	0.015	−0.054	−0.014
	(0.114)	(0.116)	(0.047)	(0.115)	(0.117)	(0.046)
100% Foreign Ownership	−1.366$^\tau$	−0.967	−0.503*	−1.238$^\tau$	−0.710	−0.402$^\tau$
	(0.719)	(0.676)	(0.233)	(0.705)	(0.634)	(0.214)
Majority Foreign Ownership	−1.490*	−1.516*	−0.693**	−1.444$^\tau$	−1.450*	−0.683**
	(0.752)	(0.762)	(0.262)	(0.736)	(0.708)	(0.242)
Location = Tbilisi	0.467	1.554**	0.331*	0.416	1.448**	0.271$^\tau$
	(0.388)	(0.487)	(0.156)	(0.390)	(0.489)	(0.152)
Respondent = Owner				0.442	0.904*	0.374**
				(0.417)	(0.393)	(0.138)
Sector Dummies	Yes	Yes	Yes	Yes	Yes	Yes
Region Dummies	Yes	Yes	Yes	Yes	Yes	Yes
Constant	2.676*	3.154*	0.050	2.499*	2.864*	−0.049
	(1.085)	(1.315)	(0.431)	(1.076)	(1.254)	(0.405)
Observations	139	140	126	139	140	126

Note: The dependent variables measure the subjective importance of each type of social tie. Standard errors in parentheses.

Linear regressions with robust standard errors.

$^\tau p < 0.10,\ ^* p < 0.05,\ ^{**} p < 0.01$

raw data, with all results short of statistical significance. The p-values on diaspora affiliation are 0.21, 0.38, and 0.20 for ties to family, ties to friends, and combined ties, respectively.

B4.7. Conclusion

Chapter 4 tests and finds support for two related claims: (1) that diaspora-affiliated firms are more socially connected than other foreign firms, and (2) that they view social ties as more important to profitability. The first claim is evaluated in 11 tests across three distinct measures of connectedness, all using the Philippines data. The second claim is evaluated in six tests, three in the Philippines and three in Georgia. Across these 17 tests, all estimated effects are in the expected direction, namely in all analyses the estimated effect of diaspora affiliation (diaspora ownership in the Georgia data) is positive. Seven of these estimated effects are statistically significant ($p < .05$). Conducting the same analyses on the raw, unimputed data, I again estimate a positive relationship between diaspora affiliation and social connectedness in all 17 tests; 6 of these results remain statistically significant. As is to be expected with a smaller sample size, the results in the raw data are, in most cases, somewhat weaker. However, the fact that the direction of effects is consistent and that six results remain statistically significant makes it clear that the effects presented in the main text are not driven by the imputation process itself.

APPENDIX C: SUPPLEMENTARY MATERIALS FOR CHAPTER 5

How Do Diaspora-Affiliated Firms Use Social Networks?

This appendix provides regression tables, technical details, and robustness checks for the results presented in chapter 5. It follows the same format as appendix B. Descriptive statistics for all variables are provided in appendix A.

C5.1. Access to Information

Figure 5.1 in the main text presents a simple bar chart of the percentage of diaspora-affiliated and nondiaspora-affiliated foreign firms that report using each of eight sources of information and what percentage of the firms in each group report that a given source of information is their most important. Table C5.1 presents the results of a regression analysis that evaluates the effect of diaspora affiliation on the probability that a firm uses each source of information, while table C5.1a examines the probability that a firm chooses each type of information as the most important. Of particular interest theoretically is the effect of diaspora affiliation on firms' use of social ties, namely their use of "friends, family and personal networks" as an information source. I predict that, because they are better connected, diaspora-affiliated firms are more likely to gather information through social ties and are more likely to view social ties as their most valuable source of information. In table C5.1, I estimate that diaspora-affiliated firms are more likely to use social ties to gather information, but the effect is neither large nor statistically significant ($p = 0.084$). I find no evidence, however, that diaspora-affiliated firms are more likely to rank social ties as their most important source of information (table C5.1a).

Table C5.1. Diaspora Affiliation and Source of Information

	(1)	(2)	(3)	(4)	(5)	(6)	(7)	(8)	(9)	(10)	(11)	(12)	(13)	(14)	(15)	(16)
	Friends, Family, Personal Networks		Internet		Newspapers		Filipino Embassy/ Consulate		Filipino Investment Promotion Agency		Home Country Embassy/Consulate		Law Firm or Consultant		Industry Associations	
Diaspora Affiliated	0.107ᵀ		0.082		−0.056		−0.168*		−0.204**		0.022		0.098		−0.017	
	(0.062)		(0.054)		(0.068)		(0.070)		(0.075)		(0.080)		(0.066)		(0.056)	
Diaspora Owned		−0.006		0.038		−0.042		−0.061		−0.127ᵀ		0.015		0.017		−0.064
		(0.060)		(0.048)		(0.068)		(0.079)		(0.075)		(0.090)		(0.064)		(0.054)
Firm Age	−0.046	−0.043	−0.016	−0.013	−0.030	−0.032	−0.032	−0.038	−0.022	−0.027	−0.043	−0.042	−0.061*	−0.059ᵀ	0.019	0.018
	(0.033)	(0.033)	(0.025)	(0.026)	(0.038)	(0.038)	(0.037)	(0.038)	(0.035)	(0.035)	(0.043)	(0.043)	(0.031)	(0.031)	(0.029)	(0.029)
Publicly Traded	−0.049	−0.035	−0.000	0.006	0.052	0.050	0.108	0.090	0.089	0.074	0.139	0.140	0.118ᵀ	0.129ᵀ	0.090	0.094ᵀ
	(0.069)	(0.070)	(0.058)	(0.058)	(0.077)	(0.076)	(0.074)	(0.075)	(0.077)	(0.078)	(0.090)	(0.090)	(0.068)	(0.068)	(0.054)	(0.054)
Size (Revenue)	0.009	0.008	0.002	0.004	0.029	0.027	−0.005	−0.007	−0.004	−0.010	−0.021	−0.020	0.038	0.039	0.002	−0.001
	(0.028)	(0.029)	(0.020)	(0.021)	(0.033)	(0.034)	(0.036)	(0.037)	(0.036)	(0.036)	(0.040)	(0.040)	(0.028)	(0.028)	(0.023)	(0.023)
Number of Employees	−0.042	−0.036	−0.061*	−0.060*	−0.038	−0.038	−0.025	−0.029	0.052	0.051	−0.017	−0.017	−0.050	−0.047	−0.017	−0.014
	(0.033)	(0.034)	(0.026)	(0.026)	(0.037)	(0.037)	(0.043)	(0.043)	(0.041)	(0.041)	(0.045)	(0.045)	(0.031)	(0.032)	(0.026)	(0.026)
100% Foreign Owned	−0.119	−0.106	0.047	0.050	−0.015	−0.014	0.193	0.185	−0.054	−0.056	0.110	0.109	0.061	0.069	0.019	0.028
	(0.095)	(0.098)	(0.073)	(0.076)	(0.106)	(0.105)	(0.126)	(0.127)	(0.101)	(0.102)	(0.125)	(0.125)	(0.095)	(0.093)	(0.086)	(0.085)
Majority Foreign Owned	0.011	0.026	−0.016	−0.011	−0.051	−0.053	0.004	−0.011	0.011	0.004	0.053	0.054	0.002	0.012	0.037	0.043
	(0.069)	(0.070)	(0.055)	(0.054)	(0.082)	(0.082)	(0.084)	(0.087)	(0.086)	(0.089)	(0.098)	(0.099)	(0.073)	(0.073)	(0.058)	(0.057)
Special Enterprise Zone	−0.016	−0.021	0.050	0.055	−0.035	−0.041	0.087	0.081	0.071	0.053	0.038	0.040	−0.033	−0.032	−0.066	−0.078
	(0.068)	(0.069)	(0.052)	(0.055)	(0.070)	(0.071)	(0.080)	(0.085)	(0.081)	(0.085)	(0.090)	(0.092)	(0.069)	(0.072)	(0.052)	(0.052)
Sector Dummies	Yes	Yes	Yes	Yes	Yes	Yes	Yes	Yes	Yes	Yes	Yes	Yes	Yes	Yes	Yes	Yes
Region Dummies	Yes	Yes	Yes	Yes	Yes	Yes	Yes	Yes	Yes	Yes	Yes	Yes	Yes	Yes	Yes	Yes
Constant	1.051**	1.100**	0.993**	1.011**	0.952**	0.947**	0.312ᵀ	0.263	−0.006	−0.047	0.464*	0.467*	0.814**	0.848**	0.916**	0.937**
	(0.155)	(0.159)	(0.151)	(0.154)	(0.197)	(0.194)	(0.167)	(0.169)	(0.144)	(0.144)	(0.223)	(0.223)	(0.173)	(0.179)	(0.145)	(0.143)
Observations	219	219	219	219	219	219	206	206	216	216	203	203	218	218	219	219

Note: Standard errors in parentheses; linear regressions with robust standard errors.
ᵀ $p < 0.10$, * $p < 0.05$, ** $p < 0.01$

The strongest effects in table C5.1 show that diaspora-affiliated firms are less likely to make use of the Philippine Investment Promotion Agency and the Philippine Embassy/Consulate. This is consistent with my theory. If diaspora-affiliated firms have an advantage gaining information via social ties, they should be less dependent on these formal sources. However, the most direct implication of my theory is with regard to the use of social ties. When I conduct this analysis using the raw data instead of the imputed data, the results are similar with regard to the Philippine Investment Promotion Agency and the Philippine Embassy/Consulate, but the estimated effect of diaspora affiliation on use of social ties is much smaller. This further undermines an already weak finding—the evidence that diaspora-affiliated firms are more likely than other foreign firms to use social ties to gather information is not convincing.

In table C5.1a, I estimate a weak, statistically insignificant negative effect of diaspora affiliation on the probability that firms' rate social ties as their most important source of information. I estimate a similar weak negative effect in the raw data. While roughly 25% of diaspora-affiliated firms report that social ties are their most important source of information, they are not more likely to report this than are other foreign firms. Gathering information does not appear to be an area where diasporans' social ties provide a clear advantage to the firms they own and manage.

C5.2. Dispute Resolution

This section presents the regression results underlying figure 5.2 in the main text. All regressions are logit regressions except those used to predict whether assistance was sought from the Special Economic Zone Authority (PEZA). Because only 6% of firms use this method, logit regressions would not converge and I was forced to use linear regression instead.

As noted in the main text, there is almost no difference between diaspora-affiliated and nondiaspora-affiliated foreign firms in their propensity to attempt resolution through the courts. However, many firms pursue resolution simultaneously through multiple channels and, consistent with my theory, diaspora-affiliated firms are more likely to attempt resolution outside the courts in general and to use social ties in particular. It is important to note that the core analysis in this section relies on a subset of 101 firms rather than on the full 223 firms in the Philippines sample. I restrict

Table C5.1a. Diaspora Affiliation and Firms' Most Important Sources of Information

	(1)	(2)	(3)	(4)	(5)	(6)
	Friends, Family, and Personal Networks		Law Firm or Consultant		Industry Association	
Diaspora Affiliated	−0.059		0.085		0.100	
	(0.074)		(0.061)		(0.070)	
Diaspora Owned		−0.029		0.026		0.100
		(0.073)		(0.059)		(0.076)
Firm Age	0.001	−0.002	−0.057$^\tau$	−0.053	0.036	0.040
	(0.036)	(0.036)	(0.033)	(0.033)	(0.035)	(0.035)
Publicly Traded	−0.062	−0.067	−0.023	−0.013	0.090	0.093
	(0.076)	(0.075)	(0.065)	(0.064)	(0.078)	(0.078)
Size (Revenue)	−0.027	−0.027	0.034	0.033	−0.013	−0.011
	(0.031)	(0.032)	(0.023)	(0.022)	(0.038)	(0.038)
Number of Employees	−0.010	−0.013	−0.004	0.001	−0.005	−0.003
	(0.039)	(0.039)	(0.030)	(0.030)	(0.043)	(0.042)
100% Foreign Owned	−0.189*	−0.193*	−0.030	−0.022	0.195	0.193
	(0.084)	(0.084)	(0.092)	(0.090)	(0.119)	(0.122)
Majority Foreign Owned	−0.018	−0.024	0.027	0.037	0.136	0.139
	(0.087)	(0.087)	(0.069)	(0.068)	(0.087)	(0.090)
Special Enterprise Zone	−0.057	−0.061	−0.065	−0.062	−0.009	0.009
	(0.072)	(0.073)	(0.058)	(0.061)	(0.075)	(0.075)
Sector Dummies	Yes	Yes	Yes	Yes	Yes	Yes
Region Dummies	Yes	Yes	Yes	Yes	Yes	Yes
Constant	0.785**	0.780**	0.072	0.087	0.054	0.038
	(0.222)	(0.224)	(0.174)	(0.187)	(0.200)	(0.201)
Observations	200	200	200	200	200	200

Note: Standard errors in parentheses; linear regressions with robust standard errors.
$^\tau p < 0.10,$ $^* p < 0.05,$ $^{**} p < 0.01$

the analysis to those firms that report having had a dispute in the past two years.

Because the sample is restricted in this manner, models 1 and 2 in table C5.2 estimate the effect of diaspora affiliation on the probability that firms report having had a dispute. Diaspora-affiliated firms are somewhat more likely to report a dispute, though the effect is not statistically significant.

In the raw data, the estimated effects of diaspora affiliation on firms' propensity to attempt resolution outside of courts and to use social ties to do so are slightly smaller than in the imputed data, causing these effects to fall just below the threshold of statistical significance ($p = 0.075$ and $p = 0.065$, respectively).

Table C5.2a supplements the analysis presented in table C5.2 and estimates the probability that firms attempted resolution through each of the

Table C5.2. Diaspora Affiliation and Dispute Resolution

	(1)	(2)	(3)	(4)	(5)	(6)	(7)	(8)
	Dispute in the Past 2 Years		Attempted to Use Courts		Attempted Resolution Outside of Courts		Used Social Ties	
Diaspora Affiliated	0.441		0.063		2.815**		1.937**	
	(0.341)		(0.541)		(1.038)		(0.651)	
Diaspora Owned		0.291		0.881		1.518*		0.425
		(0.342)		(0.611)		(0.675)		(0.600)
Firm Age	0.273	0.286	0.181	0.164	−0.385	−0.144	0.175	0.363
	(0.176)	(0.175)	(0.283)	(0.301)	(0.411)	(0.330)	(0.346)	(0.342)
Publicly Traded	0.656ᵀ	0.680ᵀ	−0.156	−0.121	−0.841	−0.248	−0.813	−0.468
	(0.373)	(0.373)	(0.616)	(0.611)	(0.845)	(0.783)	(0.680)	(0.686)
Size (Revenue)	−0.109	−0.097	0.208	0.279	−0.169	0.155	0.120	0.156
	(0.166)	(0.163)	(0.251)	(0.257)	(0.330)	(0.328)	(0.265)	(0.257)
Number of Employees	−0.034	−0.030	0.183	0.145	0.047	−0.185	−0.053	−0.137
	(0.179)	(0.178)	(0.284)	(0.290)	(0.502)	(0.386)	(0.368)	(0.328)
100% Foreign Owned	0.408	0.397	0.483	0.414	0.714	0.482	−0.025	−0.049
	(0.479)	(0.487)	(0.765)	(0.771)	(0.983)	(1.023)	(0.811)	(0.825)
Majority Foreign Owned	−0.149	−0.132	0.284	0.231	−2.906**	−2.181**	−2.063*	−1.624ᵀ
	(0.430)	(0.427)	(0.719)	(0.691)	(0.904)	(0.774)	(0.895)	(0.864)
Special Enterprise Zone	−0.527	−0.483	−0.422	−0.261	1.302	1.604ᵀ	1.100	1.065
	(0.356)	(0.359)	(0.614)	(0.628)	(1.054)	(0.941)	(0.809)	(0.743)
Sector Dummies	Yes	Yes	Yes	Yes	Yes	Yes	Yes	Yes
Region Dummies	Yes	Yes	Yes	Yes	Yes	Yes	Yes	Yes
Constant	−0.933	−0.876	−2.443	−3.094ᵀ	2.377	2.424	−2.990ᵀ	−1.975
	(0.868)	(0.859)	(1.581)	(1.778)	(2.538)	(1.962)	(1.769)	(1.692)
Observations	223	223	94	94	82	82	97	97

Note: Standard errors in parentheses; logistic regressions with robust standard errors.
ᵀ $p < 0.10$, * $p < 0.05$, ** $p < 0.01$

additional options about which they were asked (see table 5.1 in the main text for a list). Diaspora-affiliated firms are more likely to attempt resolution through international or local arbitration ($p < 0.01$) and possibly more likely to appeal to the local (Philippines) government or to the home country government ($p < 0.1$). I don't have strong theoretical expectations about either of these strategies, but as noted in the chapter, it is plausible that firms that value social ties highly prefer to resolve disputes through less-confrontational means. Arbitration may be less likely than formal adjudication to rupture the social bond between a firm and its counterpart in a dispute. Similarly, as demonstrated later in chapter 5, diaspora-affiliated firms are better connected to government officials in the host country, which may account for their increased propensity to turn to those government officials to assist in resolving disputes. Why diaspora-affiliated firms are also (pos-

Table C5.2a. Diaspora Affiliation and Dispute Resolution: Additional Strategies

	(1)	(2)	(3)	(4)	(5)	(6)	(7)	(8)	(9)	(10)	(11)	(12)
	Int'l or Local Arbitration		Appeal to Local Govt		Appeal to Home		Appeal to Well-connected Individuals		Work with Law Firm		Assistance from PEZA	
Diaspora Affiliated	2.965** (0.908)		1.737τ (0.962)		2.547τ (1.414)		1.937** (0.651)		1.033 (0.685)		0.052 (0.045)	
Diaspora Owned		2.329** (0.694)		-0.130 (0.920)		1.682τ (0.946)		0.425 (0.600)		1.334* (0.640)		0.010 (0.081)
Firm Age	0.194 (0.423)	0.439 (0.368)	0.034 (0.601)	0.285 (0.537)	-0.022 (0.898)	0.467 (0.512)	0.175 (0.346)	0.363 (0.342)	-0.108 (0.262)	-0.048 (0.267)	0.007 (0.030)	0.012 (0.030)
Publicly Traded	0.736 (0.834)	0.965 (0.767)	1.370 (1.068)	1.491 (1.181)	0.797 (0.927)	0.365 (0.813)	-0.813 (0.680)	-0.468 (0.686)	0.088 (0.604)	0.264 (0.602)	0.047 (0.046)	0.054 (0.047)
Size (Revenue)	0.771τ (0.467)	0.967* (0.400)	-0.006 (0.488)	-0.021 (0.440)	0.236 (0.357)	0.426 (0.432)	0.120 (0.265)	0.156 (0.257)	0.136 (0.256)	0.219 (0.258)	-0.008 (0.022)	-0.006 (0.021)
Number of Employees	-0.651 (0.774)	-0.877 (0.679)	-0.016 (0.495)	-0.066 (0.471)	-0.518 (0.491)	-0.866 (0.536)	-0.053 (0.368)	-0.137 (0.328)	0.016 (0.315)	-0.078 (0.301)	0.004 (0.036)	0.003 (0.035)
100% Foreign Owned	0.172 (0.771)	0.015 (0.749)	4.245** (1.386)	4.137** (1.478)	0.811 (0.995)	0.404 (1.057)	-0.025 (0.811)	-0.049 (0.825)	0.328 (0.754)	0.220 (0.765)	0.029 (0.095)	0.029 (0.098)
Majority Foreign Owned	-0.623 (0.842)	-0.667 (0.836)	-0.966 (1.278)	-0.924 (1.487)	-1.898 (1.285)	-2.095 (1.306)	-2.063* (0.895)	-1.624τ (0.864)	-0.895 (0.715)	-0.971 (0.695)	-0.032 (0.079)	-0.023 (0.082)
Special Enterprise Zone	-1.008 (0.715)	-0.022 (0.754)	0.653 (1.019)	0.676 (0.847)	-0.067 (1.654)	0.742 (1.235)	1.100 (0.809)	1.065 (0.743)	0.642 (0.680)	1.030 (0.724)	0.241* (0.098)	0.243* (0.102)
Sector Dummies	Yes	Yes	Yes	Yes	Yes	Yes	Yes	Yes	Yes	Yes	Yes	Yes
Region Dummies	Yes	Yes	Yes	Yes	Yes	Yes	Yes	Yes	Yes	Yes	Yes	Yes
Constant	-2.875τ (1.714)	-2.182 (1.891)	-18.157** (2.959)	-17.186** (2.888)	-20.837** (3.731)	-19.997** (2.521)	-2.990τ (1.769)	-1.975 (1.692)	-1.203 (1.731)	-1.394 (1.789)	-0.053 (0.109)	-0.032 (0.110)
Observations	91	91	86	86	89	89	97	97	95	95	97	97

Note: Standard errors in parentheses. Logistic regressions with robust standard errors (models 1–10); linear regressions with robust standard errors (models 11–12).

τ p < 0.10, * p < 0.05, ** p < 0.01

sibly) more likely to appeal to their home country government for help I am not sure.

Looking to the effects of the various control variables, larger firms (by revenue) are more likely to make use of arbitration and firms with a higher share of foreign ownership are more likely to pursue arbitration. Not surprisingly, firms located in special economic zones are more likely to seek assistances from the Philippines Economic Zone Authority. More counterintuitively, firms that are 100% foreign owned, and thus do not have a domestic partner, are significantly more likely to appeal to the local (i.e., Philippines) government for assistance.

C5.3. Extending and Receiving Credit

Table C5.3 matches figure 5.3 in the main text. These regressions estimate the effect of diaspora affiliation on the probability that firms either extend credit to their customers or receive credit from their suppliers. This giving and receiving of credit was more common than we expected when we wrote the survey. As noted in the main text, 77% of all firms receive credit from suppliers and 74% extend credit to customers. I find no evidence, however, that diaspora-affiliated firms have an advantage in this area. I estimate they are slightly more likely than nondiaspora-affiliated foreign firms to extend credit and slightly less likely to receive it, but neither effect is statistically significant.

Publicly traded firms are less likely to offer credit to customers ($p < .05$), and firms with larger revenues are perhaps more likely to receive it ($p < 0.1$). In the raw data, the estimated negative relationship between diaspora affiliation and receiving credit from suppliers is stronger and approaches statistical significance ($p = .076$). The estimated effect of diaspora affiliation on extending credit remains positive and statistically insignificant.

C5.4. Acquiring Real Estate

Table C5.4 matches figure 5.4 in the main text and relies on data from Georgia. I estimate that diaspora-owned firms are more likely than other foreign firms to use social ties to rent or purchase real estate. However, these results fall short of statistical significance ($p = .061$ for family ties and $p = .077$ for

Table C5.3. Diaspora Affiliation and the Giving and Receiving of Credit

	(1)	(2)	(3)	(4)
	Receives Credit from Supplier		Offers Credit to Customers	
Diaspora Affiliated	−0.246		0.507	
	(0.444)		(0.421)	
Diaspora Owned		−0.241		0.320
		(0.429)		(0.395)
Firm Age	0.003	−0.007	−0.003	0.020
	(0.223)	(0.221)	(0.185)	(0.187)
Publicly Traded	−0.512	−0.511	−0.953*	−0.913*
	(0.392)	(0.393)	(0.443)	(0.437)
Size (Revenue)	0.357ᵀ	0.342ᵀ	0.287	0.303
	(0.187)	(0.193)	(0.202)	(0.200)
Number of Employees	0.275	0.280	−0.134	−0.130
	(0.215)	(0.220)	(0.225)	(0.225)
100% Foreign Owned	0.198	0.212	0.400	0.444
	(0.650)	(0.656)	(0.778)	(0.793)
Majority Foreign Owned	0.347	0.353	−0.524	−0.474
	(0.458)	(0.456)	(0.471)	(0.452)
Special Enterprise Zone	−0.059	−0.094	−0.411	−0.378
	(0.438)	(0.455)	(0.373)	(0.377)
Sector Dummies	Yes	Yes	Yes	Yes
Region Dummies	Yes	Yes	Yes	Yes
Constant	0.217	0.222	16.546**	16.435**
	(1.204)	(1.242)	(0.958)	(0.934)
Observations	216	216	207	207

Note: Standard errors in parentheses; logistic regressions with robust standard errors.
ᵀ $p < 0.10$, * $p < 0.05$, ** $p < 0.01$

combined ties). None of the control variables have significant effects. In the raw data, the estimated positive effects of diaspora ownership on use of social ties are slightly stronger across all three dependent variables, though the effects remain short of statistical significance ($p = .060$ for family ties and $p = .055$ for combined ties).

C5.5. Government Relations

In this section I return to analysis of the Philippines data, evaluating firms' use of social ties to interact with government, as well as their propensity to attempt to influence policy and their ability to succeed in doing so.

Table C5.4. Diaspora Ownership and Acquiring Real Estate

	(1) Family Ties for Real Estate	(2) Friend Ties for Real Estate	(3) Either Family or Friend
Diaspora-Owned Firm	0.190$^\tau$	0.034	0.192$^\tau$
	(0.101)	(0.105)	(0.107)
Firm Age (logged)	−0.030	−0.086	−0.097
	(0.029)	(0.063)	(0.064)
Employees (logged)	0.011	−0.028	−0.022
	(0.019)	(0.024)	(0.026)
100% Foreign Ownership	0.024	−0.213	−0.214
	(0.081)	(0.163)	(0.156)
Majority Foreign Ownership	0.021	−0.401*	−0.407*
	(0.088)	(0.168)	(0.165)
Location = Tbilisi	−0.077	0.070	−0.039
	(0.081)	(0.075)	(0.091)
Sector Dummies	Yes	Yes	Yes
Region Dummies	Yes	Yes	Yes
Constant	0.073	0.661**	0.747**
	(0.128)	(0.234)	(0.237)
Observations	136	135	138

Note: The dependent variables measure the use of friendship or family ties in the process of renting or purchasing real estate. Standard errors in parentheses; linear regressions with robust standard errors.
$^\tau p < 0.10$, $^* p < 0.05$, $^{**} p < 0.01$

The Use of Social Ties in Government Relations

Table C5.5 matches figure 5.5 and shows that diaspora-affiliated firms are more likely to reach out to government officials via personal relationships as part of their government relations strategy. Note that the question employed here—asking which of four strategies firms employ to "improve relations with government agencies and influence government policy"—are the questions used in the modified list experiment described in appendix A3.3.

The key finding is that diaspora-affiliated firms are more likely to use social ties in this area. This finding is robust to analysis with the raw data. This result is also robust to controlling for whether the respondent is a diasporan. It is possible that diasporans might be more likely than other managers to report that their firms use social ties in this way, even holding firm behavior constant—I find that such bias is not driving these results.

Looking at the control variables in table C5.5, I estimate that firms that are 100% foreign owned are more likely to reach out via personal relation-

Table C5.5. Diaspora Affiliation and Use of Social Ties to Interact with Government

	(1)	(2)	(3)	(4)	(5)	(6)	(7)	(8)
	Reach Out via Personal Relationships		Invite Officials to Tour Facilities		Attend Business Forum		Produce Reports or White Papers	
Diaspora Affiliated	1.650**		0.365		0.740		0.374	
	(0.607)		(0.531)		(0.840)		(0.559)	
Diaspora Owned		1.422*		0.707		0.310		0.374
		(0.609)		(0.568)		(0.737)		(0.664)
Firm Age	−0.180	−0.123	0.338	0.314	1.043$^{\tau}$	1.015$^{\tau}$	0.236	0.243
	(0.332)	(0.324)	(0.296)	(0.295)	(0.553)	(0.521)	(0.297)	(0.297)
Publicly Traded	0.287	0.502	−0.243	−0.143	−0.262	−0.140	0.397	0.443
	(0.638)	(0.672)	(0.672)	(0.675)	(0.790)	(0.785)	(0.708)	(0.709)
Size (Revenue)	−0.037	0.069	0.725*	0.812*	−0.417	−0.435	−0.231	−0.207
	(0.278)	(0.290)	(0.334)	(0.362)	(0.479)	(0.425)	(0.253)	(0.257)
Number of Employees	−0.537	−0.627$^{\tau}$	−0.478	−0.578	0.323	0.407	0.043	0.019
	(0.343)	(0.369)	(0.374)	(0.386)	(0.562)	(0.525)	(0.355)	(0.358)
100% Foreign Owned	2.402*	2.157*	0.238	0.187	1.544	1.501	0.234	0.258
	(1.131)	(0.999)	(0.796)	(0.783)	(1.351)	(1.212)	(0.791)	(0.792)
Majority Foreign Owned	−0.317	−0.090	0.175	0.195	0.637	0.907	−1.673*	−1.651*
	(0.605)	(0.606)	(0.666)	(0.656)	(1.095)	(0.999)	(0.783)	(0.768)
Special Enterprise Zone	0.858	1.187*	0.051	0.162	0.433	0.403	0.338	0.404
	(0.546)	(0.593)	(0.603)	(0.613)	(0.899)	(0.902)	(0.604)	(0.598)
Sector Dummies	Yes	Yes	Yes	Yes	Yes	Yes	Yes	Yes
Region Dummies	Yes	Yes	Yes	Yes	Yes	Yes	Yes	Yes
Constant	1.427	1.312	−0.681	−0.585	13.180**	14.514**	0.305	0.304
	(1.732)	(1.754)	(1.468)	(1.483)	(1.367)	(1.391)	(1.674)	(1.655)
Observations	100	100	103	103	78	78	98	98

Note: Standard errors in parentheses; logistic regressions with robust standard errors.
$^{\tau} p < 0.10$, $^{*} p < 0.05$, $^{**} p < 0.01$

ships. Firms with larger revenues are more likely to invite officials to tour their facilities, and older firms are more likely to rely on business forums.

Attempting and Achieving Policy Influence

As noted in the main text, I examine three different dependent variables in testing the policy influence hypothesis: *attempted to influence policy, success if attempted,* and *influence policy.* The first variable takes a value of 1 if the firm attempted to influence policy at either the local or national level, 2 if the firm attempted to influence policy at both levels, and 0 otherwise. *Success if attempted* is coded 1 if a firm achieved at least some of its policy objectives at either the local or national level, 2 if a firm achieved at least some

Table C5.6. Diaspora Affiliation and Policy Influence

	(1)	(2)	(3)	(4)	(5)	(6)
	Attempted to Influence Policy		Success if Attempted		Influenced Policy	
Diaspora Affiliated	0.973**		1.772*		0.897*	
	(0.367)		(0.809)		(0.365)	
Diaspora Owned		0.723*		2.045*		1.003**
		(0.347)		(0.850)		(0.344)
Firm Age	0.094	0.118	−0.444	−0.385	−0.026	0.009
	(0.171)	(0.172)	(0.314)	(0.303)	(0.172)	(0.175)
Publicly Traded	0.032	0.099	2.080*	1.907**	0.686$^\tau$	0.663$^\tau$
	(0.363)	(0.358)	(0.844)	(0.666)	(0.387)	(0.385)
Size (Revenue)	0.092	0.119	0.408	0.456	0.012	0.059
	(0.152)	(0.158)	(0.324)	(0.295)	(0.152)	(0.158)
Number of Employees	0.086	0.086	−0.622	−0.624$^\tau$	−0.064	−0.082
	(0.172)	(0.175)	(0.394)	(0.342)	(0.163)	(0.168)
100% Foreign Owned	0.142	0.140	0.610	0.361	−0.060	−0.157
	(0.548)	(0.551)	(1.102)	(1.130)	(0.510)	(0.547)
Majority Foreign Owned	0.014	0.023	0.968	0.801	0.259	0.216
	(0.380)	(0.375)	(0.914)	(0.745)	(0.394)	(0.382)
Special Enterprise Zone	0.742*	0.819*	−0.171	0.578	0.638$^\tau$	0.783*
	(0.375)	(0.386)	(0.722)	(0.686)	(0.376)	(0.375)
Sector Dummies	Yes	Yes	Yes	Yes	Yes	Yes
Region Dummies	Yes	Yes	Yes	Yes	Yes	Yes
Cut1: Constant	−0.996	−1.099	−1.062	−0.769	0.331	0.442
	(0.875)	(0.896)	(1.692)	(1.730)	(0.871)	(0.837)
Cut2: Constant	0.344	0.227	−0.082	0.234	1.269	1.387
	(0.890)	(0.907)	(1.746)	(1.806)	(0.888)	(0.848)
Observations	217	217	84	84	207	207

Note: Standard errors in parentheses. Ordered logistic regressions with robust standard errors.
$^\tau p < 0.10$, $^* p < 0.05$, $^{**} p < 0.01$

of its policy objectives at both the local or national level, 0 if it failed to achieve its objectives, and missing if no attempt was made. Thus the test of this hypothesis has a smaller sample size—firms that did not attempt to influence policy at either level are dropped from the sample. Lastly, *influence policy* is coded the same as *success if tried* but takes a value of zero, instead of missing, if no attempt to influence policy was made. No attempt yields no success.

Table C5.6 matches figure 5.6 and shows that diaspora-affiliated firms are more likely to attempt to influence policy, more likely to succeed in influencing policy conditional on having attempted, and more likely to influence policy overall (i.e., more likely to influence policy unconditional on making an attempt). Looking at the control variables, publicly traded firms are more likely to achieve policy influence, and firms in special enterprise zones are more likely to attempt to influence policy. The estimated effects of diaspora affiliation are weaker in the raw data. All the estimated effects remain positive, but only the effect on *attempted to influence policy* remains statistically significant.

C5.6. Conclusion

Chapter 5 presents twelve distinct tests across six hypotheses, all related to the effect of diaspora affiliation on firms' use of social ties in business and their ability to influence government policy.[1] In the main analysis, I estimate effects in the expected (positive) direction in ten of these tests; five of these positive results are statistically significant. The two negative estimated effects are not significant. When I rerun this analysis using the raw, unimputed data, ten results are in the expected direction and two are statistically significant.

In comparison to chapter 4, chapter 5 is more mixed in its results. I find strong support for some hypotheses—in particular I find strong evidence that diaspora-affiliated firms are more likely than nondiaspora-affiliated firms to use social ties to influence government, and that they are more likely to attempt to influence policy and to succeed in doing so. However, I find no evidence that diaspora-affiliated firms enjoy advantages with respect to access to information or giving or receiving credit. I find evidence consistent with my hypothesis that diaspora-affiliated firms are more likely to use their social ties to acquire real estate, but the results fall just short of statistical significance.

APPENDIX D: SUPPLEMENTARY MATERIALS FOR CHAPTER 6

The Development Impact of Diaspora-Affiliated Firms

This appendix provides regression tables, technical details, and robustness checks for the results presented in chapter 6. This appendix follows the same format as appendices B and C. Descriptive statistics for all variables are provided in appendix A.

D6.1. Diaspora Ownership and Social Responsibility

The results in figure 6.1 in the chapter and table D6.1 below show that diaspora-owned firms are no more socially responsible than other foreign firms. Indeed the only statistically significant difference between diaspora-owned and nondiaspora-owned firms suggests that diaspora-owned firms may even be less socially responsible than other foreign firms. Diaspora-owned firms are more likely to agree with the statement, "This firm keeps its total labor costs as low as possible."

The estimated effect of diaspora ownership on agreement with the statement on labor cost minimization is actually slightly stronger in the raw data ($p = 0.014$). Other estimated effects are similar in the raw data. The results are also similar in analysis that controls for whether the respondent is the firm owner. The regressions in models 1–7 in table D6.1 are ordered logistic regressions, because of the ordinal nature of the dependent variables. The regression in model 8 is a logistic regression because *donations* is a binary dependent variable. Looking at the effects of the various control variables, I estimate that older firms are somewhat less socially responsible, particularly in areas related to wages and quality of life for employees. Firms located in Tbilisi are more likely to focus on minimizing labor costs and firms with more employees are more likely to make donations to charity and (possibly) pay higher salaries.

Table D6.1. Diaspora Ownership and Social Responsibility

	(1) Higher Salaries	(2) Quality of Life	(3) Professional Development	(4) Profit-Focused	(5) Minimize Labor Costs	(6) Prioritize Local Hiring	(7) Green	(8) Donations
Diaspora-Owned Firm	−0.438	−0.402	0.009	0.372	1.081**	0.682	−0.440	−0.113
	(0.598)	(0.616)	(0.466)	(0.391)	(0.419)	(0.586)	(0.510)	(0.524)
Firm Age (logged)	−0.659*	−0.724*	−0.185	−0.359	−0.243	0.407	−0.505	0.461
	(0.324)	(0.294)	(0.318)	(0.298)	(0.287)	(0.429)	(0.318)	(0.316)
Employees (logged)	0.278$^\tau$	0.188	0.185	0.055	−0.100	0.097	−0.012	0.689**
	(0.157)	(0.166)	(0.134)	(0.132)	(0.111)	(0.130)	(0.139)	(0.205)
100% Foreign Ownership	0.470	1.039	0.369	−0.218	0.213	−0.702	−0.625	−0.603
	(0.868)	(0.865)	(0.532)	(0.489)	(0.703)	(0.605)	(0.688)	(0.803)
Majority Foreign Ownership	−0.312	0.067	0.383	0.242	0.593	−1.013	−1.349$^\tau$	−0.152
	(0.932)	(0.867)	(0.627)	(0.588)	(0.712)	(0.632)	(0.754)	(0.832)
Location = Tbilisi	−0.562	−1.071*	−0.169	−0.431	1.159*	0.379	0.073	0.734
	(0.541)	(0.535)	(0.430)	(0.607)	(0.532)	(0.556)	(0.528)	(0.592)
Sector Dummies	Yes	Yes	Yes	Yes	Yes	Yes	Yes	Yes
Region Dummies	Yes	Yes	Yes	Yes	Yes	Yes	Yes	Yes
Constant								−2.344
								(1.430)
Cut 1: Constant	−4.467**	−5.768**	−3.610**	−5.468**	−1.552	−2.519*	−6.562**	
	(1.403)	(1.445)	(1.251)	(1.398)	(1.039)	(1.266)	(1.481)	
Cut 2: Constant	−4.016**	−4.761**	−3.074**	−5.050**	−0.510	−1.160	−6.145**	
	(1.302)	(1.232)	(1.122)	(1.303)	(1.057)	(1.182)	(1.439)	
Cut 3: Constant	−3.036*	−3.964**	−2.568*	−4.514**	−0.002	−0.415	−4.436**	
	(1.237)	(1.178)	(1.095)	(1.239)	(1.065)	(1.172)	(1.281)	
Cut 4: Constant	−1.099	−1.648	−0.914	−2.193$^\tau$	1.655	0.645	−3.797**	
	(1.236)	(1.150)	(1.066)	(1.138)	(1.081)	(1.207)	(1.220)	
Cut 5: Constant	0.132	−0.066	−0.057	−1.379	2.479*		−2.622*	
	(1.248)	(1.134)	(1.046)	(1.132)	(1.090)		(1.211)	
Cut 6: Constant	1.997	1.469	1.478	0.118	3.726**			
	(1.338)	(1.116)	(1.046)	(1.125)	(1.139)			
Observations	126	124	129	126	138	139	127	145

Note: Standard errors in parentheses. Ordered logistic regressions with robust standard errors (models 1–7). Logistic regression with robust standard errors (model 8).
$^\tau p < 0.10$, $^* p < 0.05$, $^{**} p < 0.01$

D6.2. Greenfield Investment, Reinvested Earnings, Export Earnings, and Employment Intensity

The tables in this section present the regression results that underlie figure 6.2 in the main text. Table D6.2 presents the results relating diaspora ownership to Greenfield entry in Georgia. Table D6.2a examines the effects of diaspora affiliation on Greenfield investment, reinvested earnings, export earnings, and employment intensity in the Philippines.

In the Georgia data, I observe no clear relationship between diaspora ownership and Greenfield entry. In the regression depicted in table D6.2, I estimate that diaspora-owned firms are slightly more likely than other foreign firms to enter via Greenfield investment, while in the raw data I estimate the reverse, namely that diaspora-owned firms are slightly less likely to enter via Greenfield investment. Neither of these estimated effects is statistically significant, and none of the control variables have significant effects either.

Table D6.2. Greenfield Investment: Georgia

	(1) Greenfield Investment
Diaspora-Owned Firm	0.070
	(0.564)
Firm Age (logged)	0.203
	(0.416)
Employees (logged)	−0.123
	(0.133)
100% Foreign Ownership	−0.577
	(0.904)
Majority Foreign Ownership	−0.518
	(0.949)
Location = Tbilisi	0.579
	(0.486)
Sector Dummies	Yes
Region Dummies	Yes
Constant	0.885
	(1.397)
Observations	154

Note: Standard errors in parentheses. Logistic regressions with robust standard errors.
$^{\tau} p < 0.10, ^{*} p < 0.05, ^{**} p < 0.01$

In table 6.2a, I consistently estimate a positive relationship between diaspora affiliation and behaviors associated with positive development spillovers in the Philippines, but none of these effects are statistically significant. In the raw data, the estimated effects of diaspora affiliation on Greenfield investment, reinvestment of earnings, and employment intensity are all more strongly positive, and the reinvestment of earnings and employment

Table D6.2a. Greenfield Investment, Reinvested Earnings, Export Earnings, and Employment Intensity: The Philippines

	(1)	(2)	(3)	(4)	(5)	(6)	(7)	(8)
	Greenfield Investment		Reinvestment of Earnings		Export Earnings		Employment	
Diaspora Affiliated	0.517		0.535		0.344		0.463	
	(0.427)		(0.391)		(0.331)		(0.324)	
Diaspora Owned		0.308		0.586		0.149		0.566^T
		(0.460)		(0.370)		(0.324)		(0.292)
Firm Age	−0.174	−0.143	−0.532**	−0.492*	−0.204	−0.189	0.445**	0.469**
	(0.249)	(0.249)	(0.205)	(0.195)	(0.182)	(0.183)	(0.171)	(0.169)
Publicly Traded	−0.323	−0.290	−0.492	−0.426	−0.224	−0.208	0.307	0.326
	(0.549)	(0.545)	(0.451)	(0.431)	(0.347)	(0.348)	(0.335)	(0.331)
Size (Revenue)	0.099	0.103	−0.134	−0.136	−0.024	−0.027	1.104**	1.119**
	(0.233)	(0.227)	(0.212)	(0.205)	(0.147)	(0.147)	(0.161)	(0.161)
Number of Employees	−0.452^T	−0.443^T	0.179	0.172	0.271	0.289		
	(0.264)	(0.265)	(0.211)	(0.207)	(0.191)	(0.186)		
100% Foreign Owned	−0.834	−0.828	−0.072	−0.090	−0.883^T	−0.867^T	−0.312	−0.363
	(0.619)	(0.616)	(0.475)	(0.469)	(0.456)	(0.469)	(0.408)	(0.400)
Majority Foreign Owned	0.434	0.457	0.702	0.698	−0.659^T	−0.635	−0.530	−0.539
	(0.654)	(0.645)	(0.481)	(0.482)	(0.394)	(0.393)	(0.403)	(0.393)
Special Enterprise Zone	0.487	0.533	−0.171	−0.062	0.276	0.294	0.857*	0.942**
	(0.501)	(0.516)	(0.350)	(0.366)	(0.340)	(0.351)	(0.332)	(0.339)
Sector Dummies	Yes	Yes	Yes	Yes	Yes	Yes	Yes	Yes
Region Dummies	Yes	Yes	Yes	Yes	Yes	Yes	Yes	Yes
Constant	19.532**	19.169**						
	(1.220)	(1.300)						
Cut 1: Constant			−4.138**	−4.111**	0.762	0.716	0.647	0.758
			(0.950)	(0.965)	(0.997)	(0.975)	(1.002)	(0.980)
Cut 2: Constant			−2.708**	−2.676**	1.701^T	1.653^T	3.304**	3.401**
			(0.922)	(0.939)	(1.015)	(0.995)	(1.055)	(1.034)
Cut 3: Constant			−1.601^T	−1.564^T	2.547*	2.494*	4.940**	5.042**
			(0.885)	(0.905)	(1.024)	(1.006)	(1.138)	(1.115)
Cut 4: Constant							6.864**	6.973**
							(1.214)	(1.192)
Observations	216	216	189	189	207	207	223	223

Note: Standard errors in parentheses. Logistic regressions with robust standard errors (models 1 & 2). Ordered logistic regressions with robust standard errors (models 3–8).
$^T p < 0.10$, $^* p < 0.05$, $^{**} p < 0.01$

intensity results are statistically significant ($p < 0.05$). This leads me to the conclusion that it is possible, and even likely, that diaspora-affiliated firms contribute somewhat more to development through these channels than do other foreign firms. However, I view the results in the imputed data as more reliable than the results in the raw data (see appendix A). Given the weakness of these results in the imputed data, it remains quite possible that there is no difference between diaspora-affiliated and nondiaspora-affiliated foreign firms with regard to these behaviors.

Looking at the effects of the control variables in table D6.2a, we see that older firms reinvest a smaller share of their earnings, which is consistent with younger firms growing more quickly. We also see that older firms, firms with larger revenues, and firms in special enterprise zones tend to be more employment intensive. These results for the control variables also hold in the raw data.

D6.3. Sensitivity to Conflict

Table D6.3 provides results from the three regressions that underlie figure 6.3 in the text, as well as from two additional regressions in which I control for *perceived likelihood of conflict*, which is a 7-point Likert scale assessment of firm perceptions of the probability of a return to violent conflict in Georgia. The addition of this extra control variable strengthens the estimated effect of diaspora affiliation on firm resilience with regard to expected profitability, but slightly weakens the relationship with regard to strategy changes. Thus adding these controls does not alter the conclusion of the main analysis—I find strong support for the war impact hypothesis, but weak support for the war risk hypothesis.

Among the control variables in table D6.3, firms located in Tbilisi are more pessimistic about the probability of a return to violence, while minority-owned firms are more likely than either 100% foreign-owned firms or majority foreign firms to expect a negative profit impact. Rerunning this analysis in the raw data, the estimated effects of diaspora ownership are remarkably similar.

Table D6.3. Conflict Likelihood, Business Strategy Effect, and Predicted Profit Impact

	(1)	(2)	(3)	(4)	(5)
	Conflict Likelihood	Business Strategy Effect	Predicted Profit Impact	Business Strategy Effect controlling for Conflict Likelihood	Predicted Profit Impact controlling for Conflict Likelihood
Diaspora-Owned Firm	−0.505	−0.622	−1.127*	−0.630	−1.308**
	(0.445)	(0.483)	(0.461)	(0.488)	(0.501)
Firm Age (logged)	−0.261	0.102	0.190	0.136	0.252
	(0.285)	(0.266)	(0.349)	(0.275)	(0.358)
Employees (logged)	0.143	−0.051	0.013	−0.041	0.041
	(0.111)	(0.122)	(0.133)	(0.140)	(0.145)
100% Foreign Ownership	−0.821	0.646	1.502$^\tau$	0.754	1.810*
	(0.820)	(0.638)	(0.810)	(0.630)	(0.876)
Majority Foreign Ownership	−0.548	1.249$^\tau$	1.772*	1.293$^\tau$	2.150*
	(0.845)	(0.668)	(0.857)	(0.689)	(0.912)
Location = Tbilisi	1.592**	0.023	0.163	−0.263	−0.018
	(0.569)	(0.519)	(0.539)	(0.616)	(0.639)
Perceived Likelihood of Conflict				0.338**	0.317$^\tau$
				(0.126)	(0.178)
Sector Dummies	Yes	Yes	Yes	Yes	Yes
Region Dummies	Yes	Yes	Yes	Yes	Yes
Cut 1: Constant	−1.593	−2.954*	0.944	−1.470	2.555
	(1.158)	(1.351)	(1.428)	(1.378)	(1.646)
Cut 2: Constant	−0.763	−2.240$^\tau$		−0.741	
	(1.146)	(1.261)		(1.250)	
Cut 3: Constant	−0.203	1.022		2.480$^\tau$	
	(1.143)	(1.284)		(1.294)	
Cut 4: Constant	1.617	1.725		3.208*	
	(1.161)	(1.282)		(1.300)	
Cut 5: Constant	2.521*	2.629*		4.188**	
	(1.195)	(1.303)		(1.319)	
Cut 6: Constant	3.427**				
	(1.247)				
Observations	137	146	144	133	132

Note: Standard errors in parentheses. Ordered logistic regressions with robust standard errors.
$^\tau p < 0.10$, $^* p < 0.05$, $^{**} p < 0.01$

D6.4. Conclusion

Chapters 4 and 5 provide the main tests of my theory of diasporans as trans-national brokers. This chapter tests implications of an alternative theory drawn from the literature and also explores the development impact and conflict sensitivity of diaspora-affiliated and nondiaspora-affiliated foreign firms. The War Risk Hypothesis (H6.2) and the War Impact Hypothesis (H6.3) both test implications of my theory of diasporans as transnational brokers. I find strong support for the war impact hypothesis but not for the war risk hypothesis. Diaspora-owned firms are less likely to expect that a return to violent conflict would negatively impact their profitability, a result that is robust to controlling for firms' perceptions about the likelihood of such a return to violence, and robust to analysis using raw, rather than im-puted, data.

NOTES

Chapter 1

1. Information on Mr. Laurel is based on an author interview conducted October 27, 2014.

2. Information on Ms. Aguas is based on an author interview conducted December 16, 2016.

3. As of 2013, 69% of migrants lived in high-income countries and 72% had departed low- or middle-income homelands (Connor et al. 2013).

4. One necessary caveat to this Chinese figure involves the role of Hong Kong. The success of Hong Kong-based firms in China during this period reflects both the regulatory advantages granted to Hong Kong-based firms as well as advantages that may have accrued to these firms via the knowledge and connections of their diaspora owners.

5. Because this estimate is based on a random sample of all the recently registered foreign firms operating in Georgia, 16% is a reliable estimate for the prevalence of diaspora ownership overall in Georgia. The Philippines sample is nonrandom, and thus this figure may not be representative of the Philippines economy at large. See chapter 3 and appendix A for details on these surveys.

6. On the relationship between political risk and FDI, see, for example, Jensen (2003), Li and Resnick (2003), or Javorcik and Wei (2009). While most scholars find a positive relationship between FDI and growth, others find evidence of a negative or mixed relationship, e.g., Borensztein, Gregorio, and Lee (1998) or Alfaro et al. (2004).

7. The 2010 United Nations Industrial Development Organization (UNIDO) Africa Investor Survey also allows such comparison, so while I remain confident that the 2009 Georgia survey was the first, there is now at least one other survey providing much needed data in this area. See Boly et al. (2014) for some analysis drawing on the UNIDO survey. As I discuss later, the UNIDO data are quite limited in their ability to shed light on differences in capabilities and strategy between diaspora-affiliated and nondiaspora-affiliated foreign firms. Additionally, I contributed to the 2012 Vietnam Provincial Competitiveness Index survey, which allows some comparisons between diaspora and nondiaspora firms (Malesky 2013).

8. For example, Safran (1988) writes, "[the] continued psychic relationship with the homeland differentiates diaspora communities from other expatriate communities." Shain (2007) identifies diasporans as "individuals who reside outside of their perceived homeland." Brinkerhoff (2016: 1) defines diasporans as "immigrants who still feel a connection to their country of origin." The Sheffer definition itself is used by several scholars, including Nielsen and Riddle (2010). The Safran definition also appears in work by Gillespie, Sayre, and Riddle (2001); the Shain definition also appears in Riddle (2008).

9. See Levitt and Waters (2002) and Soehl and Waldinger (2012) on second- and third-generation diasporans.

10. As discussed in section 4.1, this definition is difficult to apply empirically because it is difficult for the manager of a firm to know whether the owner or other managers at the firm retain "sentimental links" to the homeland. Thus the definitions given to survey respondents are somewhat simplified to consistently capture Filipinos (Georgians) who are currently living abroad or have done so in the past.

11. This is known as the Lucas Paradox, in reference to the work of Robert Lucas (1990).

12. United Nations Commission on Trade and Development (2011).

13. See Kobrin 1980, 1982; Vernon 1971; Moran 1985: 108–15; Kahler 1984: 266–315; and Frieden 1994.

14. See, for example, De Mello (1999), Acharyya (2009), and Chowdhury and Mavrotas (2006).

15. Senate bill No. 2856. http://www.senate.gov.ph/lisdata/114549691!.pdf (accessed September 30, 2014).

16. This empirical analysis answers a call, made in the academic literature, for empirical evaluation of these optimistic claims (Nielsen and Riddle 2010: 441–42).

17. While several regional and country-specific studies during this period point to specific cases in which labor emigration contributed to development, these findings received insufficient attention. For example, Chirwa (1997) notes the positive effects of labor emigration on rural sending communities in Malawi and the negative effects of the forced repatriation of those migrants.

18. Johnson (2004), cited by Clemens and Pettersson (2008: 1).

19. The economic importance of these remittances is augmented by the fact that they tend to be counter-cyclical, i.e., flows of remittances tend to increase when economic conditions in the homeland worsen (e.g., Frankel 2011).

20. Key works include Weidenbaum and Hughes (1996); Bandelj (2002); Saxenian (2006); Brinkerhoff (2008); Kapur (2010); Riddle, Hrivnak, and Nielsen (2010); Mullings (2011); Vaaler (2011); and Pandya and Leblang (2011).

21. In an analysis of US counties, Burchardi, Chaney, and Hassan (2016) find that doubling the number of individuals with ancestry from a given country increases the probability of inward FDI from that country by 4%, and increases the number of people employed by subsidiaries of firms headquartered in that country.

22. Orozco (2002) preceded this work with regard to Latin America. Earlier, pri-

marily qualitative work has also pointed to the importance of remittances in specific cases (e.g., Oberai and Singh 1980).

23. Of course, Nader ignores the fact that Yunus lived in the United States from 1965 to 1972, during which time he earned his PhD in economics at Vanderbilt and worked as an economics professor at Middle Tennessee State University. Yunus is a diasporan, and without the education he received and the social ties he developed in the United States, he may never have become the transformative force he is now.

24. Data from the World Bank's World Development Indicators (WDI).

25. Cited in Riddle and Nielsen (2010).

Chapter 2

1. These names and the firm's nationality have been changed to protect the firm's identity. This caselet is based on my initial conversation with Marcus described in the text (January 2010) and on a later follow-up interview at the business site, where I interviewed Georg (February 2010).

2. It may be that some nondiasporans also possess the ties necessary to play this brokerage role, but I expect this is not common.

3. In the sample of foreign firms in the Philippines on which I test this theory, 85% of nondiaspora-affiliated foreign firms employ at least one local Filipino manager.

4. In the Philippines survey, I draw on responses to the question, "As a business expert, can you briefly describe how your owners' and managers' social relationships affect your firm?" The enumerator guidance that accompanied this question was, "If they answer in vague terms, please prompt for a specific example from their firm." In the Georgia survey, I draw on responses to the question, "Can you briefly describe the effects that your owners' and managers' friendships and/or family relationships have on the way your firm does business?"

5. These focus groups were arranged with the assistance of the Manila Jaycees and the University of Southern California Alumni Association in Manila and included diaspora and nondiaspora managers of multinational and domestic firms. In the actual survey, we restricted the sample to firms with at least partial foreign ownership. See chapter 3 and appendix A for survey details.

6. John Dunning's (1980, 1988) "eclectic paradigm" has a foundational role in this understanding, but I choose a later departure point to focus on the role of firm capabilities.

7. Helpman, Melitz, and Yeaple (2004) and Melitz (2008) model this formally, others confirm it empirically.

8. This term was coined by Zaheer (1995).

9. See Johanson and Vahlne (2009).

10. Including social ties within my conception of firm resources is consistent with the "relational view" introduced by Dyer and Singh (1998).

11. Foreign firms may face greater scrutiny of their compliance with regulations,

leading to a de facto difference in regulatory burden even when no *de jure* difference exists (e.g., Haufler 2001: 70; Mosley and Uno 2007).

12. See, for example, Harvey, Speier, and Novicevic (2000) and Reiche (2011).

13. The literature in these areas is voluminous. Regarding access to capital, see McMillan and Woodruff (1999) and Uzzi (1996); regarding social ties and profitability more generally see Hochberg, Ljungqvist, and Lu (2007) and Musteen, Francis, and Datta (2010).

14. Blonigen, Ellis, and Fausten (2003) find that, once one member of a business group enters a given host country, other members of that business group become much more likely to enter that country. Once that first member of the group is established, other firms with few connections in the homeland can use the strong ties they have to their fellow group member to gain market and risk information, and as a starting point to establish relationships with additional firms in the new market.

15. These are contexts in which informal institutions are more important, and formal institutions less important, than in wealthy industrialized countries (e.g., Helmke and Levitsky 2006).

16. Firm BOP313, Georgia.

17. Saxenian (2006) offers a detailed account of the social ties developed by migrants working in Silicon Valley and the role those ties play in the success of migrants starting and running information technology firms back in their homelands (e.g., India and Taiwan).

18. See Granovetter (1973) on the power of weak ties; Freeman (1977) on betweenness centrality; Coleman (1988, 1990) on network closure; Burt (1992, 2000) on structural holes.

19. I expect such "truncated" social networks are less common among the wealthy, educated diasporans that are the focus of my theory (Portes 1998; Hagan 1998).

20. Hansen (1999) argues that weak ties are particularly important for knowledge transfer within firms (though he argues that the transfer of the most complex knowledge requires strong ties).

21. Philippines Firm 053, a nondiaspora-affiliated foreign advertising firm based in the United States.

22. Philippines Firm 054, a minority-foreign-owned manufacturing firm based in the Philippines.

23. Ms. Ramos's name and the name of her firm have been changed to preserve her anonymity.

24. Philippines Firm 058, a domestic consulting firm based in the Philippines. Because this firm is not foreign owned, it is excluded from the sample of firms examined in the quantitative analysis.

25. Philippines Firm 025, a nondiaspora-affiliated foreign manufacturing firm.

26. In the sample of foreign firms in the Philippines on which I test this theory, 85% of nondiaspora-affiliated foreign firms employ at least one local Filipino manager.

27. The importance of cultural knowledge is underscored by Gillespie, McBride,

and Riddle (2010), who study local managers and find that bicultural or cosmopolitan individuals are more likely to rise to upper management in Mexican firms.

28. Philippines Firm 059, a diaspora-owned graphic design firm based in the Philippines.

29. Zucker (1986) makes a similar argument. Lane and Bachmann make the related argument that "trust-based relations between buyer and supplier firms rarely evolve spontaneously on the level of individual interaction but are highly dependent on the existence of stable legal, political and social institutions" (1986: 365).

30. While domestic firms have access to local private information, they often lack the global private information that provides a competitive advantage to multinational firms (Kingsley and Graham 2017). This is likely to be particularly true of domestic firms that serve the domestic market exclusively and somewhat less true of domestic firms that export (e.g., Helpman, Melitz, and Yeaple 2004).

31. See Albuquerque, Bauer, and Schneider (2009) and Kingsley and Graham (2017).

32. See Khanna and Palepu (2013) on a lack of information analysts as a key "institutional void" in emerging markets. See Kingsley and Graham (2017) on how foreign investors can use local private information to substitute for a lack of local public information.

33. Firm BOP432, Georgia.

34. Firm MOF289, Georgia.

35. In a somewhat different context, Larson and Lewis (2016) find that social ties between coethnics are particularly effective at transmitting information, compared to ties between individuals of different ethnicities.

36. Philippines Firm 036, a nondiaspora-owned telecommunications and networking firm based in the Philippines.

37. Philippines Firm 186, a nondiaspora-owned food safety firm based in the Philippines.

38. Chen (2008) is more skeptical of migrants' abilities in this area, arguing that migrants who succeed in developing strong social ties in the country of settlement often do so at the expense of maintaining ties in the homeland, leading to failures in knowledge transfer.

39. It is interesting that one of the few existing studies to explore diaspora business advantages at the firm level, Schulte (2008), mentions a linguistic advantage but makes no reference at all to social networks. Note, however, that Schulte examines diaspora-owned firms only and does not compare them to nondiaspora-owned firms.

40. Firm owner/manager and focus group participant, Manila, May 2014.

41. Jeffries and Reed (2000) find that too much trust in a relationship, as well as too little trust, can damage a firm's ability to solve problems of adaptation in relational contracting. This is one of several findings that complicate the relationship between trust and contracting efficiency. However, the broad consensus in the literature is that higher levels of trust in business relationships is generally beneficial to both parties.

42. Philippines Firm 07, a diaspora-managed firm.

43. Wong and Boh (2010) examine managers' social networks to demonstrate the ability of third parties to serve in this capacity. Very similar to the arguments made in this section overall, Chand and Tung (2011) discuss the role of trust in diasporans' ability to use their transnational social ties to facilitate trade and investment.

44. Philippines Firm 062, a diaspora-managed firm.

45. Both Georgia and the Philippines are democracies. In a nondemocratic context, a useful distinction can still be made between government officials who make laws (i.e., who possess similar powers to elected officials in democracies) and those that simply implement those laws (i.e., bureaucrats).

46. One promising extension of this work involves a broader examination of the stakeholder groups that diaspora-affiliated firms assemble to both pursue policy change proactively and to protect themselves from adverse government action defensively. Markus (2012, 2015) details how domestic firms assemble diverse coalitions to fend off state predation, and I expect diaspora-affiliated firms engage in similar behaviors.

47. Philippines Firm 059, a diaspora-owned graphic design firm.

48. Philippines Firm 065, a diaspora-managed firm based in the United States.

49. See Kapur (2014) for a recent review of this literature.

50. My data is at the firm level, rather than the individual level, so I do not have data on the socioeconomic status class of the diasporans in my sample.

51. For example, Gai Nyok earned a master's degree in economics at the University of Illinois, while Biar Atem became a manager at The Venetian in Las Vegas and founder of the South Sudan Center of America.

52. For example, there is a well-developed subset of the literature in law and business that examines when and how executives are able to shape corporate philanthropy toward their own ends, such as by channeling donations toward non-profit organizations with which they are affiliated (e.g., Atkinson and Galaskiewicz 1988; Ladd 2004).

53. My discussion here is particularly indebted to the work of Alejandro Portes, Jennifer Brinkerhoff, and Robin Cohen.

54. However, many scholars remain skeptical about the potential of CSR to improve development outcomes (e.g., Blowfield 2005; Locke 2013).

55. See, for example, the Calvert Foundation's "Diaspora Communities" project (http://www.calvertfoundation.org/impact/initiatives/diasporas, accessed May 22, 2015) or the Diaspora Investment Alliance (formerly the Rockefeller Foundation-Aspen Institute Diaspora Program).

56. The limited scope of social insurance in less developed countries is aggravated by the fact that the welfare spending that does occur rarely targets the least well off within those countries (Rudra 2008).

57. I control in these analyses for the role of risk perception—i.e., for how likely each firm believes it is that conflict will recur.

Chapter 3

1. See Kerner (2015) for a discussion of the often poor match between these data and the theory they are employed to test.

2. For full analysis, see chapter 5.

3. Boly et al. (2014) primarily seek to contrast diaspora-affiliated firms with domestic firms, focusing specifically on variations in export behavior between these two types of firms. They find that diaspora-affiliated firms are more export-oriented than domestic firms are but perhaps slightly less export-oriented than nondiaspora foreign firms.

4. The p-value for each test indicates the probability that I would still estimate a difference this large if my theory was incorrect and there was, in fact, no difference between diaspora-affiliated and nondiaspora-affiliated foreign firms.

5. A survey of articles in top management journals found a 32% mean response rate for managerial surveys conducted by mail (Cycyota and Harrison 2006).

6. Cammett (2013) refers to this strategy as "proxy interviewing" and the methodology adopted in both the Georgia and the Philippines surveys matches closely with her description of the process.

7. The results from the Philippines survey are also exploited in some nondiaspora-related research on which these three scholars are coauthors (Cruz et al. 2016; Cruz and Graham 2017).

8. Blonigen and Wang (2004) argue that the determinants of FDI flows into developing countries are fundamentally different than the determinants of FDI flows into rich industrialized countries.

9. For these purposes I define developing countries as countries that fall below the World Bank's threshold for high income economies, which in 2013 was a gross national income per capita of US $12,746. Data on GDP per capita, growth, FDI, inequality (GINI), market capitalization, primary product exports, emigrant stock and literacy rate are all drawn from the World Development Indicators. The ease of doing business score is from the World Bank's Doing Business project. Expropriation and transfer risk data are drawn from the Credendo Group (2012), see Graham, Johnston, and Kingsley (2017). Political constraints data are drawn from Henisz (2000). Corruption data is from Transparency International, and the data on liberal democracy is from the Varieties of Democracy project (Coppedge et al. 2016). All data in figure 3.1 are accessed via version 1.5 of the IPE Data Resource (Graham and Tucker 2017).

10. World Bank, World Development Indicators, 2016.

11. Credendo Group (2012), see Graham, Johnston, and Kingsley (2017).

12. For a summary of this history, see Karnow (2010).

13. In addition to their direct effects on firms' propensity to use social ties, political conditions may also affect respondents' willingness to answer questions about sensitive topics (Li and Jensen 2010). See appendix A3.3 for a discussion of sensitive topics in these surveys.

14. Appendix A3.3 provides a more detailed and technical discussion of the Georgia sample and the scope of inference for which it allows.

15. For a discussion of political context and firm responses to sensitive questions, see Jensen, Li, and Rahman (2010). Fisman and Svensson (2007) discuss how issues related to corruption were desensitized in Uganda via government awareness-raising campaigns.

16. Work based on these prior surveys includes Cruz (2013), Cruz and Keefer (2015), and Cruz, Labonne, and Querubin (2017).

17. See, for example, Azfar and Murrell (2009) on identifying reticent respondents. We employ the *lisit* technique introduced by Corstange (2009).

Chapter 4

1. In Georgia, respondents are a mix of owners and managers, but predominantly managers. In the Philippines all respondents are managers, including some owner-managers.

2. The definition provided in the Georgian survey is more explicit about what it means to be "Georgian." In the Philippines survey we were not explicit about this. In both cases, I expect that individuals responded on the basis of their own preexisting perceptions of who is and is not Georgian (Filipino).

3. Note that these definitions also do not specify a minimum length of time that an individual must live abroad to qualify as a diasporan. If an individual lives abroad for only a short time and does not develop a substantial network of social ties in the country of settlement, he/she is less likely to be able to serve as an effective transnational broker. If such individuals are classified as diasporans, this, too, would make it more challenging for me to find empirical support for my theory.

4. As discussed in appendix A, it is also the case that the Philippines sample likely underrepresents firms with the fewest ties to other firms. If, as I theorize, diaspora-affiliated firms are better connected than their peers, diaspora-affiliated firms may be overrepresented in the sample. This overrepresentation should not bias my estimation of the differences between diaspora-affiliated and nondiaspora affiliated firms, but it does mean that we cannot necessarily infer that two-thirds of foreign firms in the Philippines are diaspora-affiliated.

5. All regressions used throughout chapters 4, 5, and 6 estimate heteroscedasticity-robust standard errors.

6. This precise interpretation hinges on some additional assumptions, including that the sample of firms be a random draw from the population (e.g., no nonresponse bias) and that there is no error in measurement.

7. Li, Meng, and Zhou (2007) show that Chinese firms owned by members of the Communist Party outperform firms owned by nonparty-members.

8. See appendix B4.3 for a complete list.

9. I first transform the two component measures into z-scores and then add them together to create the index.

10. For descriptive statistics on these control variables, see appendix B3.4.

11. Results using the raw data are stronger for some hypotheses tested in this chapter and weaker for others, but in all cases the estimated effects of diaspora affiliation are consistent with the results presented in the main text.

Chapter 5

1. In the Philippines, respondents were asked, "As a business expert, can you briefly describe how your owners' and managers' social relationships affect your firm?" In Georgia, the question was "Can you briefly describe the effects that your owners' and managers' friendships and/or family relationships have on the way your firm does business?"

2. Approximately 45% of firms report a dispute in the past two years.

3. One reason I focus on the prediction that diaspora-affiliated firms are more likely to employ noncourt options, rather than predicting that they are less likely to use the actual courts, is that it is possible that social ties also help firms prevail in formal settings (e.g., Ang and Jia 2014).

4. These differences hold up in both imputed and nonimputed data. Using imputed data, $p = 0.004$ for attempted resolution of disputes outside of court and $p = 0.007$ for use social ties to resolve disputes directly. In the raw data, the values are $p < 0.001$ and $p = 0.004$, respectively.

5. To calculate substantive effects, I compare the probability that a typical diaspora-affiliated firm engages in a particular behavior, such as using social networks to resolve a dispute, with the probability that an otherwise identical nondiaspora-affiliated foreign firm engages in the same behavior. The difference between these two probabilities is the substantive effect of diaspora affiliation. To calculate this, I estimate predicted probabilities for two hypothetical firms, one that is diaspora affiliated (i.e., *diaspora affiliated* = 1) and one that is not (i.e., *diaspora affiliated* = 0). For each of these hypothetical firms, I set the values of all other independent variables, like *firm age*, at their median. For the vectors of region and sector dummies, where median values are all zero, I assign the hypothetical firms to be manufacturing firms based in the Americas.

6. The questions employed in this section are modeled on previous survey work in Vietnam by McMillan and Woodruff (1999).

7. Rankings as of 2014.

8. For full regression results, see appendix C5.4. These predicted probabilities are calculated in the same manner as described in chapter 5, note 5. However, in the Georgia data the sector of the hypothetical firm is "Secondary" and the region is "West." Note that these predicted values vary substantially by sector. If the hypothetical firms are in the "primary" sector, i.e., agriculture/natural resources, then the predicted probabilities are 61% and 73% for nondiaspora-owned and diaspora-owned firms, respectively. The difference is the same, but the baseline probability is much higher. Overall, 32% of firms in Georgia report using friendship or family ties to secure real estate (see table A3.2b in appendix A).

9. Examining how policy objectives vary across different types of firms is a very exciting area of research, but one that is empirically challenging.

10. In contrast, questions about revenues and profitability were considered sensitive, and thus I opted to ask for ordinal responses to those questions, rather than specific values.

11. See chapter 5, note 5 for details on how this is calculated.

12. The predicted probabilities of attempting to influence policy at either the local or national level are 30% and 54% for nondiaspora-affiliated and diaspora-affiliated firms, respectively. The probabilities of achieving success at one or both levels are 23% and 59%. Predicted probabilities are based on logistic regressions with binary versions of the dependent variables. See chapter 5, note 5.

Chapter 6

1. Mr. Ocampo's name and the names of the firms he worked for have been changed to protect his anonymity.

2. See Blowfield and Frynas (2005) for a discussion of the role of CSR in development.

3. The empirical results discussed in this section were first published in Graham (2014).

4. The business literature generally concludes that, while CSR may be part of a firm strategy aimed at enhancing firm profitability, there is no reason to expect that, on average, firms that are more socially responsible are more profitable than firms that are not (e.g., McWilliams and Siegel 2001).

5. Existing studies tend to draw their samples from the S&P 500 or similar lists of prominent firms.

6. For a range of definitions, see Garriga and Melé (2004).

7. The literature on CSR and development stresses the need for firms to respond to the specific needs of local stakeholders, which vary greatly from community to community (see Newell and Frynas 2007; Moon 2007).

8. Respondents were shown a card with this scale presented visually.

9. These Likert-scale responses are analyzed using ordered logistic regressions, while the binary responses on donations are analyzed with logistic regressions. All models include controls for firm age, firm size, share of foreign ownership, and a dummy variable capturing whether the firm is located in the capital city of Tbilisi. I also control for sector and for home region.

10. I would like to thank Daniel Naujoks in particular for advice regarding this component of the analysis. For some of his excellent work in this area, see Naujoks (2013).

11. Further complicating this relationship, Lee, Biglaiser, and Staats (2014) argue that high levels of institutional development in the investment host country are critical in protecting foreign firms against the special risks associated with M&A entry.

12. Employment may be a particularly important political issue with regard to

FDI, as organized labor interests in the investment host country are generally opposed to FDI (Owen 2013, 2015).

13. While there has also been some political violence in the Philippines, this is almost exclusively located in Mindinao, a region far from Manila, in and around which all the firms in our sample are based. Thus I opted to focus on war risk only in the Georgia survey.

14. See, for example, Asmus (2010); Buzard, Graham, and Horne (2017).

15. This figure is based on version 3.0 of the PRIO Battledeaths Dataset (Lacina and Gleditsch 2005).

16. The question asks, "How important is the possibility of **future** violent conflict over Abkhazia and South Ossetia to your firm's business strategy over the next three years?"

Chapter 7

1. Some of these perceived threats to culture have explicitly racist or xenophobic roots. However, writers like Ross Douthat (2016) focus on the fact that new immigrant voters may have policy preferences, particularly related to family law and the separation of church and state, that do not match those of citizens in the country of settlement.

2. See Berthelemy, Beuran, and Maurel (2009) for a discussion under which foreign aid and migration are complements or substitutes. See De Haas (2005, 2007) for a discussion of why increases in foreign aid are unlikely to decrease migration. Particularly in the short run, economic development in poor countries is likely to increase, rather than reduce, outward migration (Clemens 2015).

3. For an example of the type of initiatives seeking to bolster the capacity of diasporans to promote development in their homelands, see the European Commission-United Nations Joint Migration and Development Initiative.

4. See Agunias and Newland (2007) for a broader discussion of diaspora engagement efforts by developing-country governments.

5. For recent work in this area, see Elo (2016), Lin and Yang (2017), Pruthi et al. (2018), and Sommer and Gamper (2017).

6. See also Wahba and Zenou (2012).

7. A foundation for future examination of this topic has been laid by the work of several scholars, including Brinkerhoff (2016) and Kshetri (2013), who explore the role of diaspora entrepreneurs as agents of institutional change in the homeland, and Ye (2014), who describes the role of the diaspora in shifting economic policy toward greater openness in China and India.

8. This has been shown to be true in certain extreme cases. For example, Guidolin and La Ferrara (2007) show that the sudden end of the civil war in Angola in 2002 actually lowered the stock prices of those diamond mining firms that had been able to operate successfully while the conflict was ongoing. This is also, in some sense, the flip side of the argument made by Garcia-Johnson (2000) with regard to environmental regulation in Brazil and Mexico. She argues that MNCs have a com-

petitive advantage over domestic firms when it comes to complying with environmental regulations, and thus MNCs advocate for stricter regulation to give themselves an edge over domestic competitors.

9. This is a research area that seems ripe for new work more broadly. For example, while conventional wisdom holds that foreign investment generally reduces corruption, Malesky, Gueorguiev, and Jensen (2015) argue that foreign firms sometimes use bribes to enter protected industries in search of rents. The relationship between FDI and corruption is clearly contingent on the capabilities of foreign firms and the constraints facing them in the investment host country, but much work remains to be done to understand these interactions fully.

10. Most high-skilled migrants continue to seek out wealthy destination countries, though recent evidence suggests that the pool of countries receiving high-skilled migrants is diversifying (e.g., Chacko and Gebre 2013; Artuc et al. 2014). The arguments in this section apply to any country to which educated, wealthy, and/or politically connected individuals seek to migrate.

11. Only 6% of foreign firms in my sample have no diaspora affiliation and no local manager.

Appendix A

1. In the Philippines we restrict respondents to managers to increase consistency in respondents' roles across firms. In the Georgia analysis I control for whether the respondent is a firm owner.

2. Some firms on the Ministry of Finance list also turned out to be registered before the year 2000, but had been reregistered after that date.

3. Georgia has no up-to-date telephone or address directories and few of the firms operating in Georgia maintain websites, making it difficult to contact those firms that had moved within the past few years.

4. Firms from Azerbaijan, France, Israel, the Netherlands, and the United States were more likely than average to refuse to participate in the survey, but there is no obvious common characteristic across these countries that appears to drive nonresponse. Note that Graham (2014) includes a supplemental nonrandom sample of seven additional diaspora-owned firms. This nonrandom supplement is not used in the analysis in this book.

5. In addition to helping collect the data used in this book, this collaboration produced an article on the preparations and concerns of foreign firms in the lead up to ASEAN 2015 (Cruz et al. 2016).

6. The practice of using professional organizations to establish researcher credibility is quite common in firm-level research (e.g., Fisman and Svensson 2007).

7. In 2010, the Philippines Securities and Exchange Commission (SEC) compiled a list of the 25,000 largest firms in the Philippines, of which 1,224 have at least partial foreign ownership. This list provides information on the sector, revenue, profitability, and investor home country of each firm, allowing us to compare our sample with the firms on that list in each of these dimensions.

8. The figures and discussion in this section are adapted from the online appendix that accompanies Cruz et al. (2016). Our data on the distribution of economic activity across sectors in the Philippines economy as a whole comes from the National Statistics Coordination Board. Data are from Q3 2014.

9. This includes both foreign and domestic firms.

10. The list from the SEC was, unfortunately, several years out of date and more recent data was not available.

11. Rosenfeld, Imai, and Shapiro (2016) perform a validation test of list experiments and find evidence that they reduce, though do not entirely eliminate, underreporting of sensitive behaviors.

12. Half the firms in the sample were randomly assigned to each group. Three of the firms asked the protected version declined to answer, resulting in 151 responses from firms in the direct response group and 148 responses from the shielded response group.

13. The coefficients of interest are similar in analyses using list-wise deletion.

14. This is implemented using the MI suite of commands in Stata 14. I run the imputations for Georgia and the Philippines separately and in each case I create 10 imputed versions of the data for analysis.

Appendix B

1. See section 1.3 in the main text for this conceptual discussion.

Appendix C

1. While I compare diaspora-affiliated and nondiaspora-affiliated foreign firms in their use of four different strategies for managing relationships with government officials, only one of those comparisons constitutes a test of my theory (i.e., use of social ties for this purpose). Similarly, I do not count *success if attempted* as a test as there is no clear *ex ante* theoretical expectation.

REFERENCES

Abbott, Walter F., and R. Joseph Monsen. 1979. "On the Measurement of Corporate Social Responsibility: Self-Reported Disclosures as a Method of Measuring Corporate Social Involvement." *Academy of Management Journal* 22 (3): 501–15.

Acharyya, Joysri. 2009. "FDI, Growth and the Environment: Evidence from India on CO2 Emission During the Last Two Decades." *Journal of Economic Development* 34 (1): 43–58.

Adler, Paul S. 2001. "Market, Hierarchy, and Trust: The Knowledge Economy and the Future of Capitalism." *Organization Science* 12 (2): 215–34.

Agosin, M. R., and Ricardo Mayer. 2000. "Foreign Investment in Developing Countries: Does it Crowd in Domestic Investment?" *UNCTAD Discussion Paper* 146.

Agunias, Dovelyn Rannveig. 2006. *Remittances and Development: Trends, Impacts, and Policy Options: A Review of the Literature.* Washington, DC: Migration Policy Institute.

Agunias, Dovelyn Rannveig, and Kathleen Newland. 2007. *Circular Migration and Development: Trends, Policy Routes, and Ways Forward.* Washington, DC: Migration Policy Institute.

Aharoni, Yair. 1966. "The Foreign Investment Decision Process." *Thunderbird International Business Review* 8 (4): 13–14.

Ahearne, Alan G, William L. Griever, and Francis E. Warnock. 2004. "Information Costs and Home Bias: An Analysis of US Holdings of Foreign Equities." *Journal of International Economics* 62 (2): 313–36.

Albuquerque, Rui, Gregory H. Bauer, and Martin Schneider. 2009. "Global Private Information in International Equity Markets." *Journal of Financial Economics* 94 (1): 18–46.

Aldrich, John H., James E. Alt, and Arthur Lupia. 2008. "The EITM Approach: Origins and Interpretations." *The Oxford Handbook of Political Methodology*, edited by Janet M. Box-Steffensmeier, Henry E. Brady, and David Collier. New York: Oxford University Press.

Alfaro, Laura, Areendam Chanda, Sebnem Kalemli-Ozcan, and Selin Sayek. 2004. "FDI and Economic Growth: The Role of Local Financial Markets." *Journal of International Economics* 64 (1): 89–112.

Alfaro, Laura, Sebnem Kalemli-Ozcan, and Vadym Volosovych. 2008. "Why

Doesn't Capital Flow from Rich to Poor Countries? An Empirical Investigation." *Review of Economics and Statistics* 90 (2): 347–68.

Alonso, Alexandra Delano, and Harris Mylonas. 2017. "The Microfoundations of Diaspora Politics: Unpacking the State and Disaggregating the Diaspora." *Journal of Ethnic and Migration Studies*. Online. Available at https://www.tandfon line.com/doi/full/10.1080/1369183X.2017.1409160

Ang, Alvin P. 2007. "Workers' Remittances and Economic Growth in the Philippines." Paper read at DEGIT Conference Papers.

Antwi-Boateng, Osman. 2011. "The Political Participation of the U.S.-Based Liberian Diaspora and Its Implication for Peace Building." *Africa Today* 58 (1): 3–26.

Artuç, Erhan, Frédéric Docquier, Çaglar Özden, and Christopher Parsons. 2015. "A Global Assessment of Human Capital Mobility: The Role of Non-OECD Destinations." *World Development* 65: 6–26.

Asmus, Ronald. 2010. *A Little War that Shook the World: Georgia, Russia, and the Future of the West*. New York: Palgrave Macmillan.

Atkinson, Lisa, and Joseph Galaskiewicz. 1988. "Stock Ownership and Company Contributions to Charity." *Administrative Science Quarterly* 33 (1): 82–100.

Aupperle, Kenneth E., Archie B. Carroll, and John D. Hatfield. 1985. "An Empirical Examination of the Relationship Between Corporate Social Responsibility and Profitability." *Academy of Management Journal* 28 (2): 446–63.

Aykut, Dilek, and Andrea Goldstein. 2007. "Developing Country Multinationals: South-South Investment Comes of Age." *Industrial Development for the 21st Century: Sustainable Development Perspectives*, 85–116. New York: OECD Press.

Azfar, Omar, and Peter Murrell. 2009. "Identifying Reticent Respondents: Assessing the Quality of Survey Data on Corruption and Values." *Economic Development and Cultural Change* 57 (2): 387–411.

Bandelj, Nina. 2002. "Embedded Economies: Social Relations as Determinants of Foreign Direct Investment in Central and Eastern Europe." *Social Forces* 81 (2): 411–44.

Bandelj, Nina. 2008. *From Communists to Foreign Capitalists*. Princeton: Princeton University Press.

Banerjee, Biswajit. 1983. "Social Networks in the Migration Process: Empirical Evidence on Chain Migration in India." *Journal of Developing Areas* 17 (2): 185–96.

Barney, Jay. 1991. "Firm Resources and Sustained Competitive Advantage." *Journal of Management* 17 (1): 99–120.

Barney, Jay B., and Mark H. Hansen. 1994. "Trustworthiness as a Source of Competitive Advantage." *Strategic Management Journal* 15 (S1): 175–90.

Bartlett, Christopher A., and Sumantra Ghoshal. 1989. *Managing Across Borders: The Transnational Solution*. Cambridge, MA: Harvard Business School Press.

Bavelas, Alex. 1948. "A Mathematical Model for Group Structure." *Applied Anthropology* 7:16–30.

Beamer, Linda. 1992. "Learning Intercultural Communication Competence." *Journal of Business Communication* 29 (3): 285–303.

Beilock, Richard. 2003. "Helping Armenia without Helping the Blockade." *Armenian Journal of Public Policy* 1 (1): 79–112.

Beine, Michel, Frédéric Docquier, and Hillel Rapoport. 2001. "Brain Drain and Economic Growth: Theory and Evidence." *Journal of Development Economics* 64 (1): 275–89.

Bénassy Quéré, A., M. Coupet, and T. Mayer. 2007. "Institutional Determinants of Foreign Direct Investment." *World Economy* 30 (5): 764–82.

Berry, Sara. 1993. *No Condition is Permanent: The Social Dynamics of Agrarian Change in Sub-Saharan Africa.* Madison: University of Wisconsin Press.

Berthélemy, Jean-Claude, Monica Beuran, and Mathilde Maurel. 2009. "Aid and Migration: Substitutes or Complements?" *World Development* 37 (10): 1589–99.

Bertoli, Simone, and Francesca Marchetta. 2015. "Bringing It All Back Home— Return Migration and Fertility Choices." *World Development* 65:27–40.

Bhagwati, Jagdish, and Koichi Hamada. 1974. "The Brain Drain, International Integration of Markets for Professionals and Unemployment: A Theoretical Analysis." *Journal of Development Economics* 1 (1): 19–42.

Biglaiser, Glen, Hoon Lee, and Joseph L. Staats. 2016. "The Effects of the IMF on Expropriation of Foreign Firms." *Review of International Organizations* 11 (1): 1–23.

Black, Richard, and Adriana Castaldo. 2009. "Return Migration and Entrepreneurship in Ghana and Côte d'Ivoire: The Role of Capital Transfers." *Tijdschrift voor economische en sociale geografie* 100 (1): 44–58.

Blomström, Magnus, Ari Kokko, and Jean-Louis Mucchielli. 2003. "The Economics of Foreign Direct Investment Incentives." *Foreign Direct Investment in the Real and Financial Sector of Industrial Countries*, edited by H. Herrmann and R. Lipsey, 37–60. Berlin: Springer.

Blonigen, Bruce A., and Miao Wang. 2004. "Inappropriate Pooling of Wealthy and Poor Countries in Empirical FDI Studies." Working Paper. National Bureau of Economic Research, March 2004.

Blonigen, Bruce A., and Rossitza B. Wooster. 2003. "CEO Turnover and Foreign Market Participation. National Bureau of Economic Research." Working Paper. National Bureau of Economic Research, March 2003.

Bloom, Nicholas, and John Van Reenen. 2010. "Why Do Management Practices Differ Across Firms and Countries?" *Journal of Economic Perspectives* 24 (1): 203–24.

Blowfield, Michael, and Jedrzej George Frynas. 2005. "Setting New Agendas: Critical Perspectives on Corporate Social Responsibility in the Developing World." *International Affairs (Royal Institute of International Affairs)* 81 (3): 499–513.

Boly, Amadou, Nicola Daniele Coniglio, Francesco Prota, and Adnan Seric. 2014. "Diaspora Investments and Firm Export Performance in Selected Sub-Saharan African Countries." *World Development* 59:422–33.

Borensztein, Eduardo, Jose De Gregorio, and Jong-Wha Lee. 1998. "How Does Foreign Direct Investment Affect Economic Growth?" *Journal of International Economics* 45 (1): 115–35.

Borjas, George. 2013. "Immigration and the American Worker: A Review of the Academic Literature." Center for Immigration Studies, April 2013. Available at http://cis.org/sites/cis.org/files/borjas-economics.pdf

Bowen, Howard. 1953. *Social Responsibilities of the Businessman*. New York: Harper & Row.

Boyd, Monica. 1989. "Family and Personal Networks in International Migration: Recent Developments and New Agendas." *International Migration Review* 23 (3): 638–70.

Brinkerhoff, Jennifer M. 2004. "Digital Diasporas and International Development: Afghan-Americans and the Reconstruction of Afghanistan." *Public Administration and Development* 24 (5): 397–413.

Brinkerhoff, Jennifer M. 2007. "Diasporas and Development: What Role for Foreign Aid?" *Foreign Aid and Foreign Policy: Lessons for the Next Half-Century*, edited by Louis Picard, Robert Groelsema, and Terry F. Buss, 375–93. Armonk, NY: ME Sharpe.

Brinkerhoff, Jennifer M. 2008. "Diaspora Philanthropy in an At-Risk Society: The Case of Coptic Orphans in Egypt." *Nonprofit and Voluntary Sector Quarterly* 37 (3): 411–33.

Brinkerhoff, Jennifer M. 2009. *Digital Diasporas: Identity and Transnational Engagement*. Cambridge: Cambridge University Press.

Brinkerhoff, Jennifer M. 2014. "Diaspora Philanthropy: Lessons from a Demographic Analysis of the Coptic Diaspora." *Nonprofit and Voluntary Sector Quarterly* 43 (6): 969–92.

Brinkerhoff, Jennifer M. 2016. *Institutional Reform and Diaspora Entrepreneurs: The In-Between Advantage*. New York: Oxford University Press.

Brudney, Victor, and Allen Ferrell. 2002. "Corporate Charitable Giving." *University of Chicago Law Review* 69 (3): 1191–1218.

Burchardi, Konrad B., Thomas Chaney, and Tarek A. Hassan. 2016. "Migrants, Ancestors, and Investments." Working Paper. National Bureau of Economic Research, January 2016. Available at http://www.nber.org/papers/w21847

Burt, Ronald S. 1992. *Structural Holes: The Structure of Competition*. Cambridge, MA: Harvard University Press.

Burt, Ronald S. 2000. "The Network Structure of Social Capital." *Research in Organizational Behavior* 22:345–423.

Burton, Brian K., and Michael Goldsby. 2009. "Corporate Social Responsibility Orientation, Goals, and Behavior." *Business & Society* 48 (1): 88–104.

Butcher, Mike. 2014. "Ostrovok Raises New $12M Series C Round To Expand Outside Russia." *TechCrunch*, June 18, 2014. Available at http://techcrunch.com/2014/06/18/ostrovok-raises-new-12m-series-c-round-to-expand-outside-russia

Buzard, Kristy, Benjamin A. T. Graham, and Ben Horne. 2017. "Unrecognized States: A Theory of Self-Determination and Foreign Influence." *Journal of Law, Economics, and Organization* 33 (3): 578–611.

Cammett, Melani. 2013. "Using Proxy Interviewing to Address Sensitive Topics."

Interview Research in Political Science, edited by Layna Mosley, 125–43. Ithaca: Cornell University Press.

Carroll, Archie B. 1979. "A Three-Dimensional Conceptual Model of Corporate Performance." *Academy of Management Review* 4 (4): 497–505.

Chacko, Elizabeth, and Peter H. Gebre. 2013. "Leveraging the Diaspora for Development: Lessons from Ethiopia." *GeoJournal* 78 (3): 495–505.

Chakhalyan, Hasmik. 2007. "The Role of the Armenian Diaspora in Homeland Economic Development: Challenges and Opportunities." Masters thesis, Central European University. http://www.etd.ceu.hu/2008/chakhalyan_hasmik.pdf

Chan, Kalok, and Allaudeen Hameed. 2006. "Stock Price Synchronicity and Analyst Coverage in Emerging Markets." *Journal of Financial Economics* 80 (1): 115–47.

Chand, Masud, and Rosalie L. Tung. 2011. "Diaspora as the Boundary-Spanners: The Role of Trust in Business Facilitation." *Journal of Trust Research* 1 (1): 107–29.

Chen, Yun-Chung. 2008. "The Limits of Brain Circulation: Chinese Returnees and Technological Development in Beijing." *Pacific Affairs* 81 (2): 195–215.

Child, John, and Guido Möllering. 2003. "Contextual Confidence and Active Trust Development in the Chinese Business Environment." *Organization Science* 14 (1): 69–80.

Chirwa, Wiseman Chijere. 1997. "'No TEBA . . . Forget TEBA': The Plight of Malawian Ex-Migrant Workers to South Africa, 1988–1994." *International Migration Review* 31 (3): 628–54.

Choudhury, Prithwiraj Raj. 2010. "Knowledge Creation in Multinationals and Return Migration: Evidence from Micro Data." *Academy of Management Proceedings* 2010 (1): 1–6.

Chow, Simeon, and Reed Holden. 1997. "Toward an Understanding of Loyalty: The Moderating Role of Trust." *Journal of Managerial Issues* 9 (3): 275–98.

Chowdhury, Abdur, and George Mavrotas. 2006. "FDI and Growth: What Causes What?" *World Economy* 29 (1): 9–19.

Clemens, Michael A. 2011. "Economics and Emigration: Trillion-Dollar Bills on the Sidewalk?" *Journal of Economic Perspectives* 25 (3): 83–106.

Clemens, Michael A. 2015. "Does Development Reduce Migration?" *International Handbook on Migration and Economic Development*, edited by Robert E. B. Lucas, 152–85. London: Edward Elgar.

Clemens, Michael A., and Gunilla Pettersson. 2008. "New Data on African Health Professionals Abroad." *Human Resources for Health* 6 (1): 1–11.

Cochran, Philip L., and Robert A. Wood. 1984. "Corporate Social Responsibility and Financial Performance." *Academy of Management Journal* 27 (1): 42–56.

Cohen, R. 1997. *Global Diasporas: An Introduction*. Seattle: University of Washington Press.

Coleman, James S. 1988. "Social Capital in the Creation of Human Capital." *American Journal of Sociology* 94: S95–S120.

Coleman, James S. 1990. *Foundations of Social Theory*. Cambridge, MA: Harvard University Press.

Collins, Harry M. 2001. "Tacit Knowledge, Trust and the Q of Sapphire." *Social Studies of Science* 31 (1): 71–85.

Collyer, Michael. 2013. "A Geography of Extra-Territorial Citizenship: Explanations of External Voting." *Migration Studies* 2 (1): 55–72.

Connor, Phillip, D'vera Cohn, Ana Gonzalez-Barrerra, and Russ Oates. 2013. "Changing Patterns of Global Migration and Remittances: More Migrants in U.S. and Other Wealthy Countries; More Money in Middle-Income Countries." Washington, DC: Pew Research Center.

Cooper, Russell, Douglas V. DeJong, Robert Forsythe, and Thomas W. Ross. 1992. "Communication in Coordination Games." *Quarterly Journal of Economics* 107 (2): 739–71.

Coppedge, Michael, John Gerring, Staffan I. Lindberg, Svend-Erik Skaaning, Jan Teorell, David Altman, Frida Andersson, Michael Bernhard, M. Steven Fish, Adam Glynn, Allen Hicken, Carl Henrik Knutsen, Kelly McMann, Valeriya Mechkova, Farhad Miri, Pamela Paxton, Daniel Pemstein, Rachel Sigman, Jeffrey Staton, and Brigitte Zimmerman. 2016. "V-Dem Codebook v6." Varieties of Democracy (VDem) Project.

Corstange, Daniel. 2009. "Sensitive Questions, Truthful Answers? Modeling the List Experiment with LISTIT." *Political Analysis* 17 (1): 45–63.

Coval, Joshua D., and Tobias J. Moskowitz. 1999. "Home Bias at Home: Local Equity Preference in Domestic Portfolios." *Journal of Finance* 54 (6): 2045–73.

Crawford, Vincent. 1998. "A Survey of Experiments on Communication Via Cheap Talk." *Journal of Economic theory* 78 (2): 286–98.

Cruz, Cesi. 2013. "Social Networks and the Targeting of Vote Buying." Working Paper.

Cruz, Cesi, and Benjamin A. T. Graham. 2017. "Network Ties and the Political Strategies of Firms." Working Paper. Available at https://ssrn.com/abstract=2972801

Cruz, Cesi, Benjamin A. T. Graham, Prudenciano Gordoncillo, Jeanette Madamba, and Jewel Cabardo. 2016. "Who's Ready for ASEAN 2015? Firm Expectations and Preparations in the Philippines." *Pacific Affairs* 89 (2): 259–85.

Cruz, Cesi, J. Labonne, and P. Querubin. 2017. "Politician Family Networks and Electoral Outcomes: Evidence from the Philippines." *American Economic Review*. Online. Available at https://www.aeaweb.org/articles?id=10.1257/aer.20150343

Cruz, Cesi, and Philip Keefer. 2015. "Political Parties, Clientelism, and Bureaucratic Reform." *Comparative Political Studies* 48 (14): 1942–73.

Cycyota, Cynthia S., and David A. Harrison. 2006. "What (Not) to Expect When Surveying Executives a Meta-analysis of Top Manager Response Rates and Techniques Over Time." *Organizational Research Methods* 9 (2): 133–60.

Debass, Thomas, and Michael Ardovino. 2009. "Diaspora Direct Investment (DDI): The Untapped Resource." Washington, DC: United States Agency for International Development.

De Haas, Hein. 2005. "International Migration, Remittances and Development: Myths and Facts." *Third World Quarterly* 26 (8): 1269–84.

De Haas, Hein. 2007. "Morocco's Migration Experience: A Transitional Perspective1." *International Migration* 45 (4): 39–70.

De Haas, Hein. 2012. "The Migration and Development Pendulum: A Critical View on Research and Policy." *International Migration* 50 (3): 8–25.

De Mello, L. R. 1999. "Foreign Direct Investment-Led Growth: Evidence from Time Series and Panel Data." *Oxford Economic Papers* 51 (1): 133–51.

Desai, Mihir A., C. Fritz Foley, and James R. Hines Jr. 2006. "The Demand for Tax Haven Operations." *Journal of Public Economics* 90 (3): 513–31.

De Simone, Gianfranco, and Miriam Manchin. 2012. "Outward Migration and Inward FDI: Factor Mobility between Eastern and Western Europe." *Review of International Economics* 20 (3): 600–15.

Djajić, Slobodan, and Alexandra Vinogradova. 2015. "Overshooting the Savings Target: Temporary Migration, Investment in Housing and Development." *World Development* 65:110–21.

Docquier, Frédéric, and Elisabetta Lodigiani. 2010. "Skilled Migration and Business Networks." *Open Economies Review* 21 (4): 565–88.

Docquier, Frédéric, Elisabetta Lodigiani, Hillel Rapoport, and Maurice Schiff. 2011. "Emigration and Democracy." *Development Studies Working Paper*, No. 2011-02. Turin, Italy: Centro Studi Luca d'Agliano. Available at http://hdl.handle.net/10419/96047

Docquier, Frédéric, and Hillel Rapoport. 2012. "Globalization, Brain Drain, and Development." *Journal of Economic Literature* 50 (3): 681–730.

Donaldson, Thomas, and Lee E. Preston. 1995. "The Stakeholder Theory of the Corporation: Concepts, Evidence, and Implications." *Academy of Management Review* 20 (1): 65–91.

Douthat, Ross. 2016. "Ten Theses on Immigration." *New York Times*, January 13.

Duanmu, Jing-Lin, and Yilmaz Guney. 2013. "Heterogeneous Effect of Ethnic Networks on International Trade of Thailand: The Role of Family Ties and Ethnic Diversity." *International Business Review* 22 (1): 126–39.

Dunning, John H. 1980. "Toward an Eclectic Theory of International Production: Some Empirical Tests." *Journal of International Business Studies* 11 (1): 9–31.

Dunning, John H. 1988. "The Eclectic Paradigm of International Production: A Restatement and Some Possible Extensions." *Journal of International Business Studies* 19 (1): 1–31.

Dunning, John H., and Sarianna M. Lundan. 2008. *Multinational Enterprises and the Global Economy*. Northampton, MA: Edward Elgar.

Dyer, Jeffrey H., and Harbir Singh. 1998. "The Relational View: Cooperative Strategy and Sources of Interorganizational Competitive Advantage." *Academy of Management Review* 23 (4): 660–79.

Eckstein, Harry. 2000. "Case Study and Theory in Political Science." *Case Study Method: Key Issues, Key Texts*, edited by Roger Gomm, Martyn Hammersley, and Peter Foster, 119–64. London: Sage Publications.

Ellis, Christopher J., Bruce Aloysius Blonigen, and Dietrich Fausten. 2003. "Industrial Groupings and Foreign Direct Investment." *Journal of International Economics* 65 (1): 75–91.

Elo, Maria. 2016. "Typology of Diaspora Entrepreneurship: Case Studies in Uzbekistan." *Journal of International Entrepreneurship* 14 (1): 121–55.

Erickson, Bonnie H. 1979. "Some Problems of Inference from Chain Data." *Sociological Methodology* 10: 276–302.

Esipova, Neli, Julie Ray, and Anita Pugliese. 2011. "Gallup World Poll: The Many Faces of Global Migration." Research Series No. 43, Grand-Saconnex, Switzerland: International Organization of Migration. http://publications.iom.int/sys tem/files/pdf/mrs43.pdf

Faccio, Mara, Ronald W. Masulis, and John J. McConnell. 2006. "Political Connections and Corporate Bailouts." *Journal of Finance* 61 (6): 2597–2635.

Filatotchev, Igor, Xiaohui Liu, Jiangyong Lu, and Mike Wright. 2011. "Knowledge Spillovers Through Human Mobility Across National Borders: Evidence from Zhongguancun Science Park in China." *Research Policy* 40 (3): 453–62.

Fisman, Raymond, and Jakob Svensson. 2007. "Are Corruption and Taxation Really Harmful to Growth? Firm Level Evidence." *Journal of Development Economics* 83 (1): 63–75.

Foner, Nancy. 1997. "What's New About Transnationalism? New York Immigrants Today and at the Turn of the Century." *Diaspora: A Journal of Transnational Studies* 6 (3): 355–75.

Foreign Services Institute. 2010. *Engaging with Diaspora Communities: Focus on EAP, EUR and NEA.* Washington, DC: Foreign Policy Institute, Office of the Secretary of State.

Fox, Tom. 2004. "Corporate Social Responsibility and Development: In Quest of an Agenda." *Development* 47 (3): 29–36.

Frankel, Jeffrey. 2011. "Are Bilateral Remittances Countercyclical?" *Open Economies Review* 22 (1): 1–16.

Freeman, R. Edward. 1984. *Strategic Management: A Stakeholder Approach.* London: Pitman Publishing.

Freinkman, Lev. 2002. "Role of the Diasporas in Transition Economies: Lessons from Armenia." *Munich Personal RePEc Archive.* The World Bank. Available at https://mpra.ub.uni-muenchen.de/10013/1/MPRA_paper_10013.pdf

French, Kenneth R., and James M. Poterba. 1991. "Investor Diversification and International Equity Markets." *American Economic Review* 81 (2): 222–26.

Frieden, Jeffry A. 1994. "International Investment and Colonial Control: A New Interpretation." *International Organization* 48 (4): 559–93.

Gamlen, A., M. Cummings, and Paul M. Vaaler. 2017. "Explaining the Rise of Diaspora Institutions." *Journal of Ethnic and Migration Studies.* Online. Available at https://www.tandfonline.com/doi/full/10.1080/1369183X.2017.1409163?scroll =top&needAccess=true

Garchitorena, Victoria. 2007. "Diaspora Philanthropy: The Philippine Experience." Prepared for The Philanthropic Initiative, Inc., and the Global Equity Initiative, Harvard University. Online. Available at https://www.cbd.int/financial/charity/ philippines-diaspora.pdf

Garcia-Johnson, Ronie. 2000. *Exporting Environmentalism: US Multinational Chemical Corporations in Brazil and Mexico.* Cambridge, MA: MIT Press.

Garnaut, John. 2010. "The Princelings." *Sydney Morning Herald.* October 2. Available at http://www.smh.com.au/business/the-princelings-20101001-16131.html

Garriga, Elisabet, and Domènec Melé. 2004. "Corporate Social Responsibility Theories: Mapping the Territory." *Journal of Business Ethics* 53 (1): 51–71.

Gehrig, Thomas. 1993. "An Information Based Explanation of the Domestic Bias in International Equity Investment." *Scandinavian Journal of Economics* 95 (1): 97–109.

George, Alexander L., and Andrew Bennett. 2005. *Case Studies and Theory Development in the Social Sciences.* Cambridge, MA: MIT Press.

Ghemawat, Pankaj. 2001. "Distance Still Matters: The Hard Reality of Global Expansion." *Harvard Business Review.* September 2001.

Gillespie, Kate, Edward Sayre, and Liesl Riddle. 2001. "Palestinian Interest in Homeland Investment." *Middle East Journal* 55 (2): 237–55.

Gillespie, Kate, J. Brad McBride, and Liesl Riddle. 2010. "Globalization, Biculturalism and Cosmopolitanism: The Acculturation Status of Mexicans in Upper Management." *International Journal of Cross Cultural Management* 10 (1): 37–53.

Gillespie, Kate, Liesl Riddle, Edward Sayre, and David Sturges. 1999. "Diaspora Interest in Homeland Investment." *Journal of International Business Studies* 30 (3): 623–34.

Giuliano, Paola, and Marta Ruiz-Arranz. 2009. "Remittances, Financial Development, and Growth." *Journal of Development Economics* 90 (1): 144–52.

Globerman, Steven, and Daniel M. Shapiro. 1999. "The Impact of Government Policies on Foreign Direct Investment: The Canadian Experience." *Journal of International Business Studies* 30 (3): 513–32.

Goodman, Leo A. 1961. "Snowball Sampling." *Annals of Mathematical Statistics* 32 (1): 148–70.

Gooptu, Biswarup. 2014. "Snapdeal Co-found Kunal Bahl: A Rising Star of India's E-Commerce Space." *Economic Times*, February 28. Available at https://economictimes.indiatimes.com/tech/internet/snapdeal-co-founder-kunal-bahl-a-rising-star-of-indias-e-commerce-space/articleshow/31125419.cms

Gordon, Roger H., and A. Lans Bovenberg. 1996. "Why Is Capital So Immobile Internationally? Possible Explanations and Implications for Capital Income Taxation." *American Economic Review* 86 (5): 1057–75.

Graham, Benjamin A. T. 2014. "Diaspora-Owned Firms and Social Responsibility." *Review of International Political Economy* 21 (2): 432–66.

Graham, Benjamin A. T., and Jacob R. Tucker. 2017. "The International Political Economy Data Resource." *Review of International Organizations.* https://doi.org/10.1007/s11558-017-9285-0

Graham, Benjamin A. T., Noel P. Johnston, and Allison F. Kingsley. 2017. "Even Constrained Governments Steal: The Domestic Politics of Transfer and Expropriation Risks." *Journal of Conflict Resolution.* Online. Available at http://journals.sagepub.com/eprint/juMGMBbii7qyHGqsJ2Dc/full

Graham, John W. 2009. "Missing Data Analysis: Making it Work in the Real World." *Annual Review of Psychology* 60:549–76.

Granovetter, Mark S. 1973. "The Strength of Weak Ties." *American Journal of Sociology* 78 (6): 1360.

Granovetter, Mark S. 1985. "Economic Action and Social Structure: The Problem of Embeddedness." *American Journal of Sociology* 91 (3): 481–510.

Granovetter, Mark S. 1992. "Economic Institutions as Social Constructions: A Framework for Analysis." *Acta Sociologica* 35 (1): 3–11.

Grant, Robert M. 1996. "Toward a Knowledge-Based Theory of the Firm." *Strategic Management Journal* 17 (S2): 109–22.

Greenland, Sander, and William D. Finkle. 1995. "A Critical Look at Methods for Handling Missing Covariates in Epidemiologic Regression Analyses." *American Journal of Epidemiology* 142 (12): 1255–64.

Greif, Avner. 1993. "Contract Enforceability and Economic Institutions in Early Trade: The Maghribi Traders' Coalition." *American Economic Review* 83 (3): 525–48.

Gudykunst, William B., and Young Yun Kim. 1984. *Methods for Intercultural Communication Research. International and Intercultural Communication Annual, Volume VIII.* Thousand Oaks, CA: SAGE Publications.

Guidolin, Massimo, and Eliana La Ferrara. 2007. "Diamonds Are Forever, Wars Are Not." *American Economic Review* 97 (5): 1978–93.

Gulati, Ranjay. 1995. "Does Familiarity Breed Trust? The Implications of Repeated Ties for Contractual Choice in Alliances." *Academy of Management Journal* 38 (1): 85–112.

Gulatti, Leela. 1995. "Myth and Reality: In the Context of Poor Working Women in Kerala." *Indian Women: Myth and Reality*, edited by Jasodhara Bagchi. Hyderabad, India: Sangam Books.

Gupta, Sanjeev, Catherine A. Pattillo, and Smita Wagh. 2009. "Effect of Remittances on Poverty and Financial Development in Sub-Saharan Africa." *World Development* 37 (1): 104–15.

Hagan, Jacqueline Maria. 1998. "Social Networks, Gender, and Immigrant Incorporation: Resources and Constraints." *American Sociological Review* 63 (1): 55–67.

Hagen, James M., and Soonkyoo Choe. 1998. "Trust in Japanese Interfirm Relations: Institutional Sanctions Matter." *Academy of Management Review* 23 (3): 589–600.

Haikkola, Lotta. 2011. "Making Connections: Second-Generation Children and the Transnational Field of Relations." *Journal of Ethnic and Migration Studies* 37 (8): 1201–17.

Haller, William, and Patricia Landolt. 2005. "The Transnational Dimensions of Identity Formation: Adult Children of Immigrants in Miami." *Ethnic and Racial Studies* 28 (6): 1182–1214.

Hammer, Muriel. 1984. "Explorations into the Meaning of Social Network Interview Data." *Social Networks* 6 (4): 341–71.

Hansen, Morten T. 1999. "The Search-Transfer Problem: The Role of Weak Ties in Sharing Knowledge Across Organization Subunits." *Administrative Science Quarterly* 44 (1): 82–111.

Hansen, Wendy L., Neil J. Mitchell, and Jeffrey M. Drope. 2005. "The Logic of Private and Collective Action." *American Journal of Political Science* 49 (1): 150–67.

Harding, Torfinn, and Beata S. Javorcik. 2011. "Roll Out the Red Carpet and They Will Come: Investment Promotion and FDI Inflows." *Economic Journal* 121 (557): 1445–76.

Harkness, Janet A., and Alicia Schoua-Glusberg. 1998. "Questionnaires in Translation." *ZUMA-Nachrichten Spezial* 3 (1): 87–127.

Harms, Philipp, and Pierre-Guillaume Méon. 2011. "An FDI Is an FDI Is an FDI? The Growth Effects of Greenfield Investment and Mergers and Acquisitions in Developing Countries." Working Paper No. 11.10, Gerzensee, Switzerland, Study Center Gerzensee. http://hdl.handle.net/10419/128070

Harvey, Michael G., Cheri Speier, and Milorad M. Novicevic. 2000. "Strategic Global Human Resource Management: The Role of Inpatriate Managers." *Human Resource Management Review* 10 (2): 153–75.

Haufler, Virginia. 2001. *A Public Role for the Private Sector: Industry Self-Regulation in a Global Economy*. Washington, DC: Carnegie Endowment for International Peace.

Hear, Nicholas Van, Frank Pieke, and Steven Vertovec. 2004. "The Contribution of UK-Based Diasporas to Development and Poverty Reduction." A Report by the ESRC Centre on Migration, Policy and Society (COMPAS). Online. Available at http://www.ssap.org.uk/wp-content/uploads/2012/09/NVH1_DFID-diaspora-report.pdf

Hedlund, Gunnar. 1994. "A Model of Knowledge Management and the N-form Corporation." *Strategic Management Journal* 15 (S2): 73–90.

Helmke, Gretchen, and Steven Levitsky. 2006. *Informal Institutions and Democracy: Lessons from Latin America*. Baltimore: Johns Hopkins University Press.

Helpman, Elhanan, Marc J. Melitz, and Stephen R. Yeaple. 2004. "Export Versus FDI with Heterogeneous Firms." *American Economic Review* 94 (1): 300–316.

Hemingway, Christine A., and Patrick W. Maclagan. 2004. "Managers' Personal Values as Drivers of Corporate Social Responsibility." *Journal of Business Ethics* 50: 33–44.

Hemphill, Thomas A. 1997. "Legislating Corporate Social Responsibility." *Business Horizons* 40 (2): 53–58.

Henisz, Witold J. 2000. "The Institutional Environment for Multinational Investment." *Journal of Law, Economics, and Organization* 16 (2): 334–64.

Herrmann, Pol, and Deepak K. Datta. 2006. "CEO Experiences: Effects on the Choice of FDI Entry Mode." *Journal of Management Studies* 43 (4): 755–78.

Hochberg, Yael V., Alexander Ljungqvist, and Yang Lu. 2007. "Whom You Know Matters: Venture Capital Networks and Investment Performance." *Journal of Finance* 62 (1): 251–301.

Holburn, Guy L. F., and Bennet A. Zelner. 2010. "Political Capabilities, Policy Risk, and International Investment Strategy: Evidence from the Global Electric Power Generation Industry." *Strategic Management Journal* 31 (12): 1290–1315.

Hollyer, James R., B. Peter Rosendorff, and James Raymond Vreeland. 2014. "Measuring Transparency." *Political Analysis* 22 (4): 413–34.

Holste, J. Scott, and Dail Fields. 2010. "Trust and Tacit Knowledge Sharing and Use." *Journal of Knowledge Management* 14 (1): 128–40.

Hoskisson, Robert E., Lorraine Eden, Chung Ming Lau, and Mike Wright. 2000. "Strategy in Emerging Economies." *Academy of Management Journal* 43 (3): 249–67.

Huang, Ye. 2003. *Selling China: Foreign Direct Investment During the Reform Era.* Cambridge: Cambridge University Press.

Huberman, Gur. 2001. "Familiarity Breeds Investment." *Review of Financial Studies* 14 (3): 659–80.

Hymer, Stephen. 1982. "The Multinational Corporation and the Law of Uneven Development." *Introduction to the Sociology of "Developing Societies,"* edited by Hamza Alavi and Teodor Shanin, 128–52. London: Palgrave.

International Monetary Fund. 2013. "Coordinated Direct Investment Survey." International Monetary Fund. Direction of Trade Statistics (DOTS).

International Office of Migration. 2005. "Return and Reintegration of Rejected Asylum Seekers and Irregular Migrants." *IOM Migration Research Series.* International Organization for Migration.

Iskandaryan, Alexander. 2010. "Armenia-Turkey Reconciliation: Motives and Impediments." In *Prospects for Reconciliation: Theory and Practice*, Proceedings of the International Workshop, Yerevan, November 27, 39–46. http://www.arme nia-turkey.net/files/2014-08/fxwimxJTvjnYy1yyHjusZVosqL.pdf#page=39

Jamali, Dima, and Ramez Mirshak. 2007. "Corporate Social Responsibility (CSR): Theory and Practice in a Developing Country Context." *Journal of Business Ethics* 72 (3): 243–62.

Javorcik, Beata S., Çaglar Özden, Mariana Spatareanu, and Cristina Neagu. 2011. "Migrant Networks and Foreign Direct Investment." *Journal of Development Economics* 94 (2): 231–41.

Javorcik, Beata S., and Shang-Jin Wei. 2009. "Corruption and Cross-Border Investment in Emerging Markets: Firm-Level Evidence." *Journal of International Money and Finance* 28 (4): 605–24.

Jeffries, Frank L., and Richard Reed. 2000. "Trust and Adaptation in Relational Contracting." *Academy of Management Review* 25 (4): 873–82.

Jensen, M. 2003. "The Role of Network Resources in Market Entry: Commercial Banks' Entry Investment Banking, 1991–1997." *Administrative Science Quarterly* 48 (3): 466–97.

Jensen, Nathan M. 2006. *Nation-States and the Multinational Corporation: A Political Economy of Foreign Direct Investment.* Princeton: Princeton University Press.

Jensen, Nathan. 2012. "Firm Level Responses to Political Risk: Political Institutions and the Operations of U.S. Multinationals." Working Paper. Washington University in St. Louis.

Jensen, Nathan, Quan Li, and Aminur Rahman. 2010. "Understanding Corruption and Firm Responses in Cross-National Firm-Level Surveys." *Journal of International Business Studies* 41 (9): 1481–1504.

Jensen, Nathan M., Edmund J. Malesky, and Matthew Walsh. 2015. "Competing for

Global Capital or Local Voters? The Politics of Business Location Incentives." *Public Choice* 164 (3–4): 331–56.

Jerven, Morten. 2013. *Poor Numbers: How We Are Misled by African Development Statistics and What to Do About It.* Ithaca: Cornell University Press.

Johanson, Jan, and Jan-Erik Vahlne. 2009. "The Uppsala Internationalization Process Model Revisited: From Liability of Foreignness to Liability of Outsidership." *Journal of International Business Studies* 40 (9): 1411–31.

Johns, Leslie, and Rachel L. Wellhausen. 2016. "Under One Roof: Supply Chains and the Protection of Foreign Investment." *American Political Science Review* 110 (1): 31–51.

Johnson, James. 2004. Speech to Annual Representative Meeting of the British Medical Association.

Johnson, Paula Doherty. 2007. "Diaspora Philanthropy: Influences, Initiatives, and Issues." The Philanthropic Initiative, Inc. and the Global Equity Initiative, Boston. Available online at http://www.philanthropy.org/SEMINARS/documents/Johnson_Diaspora_Philanthropy_FinalMay2007.pdf

Johnston, Alastair Iain. 2012. "What (if Anything) Does East Asia Tell Us About International Relations Theory?" *Annual Review of Political Science* 15:53–78.

Jones, Candace, William S. Hesterly, and Stephen P. Borgatti. 1997. "A General Theory of Network Governance: Exchange Conditions and Social Mechanisms." *Academy of Management Review* 22 (4): 911–45.

Jones, Marc T. 1999. "The Institutional Determinants of Social Responsibility." *Journal of Business Ethics* 20 (2): 163–79.

Jongwanich, Juthathip. 2007. *Workers' Remittances, Economic Growth and Poverty in Developing Asia and the Pacific Countries.* UNESCAP Working Paper, WP/07/01. United Nations Publications, Bangkok.

Juholin, Elisa. 2004. "For Business of the Good of All? A Finnish Approach to Corporate Social Responsibility." *Corporate Governance* 4 (3): 30–31.

Kahler, Miles. 1984. *Decolonization in Britain and France: The Domestic Consequences of International Relations.* Princeton: Princeton University Press.

Kang, Jun-Koo, and René M. Stulz. 1997. "Why Is There a Home Bias? An Analysis of Foreign Portfolio Equity Ownership in Japan." *Journal of Financial Economics.* 46 (1): 3–28.

Kapur, Devesh. 2004. "Remittances: The New Development Mantra?" *G-24 Discussion Paper Series.* New York: United Nations.

Kapur, Devesh. 2010. *Diaspora Development and Democracy: The Domestic Impact of International Migration from India.* Princeton: Princeton University Press.

Kapur, Devesh. 2012. "Indian Higher Education." *The Globalization of Higher Education*, edited by Christine T. Ennew and David Greenaway, 177–208. London: Palgrave Macmillan.

Kapur, Devesh. 2014. "Political Effects of International Migration." *Annual Review of Political Science* 17 (1): 479–502.

Kapur, Devesh, and John McHale. 2006. "What Is Wrong with Plan B? International Migration as an Alternative to Development Assistance." Paper Read at Brookings Trade Forum.

Karnow, Stanley. 2010. *In Our Image: America's Empire in the Philippines*. New York: Ballantine Books.

Kaufman, Robert, and Alex Segura-Ubiergo. 2001. "Globalization, Domestic Politics, and Social Spending in Latin America: A Time-Series Cross-Section Analysis 1973–97." *World Politics* 53 (4): 553–87.

Keefer, Phillip, and Stephen Knack. 1996. "Polarization, Property Rights, and the Links Between Inequality and Growth." Open Knowledge Repository, The World Bank and University of Maryland. Available at https://openknowledge. worldbank.org/bitstream/handle/10986/19802/multi_page.pdf?sequence= 1&isAllowed=y

Kerner, Andrew. 2009. "Why Should I Believe You? The Costs and Consequences of Bilateral Investment Treaties." *International Studies Quarterly* 53 (1): 73–102.

Kerner, Andrew. 2015. "Can Foreign Stock Investors Influence Policymaking?" *Comparative Political Studies* 48 (1): 35–64.

Kerner, Andrew, and Jane Lawrence. 2013. "What's the Risk? Bilateral Investment Treaties, Political Risk and Fixed Capital Accumulation." *British Journal of Political Science* 44:107–21.

Khanna, Tarun, and Krishna Palepu. 2013. *Winning in Emerging Markets: A Road Map for Strategy and Execution*. Cambridge, MA: Harvard Business Press.

Khwaja, Asim Ijaz, and Atif Mian. 2005. "Do Lenders Favor Politically Connected Firms? Rent Provision in an Emerging Financial Market." *Quarterly Journal of Economics* 120 (4): 1371–1411.

Kiessling, Timothy, and Michael Harvey. 2006. "Global Organizational Control: A New Role by Inpatriates." *Multinational Business Review* 14 (2): 1–27.

King, Gary, James Honaker, Anne Joseph, and Kenneth Scheve. 2001. "Analyzing Incomplete Political Science Data: An Alternative Algorithm for Multiple Imputation." *American Political Science Review* 95 (1): 49–69.

King, Gary, Christopher J. L. Murray, Joshua A. Salomon, and Ajay Tandon. 2004. "Enhancing the Validity and Cross-Cultural Comparability of Measurement in Survey Research." *American Political Science Review* 98 (1): 191–207.

Kingsley, Allison F., and Benjamin A. T. Graham. 2017. "The Capital Effects of Information Voids in Emerging Markets." *Journal of International Business Studies* 48 (3): 324–43.

Kinloch, Patricia, and Joan Metge. 2014. *Talking Past Each Other: Problems of Cross Cultural Communication*. Wellington, New Zealand: Victoria University Press.

Knight, Frank H. 1921. *Risk, Uncertainty and Profit*. Boston and New York: Houghton Mifflin.

Kobrin, Stephen J. 1980. "Foreign Enterprise and Forced Divestment in LDCs." *International Organization* 34 (1): 65–88.

Kobrin, Stephen J. 1987. "Testing the Bargaining Hypothesis in the Manufacturing Sector in Developing Countries." *International Organization* 41 (4): 609–38.

Kobrin, Stephen Jay. 1982. *Managing Political Risk Assessment: Strategic Response to Environmental Change*. Vol. 8. Berkeley and Los Angeles: University of California Press.

Kogut, Bruce, and Udo Zander. 1992. "Knowledge of the Firm, Combinative Capabilities, and the Replication of Technology." *Organization Science* 3 (3): 383–97.

Kshetri, Nir. 2013. "The Diaspora as a Change Agent in Entrepreneurship-Related Institutions in Sub-Saharan Africa." *Journal of Developmental Entrepreneurship* 18 (3). Online. Available at https://papers.ssrn.com/sol3/papers.cfm?abstract_id=2350440

Kugler, Maurice, and Hillel Rapoport. 2007. "International Labor and Capital Flows: Complements or Substitutes?" *Economics Letters* 94 (2): 155–62.

Ladd, Benjamin E. 2004. "Devil Disguised as a Corporate Angel: Questioning Corporate Charitable Contributions to Independent Directors' Organizations." *William & Mary Law Review* 46 (6): 2109–93.

Laguerre, Michel S. 2006. *Diaspora, Politics, and Globalization*. New York: Palgrave Macmillan.

Larson, Andrea. 1992. "Network Dyads in Entrepreneurial Settings: A Study of the Governance of Exchange Relationships." *Administrative Science Quarterly* 37 (1): 76–104.

Larson, Jennifer M., and Janet I. Lewis. 2016. "Ethnic Networks." *American Journal of Political Science*. https://doi.org/10.1111/ajps.12282

Law, David, Murat Genç, and John Bryant. 2013. "Trade, Diaspora and Migration to New Zealand." *World Economy* 36 (5): 582–606.

Leblang, David. 2010. "Familiarity Breeds Investment: Diaspora Networks and International Investment." *American Political Science Review* 104 (3): 584–600.

Lee, Hoon, Glen Biglaiser, and Joseph L. Staats. 2014. "The Effects of Political Risk on Different Entry Modes of Foreign Direct Investment." *International Interactions* 40 (5): 683–710.

Leonard, H. Jeffrey. 1980. "Multinational Corporations and Politics in Developing Countries." *World Politics* 32:454–83.

Levin, Daniel Z., and Rob Cross. 2004. "The Strength of Weak Ties You Can Trust: The Mediating Role of Trust in Effective Knowledge Transfer." *Management Science* 50 (11): 1477–90.

Levitt, Peggy, and Mary C. Waters. 2002. *The Changing Face of Home: The Transnational Lives of the Second Generation*. New York: Russell Sage Foundation.

Levy, Jack S. 2008. "Case Studies: Types, Designs, and Logics of Inference." *Conflict Management and Peace Science* 25 (1): 1–18.

Li, Hongbin, Lingsheng Meng, Qian Wang, and Li-An Zhou. 2008. "Political Connections, Financing and Firm Performance: Evidence from Chinese Private Firms." *Journal of Development Economics* 87:283–99.

Li, Julie Juan, Kevin Zheng Zhou, Simon S. K. Lam, and David K. Tse. 2006. "Active Trust Development of Local Senior Managers in International Subsidiaries." *Journal of Business Research* 59 (1): 73–80.

Li, Quan, and Adam Resnick. 2003. "Reversal of Fortunes: Democratic Institutions and Foreign Direct Investment Inflows to Developing Countries." *International Organization* 57 (1): 175–211.

Licuanan, Victoria, Toman Omar Mahmoud, and Andreas Steinmayr. 2012.

"The Drivers of Diaspora Donations for Development: Evidence from the Philippines." *Kiel Working Papers*. Kiel, Germany: Kiel Institute for the World Economy.

Licuanan, Victoria, Toman Omar Mahmoud, and Andreas Steinmayr. 2015. "The Drivers of Diaspora Donations for Development: Evidence from the Philippines." *World Development* 65: 94–109.

Lin, Xiaohua, and Xiyan Yang. 2017. "From Human Capital Externality to Entrepreneurial Aspiration: Revisiting the Migration-Trade Linkage." *Journal of World Business* 52 (3): 360–71.

Linton, C. Freeman. 1977. "A Set of Measures of Centrality Based on Betweenness." *Sociometry* 40 (1): 35–41.

Lipset, Seymour Martin. 1959. "Some Social Requisites of Democracy: Economic Development and Political Legitimacy." *American Political Science Review* 53 (1): 69–105.

Liu, Xiaohui, Lan Gao, Jiangyong Lu, and Yingqi Wei. 2015. "The Role of Highly Skilled Migrants in the Process of Inter-Firm Knowledge Transfer Across Borders." *Journal of World Business* 50 (1): 56–68.

Locke, Richard M. 2013. *The Promise and Limits of Private Power: Promoting Labor Standards in a Global Economy*. Cambridge: Cambridge University Press.

Lodigiani, Elisabetta, and Sara Salomone. 2015. "Migration-Induced Transfers of Norms: The Case of Female Political Empowerment." *University Ca' Foscari of Venice, Dept. of Economics Research Paper Series No. 19/WP/2015*.

Lucas, Robert E., Jr. 1990. "Why Doesn't Capital Flow from Rich to Poor Countries?" *American Economic Review* 80 (2): 92–96.

Lücke, Matthias, Toman Omar Mahmoud, and Christian Peuker. 2012. "Identifying the Motives of Migrant Philanthropy." *Kiel Working Papers*. Kiel, Germany: Kiel Institute for the World Economy.

Lyons, Terrence. 2004. "Engaging Diasporas to Promote Conflict Resolution: Transforming Hawks into Doves." Working Paper. Washington, DC: Institute of Conflict Analysis and Resolution, George Mason University.

MacDonald, John S., and Leatrice D. MacDonald. 1964. "Chain Migration Ethnic Neighborhood Formation and Social Networks." *Milbank Memorial Fund Quarterly* 42 (1): 82–97.

Mahmoud, Omar, Hillel Rapoport Toman, Andreas Steinmayr, and Christoph Trebesch. 2012. "Emigration and Political Change." Working Paper.

Maimbo, Samuel Muzele, and Dilip Ratha. 2005. *Remittances: Development Impact and Future Prospects*. Washington, DC: The World Bank.

Malesky, Edmund. 2013. "The Vietnam Provincial Competitiveness Index: Measuring Economic Governance for Private Sector Development: 2012 Final Report." *Vietnam Competitiveness Initiative Policy Paper #17*. Ha Noi, Vietnam: Vietnam Chamber of Commerce and Industry and United States Agency for International Development's Vietnam Competitiveness Initiative.

Malesky, Edmund, Dimitar D. Gueorguiev, and Nathan M. Jensen. 2015. "Monopoly Money: Foreign Investment and Bribery in Vietnam, a Survey Experiment." *American Journal of Political Science* 59 (2): 419–39.

Malesky, Edmund, Tran Huu Huynh, Dau Anh Tuan, Le Thanh Ha, Do Le Thu Ngoc, Ton Nhat Quang, Le Thu Hien, Janice Stallard, and Natasha Hanshaw. 2007. "The Vietnam Provincial Competiveness Index 2007: Measuring Economic Governance for Private Sector Development." US Agency for International Development and Vietnam Chamber of Commerce and Industry, Hanoi.

Manev, Ivan M., and William B. Stevenson. 2001. "Nationality, Cultural Distance, and Expatriate Status: Effects on the Managerial Network in a Multinational Enterprise." *Journal of International Business Studies* 32 (2): 285–303.

Marinova, Nadejda. 2010. "Transnational Homeland Involvement of the US-Based Lebanese Diaspora." *Center for Global Studies Working Paper* 15:1–13.

Markus, Stanislav. 2012. "Secure Property as a Bottom-Up Process: Firms, Stakeholders, and Predators in Weak States." *World Politics* 64 (2): 242–77.

Markus, Stanislav. 2015. *Property, Predation, and Protection.* Cambridge: Cambridge University Press.

Marsden, Peter V., and Karen E. Campbell. 1984. "Measuring Tie Strength." *Social Forces* 63 (2): 482–501.

Marsden, Peter V. 1990. "Network Data and Measurement." *Annual Review of Sociology* 16:435–63.

Massey, Douglas S. 1990. "Social Structure, Household Strategies, and the Cumulative Causation of Migration." *Population Index* 56 (1): 3–26.

Mayer, Thierry, and Soledad Zignago. 2011. "Notes on CEPII's Distance Measures: The GeoDist Database." CEPII Working Paper 2011–25. Available at http://www.cepii.fr/PDF_PUB/wp/2011/wp2011-25.pdf

McDermott, John. 2014. "The New Baby Boom." *Financial Times Magazine.*

McEvily, Bill, and Akbar Zaheer. 1999. "Bridging Ties: A Source of Firm Heterogeneity in Competitive Capabilities." *Strategic Management Journal* 20 (12): 1133–56.

McFadyen, M. Ann, Matthew Semadeni, and Albert A. Cannella Jr. 2009. "Value of Strong Ties to Disconnected Others: Examining Knowledge Creation in Biomedicine." *Organization Science* 20: 552–64.

McGuire, Jean B., Alison Sundgren, and Thomas Schneeweis. 1988. "Corporate Social Responsibility and Firm Financial Performance." *Academy of Management Journal* 31 (4): 854–72.

McMillan, John. 1997. "Markets in Transition." *Advances in Economics and Econometrics: Theory and Applications,* edited by David M. Kreps and Kenneth F. Wallis, 210–39. Cambridge: Cambridge University Press.

McMillan, John, and Christopher Woodruff. 1999. "Interfirm Relationships and Informal Credit in Vietnam." *Quarterly Journal of Economics* 114 (4): 1285–1320.

McWilliams, Abagail, and Donald Siegel. 2001. "Corporate Social Responsibility: A Theory of the Firm Perspective." *Academy of Management Review* 26 (1): 117–27.

Melitz, Marc J. 2003. "The Impact of Trade on Intra-Industry Reallocations and Aggregate Industry Productivity." *Econometrica* 71 (6): 1695–1725.

Melitz, Marc J. 2008. "International Trade and Heterogeneous Firms." *The New Palgrave Dictionary of Economics.* London: Palgrave Macmillan.

Mencinger, Jože. 2003. "Does Foreign Direct Investment Always Enhance Economic Growth?" *Kyklos* 56 (4): 491–508.

Mercier, Marion. 2013. "The Return of the Prodigy Son: Do Return Migrants make Better Leaders?" Institute for the Study of Labor, Bonn, Germany. Discussion Paper Series, 7780: 1–38.

Mghebrishvili, Nana. 2012. "Challenges and Opportunities for Real Estate Investors in Georgia." *The Financial Channel* (Tbilisi, Georgia). https://www.finchannel. com/business/realestate/33876-

Miyagiwa, Kaz. 1991. "Scale Economies in Education and the Brain Drain Problem." *International Economic Review* 32 (3): 743–59.

Moon, Jeremy. 2007. "The Contribution of Corporate Social Responsibility to Sustainable Development." *Sustainable Development* 15 (5): 296–306.

Moran, Theodore H. 1985. "International Political Risk Assessment, Corporate Planning and Strategies to Offset Political Risk." *Multinational Corporations: The Political Economy of Foreign Direct Investment*, edited by Theodore Moran, 107–17. Lexington, MA: Lexington Books.

Morris, Shad S., Bijuan Zhong, and Mona Makhija. 2015. "Going the Distance: The Pros and Cons of Expanding Employees' Global Knowledge Reach." *Journal of International Business Studies* 46 (5): 552–73.

Mosley, Layna, and Saika Uno. 2007. "Racing to the Bottom or Climbing to the Top? Economic Globalization and Collective Labor Rights." *Comparative Political Studies* 40 (8): 923–48.

Mountford, Andrew. 1997. "Can a Brain Drain Be Good for Growth in the Source Economy?" *Journal of Development Economics* 53 (2): 287–303.

Mullings, Beverley. 2011. "Diaspora Strategies, Skilled Migrants and Human Capital Enhancement in Jamaica." *Global Networks* 11 (1): 24–42.

Musteen, Martina, John Francis, and Deepak K. Datta. 2010. "The Influence of International Networks on Internationalization Speed and Performance: A Study of Czech SMEs." *Journal of World Business* 45 (3): 197–205.

Nader, Ralph. 2014. "Why US Brain Drain Harms Developing Countries." *Aljazeera*, January 19.

Naujoks, Daniel. 2013. *Migration, Citizenship, and Development: Diasporic Membership Policies and Overseas Indians in the United States*. Oxford: Oxford University Press.

Newell, Peter, and Jedrzej George Frynas. 2007. "Beyond CSR? Business, Poverty and Social Justice: An Introduction." *Third World Quarterly* 28 (4): 669–81.

Newland, Kathleen, Aaron Terrazas, and Roberto Munster. 2010. "Diaspora Philanthropy: Private Giving and Public Policy." Washington, DC: Migration Policy Institute.

Newland, Kathleen, and Carylanna Taylor. 2010. *Heritage Tourism and Nostalgia Trade: A Diaspora Niche in the Development Landscape*. Washington, DC: Migration Policy Institute.

Nielsen, Tjai, and Liesl Riddle. 2010. "Investing in Peace: The Motivational Dynamics of Diaspora Investment in Post-Conflict Economies." *Journal of Business Ethics* 89 (4): 435–48.

Nixon, Ron. 2016. "Arrest of Refugees Fuels U.S. Debate on Immigration Policy."

New York Times. Available at http://www.nytimes.com/2016/02/20/us/politics/us-immigration-policy-screening.html

Nonaka, Ikujiro. 1994. "A Dynamic Theory of Organizational Knowledge Creation." *Organization Science* 5 (1): 14–37.

Norbäck, Pehr-Johan, and Lars Persson. 2007. "Investment Liberalization—Why a Restrictive Cross-Border Merger Policy Can Be Counterproductive." *Journal of International Economics* 72 (2): 366–80.

Nyberg-Sørensen, Ninna. 2007. "Living Across Worlds: Diaspora, Development, and Transnational Engagement." International Organization for Migration.

Oberai, A. S., and H. K. Manmohan Singh. 1980. "Migration, Remittances and Rural Development: Findings of a Case Study in the Indian Punjab." *International Labour Review* 119 (2): 229–42.

OECD. 2008. *Benchmark Definition of Foreign Direct Investment.* Fourth Ed. Available at https://www.oecd.org/daf/inv/investmentstatisticsandanalysis/4019373 4.pdf

OECD. 2016. Stat. FDI Flows by Partner Country. Available at https://stats.oecd.org/Index.aspx?DataSetCode=FDI_FLOW_PARTNER (accessed May 15, 2016).

Olson, Mancur. 1965. *The Logic of Collective Action: Public Goods and the Theory of Collective Action.* Cambridge, MA: Harvard University Press.

Orozco, Manuel. 2002. "Globalization and Migration: The Impact of Family Remittances in Latin America." *Latin American Politics and Society* 44 (2): 41–66.

Orozco, Manuel, and Michelle Lapointe. 2004. "Mexican Hometown Associations and Development Opportunities." *Journal of International Affairs* 57 (2): 31–51.

Owen, Erica. 2013. "Unionization and Restrictions on Foreign Direct Investment." *International Interactions* 39 (5): 723–47.

Owen, Erica. 2015. "The Political Power of Organized Labor and the Politics of Foreign Direct Investment in Developed Democracies." *Comparative Political Studies* 48 (13): 1746–80.

Özer, Özalp, Yanchong Zheng, and Kay-Yut Chen. 2011. "Trust in Forecast Information Sharing." *Management Science* 57 (6): 1111–37.

Pandya, Sonal, and David Leblang. 2011. "Deal or No Deal: The Growth of International Venture Capital Investment." Working Paper. Available at http://citeseerx.ist.psu.edu/viewdoc/download?doi=10.1.1.404.2003&rep=rep1&type=pdf

Pandya, Sonal, and David Leblang. 2012. "Deal or No Deal: Explaining the Rise of International Venture Capital Investment." Working Paper. Charlottesville: University of Virginia.

Pandya, Sonal S. 2014. "Democratization and Foreign Direct Investment Liberalization, 1970–2000." *International Studies Quarterly* 58 (3): 475–88.

Patel, Sandeep A., Amra Balic, and Liliane Bwakira. 2002. "Measuring Transparency and Disclosure at Firm-Level in Emerging Markets." *Emerging Markets Review* 3 (4): 325–37.

Pearce, Jone L. 2001. *Organization and Management in the Embrace of Government.* Mahwah, NJ: Lawrence Erlbaum Associates.

Penn World Tables. Version 8.0.

Perrone, Vincenzo, Akbar Zaheer, and Bill McEvily. 2003. "Free to Be Trusted? Organizational Constraints on Trust in Boundary Spanners." *Organization Science* 14: 422–39.

Podolny, J. M. 1994. "Market Uncertainty and the Social Character of Economic Exchange." *Administrative Science Quarterly* 39 (3): 458–83.

Polanyi, Michael. 1966. *The Tacit Dimension, The Terry Lectures, Yale University.* New York: Doubleday.

Porter, Michael E., and Mark R. Kramer. 2002. "The Competitive Advantage of Corporate Philanthropy." *Harvard Business Review* 80 (12): 56–68.

Portes, Alejandro. 1998. "Divergent Destinies: Immigration, the Second Generation, and the Rise of Transnational Communities." *Paths to Inclusion: The Integration of Migrants in the United States and Germany,* edited by Peter H. Schuck and Rainer Münz. New York: Berghahn.

Portes, Alejandro, ed. 1998. *The Economic Sociology of Immigration: Essays on Networks, Ethnicity, and Entrepreneurship.* New York: Russell Sage Foundation.

Portes, Alejandro, and L. E. Guarnizo. 1990. "Tropical Capitalists: US Bound Immigration and Small Enterprise Development in the Dominican Republic." *Migration, Remittances, and Small Business Development: Mexico and Caribbean Basin Countries,* edited by S. Diaz-Briquets and S. Weintraub, 101–31. Boulder, CO: Westview Press.

Portes, Alejandro, Luis E. Guarnizo, and Patricia Landolt. 1999. "The Study of Transnationalism: Pitfalls and Promise of an Emergent Research Field." *Ethnic and Racial Studies* 22 (2): 217–37.

Portes, Richard, and Hélène Rey. 2005. "The Determinants of Cross-Border Equity Flows." *Journal of International Economics* 65 (2): 269–96.

Premaratne, S. P. 2001. "Networks, Resources, and Small Business Growth: The Experience in Sri Lanka." *Journal of Small Business Management* 39 (4): 363–71.

Pruthi, Sarika, Anuradha Basu, and Mike Wright. 2018. "Ethnic Ties, Motivations, and Home Country Entry Strategy of Transnational Entrepreneurs." *Journal of International Entrepreneurship.* Online. https://doi.org/10.1007/s1084

Raghunathan, Trivellore E., James M. Lepkowski, John Van Hoewyk, and Peter Solenberger. 2001. "A Multivariate Technique for Multiply Imputing Missing Values Using a Sequence of Regression Models." *Survey Methodology* 27 (1): 85–96.

Ratha, Dilip, and Jan Riedberg. 2005. "On Reducing Remittance Costs." Unpublished Paper. Development Research Group, World Bank, Washington, DC.

Rauch, James, and Allessandra Cassella. 2003. "Overcoming Informational Barriers to International Resource Allocation: Prices and Ties." *Economic Journal* 113: 21–42.

Rauch, James E., and Vitor Trindade. 2002. "Ethnic Chinese Networks in International Trade." *Review of Economics and Statistics* 84 (1): 116–30.

Raveloharimisy, Joel, Liesl Riddle, and Tjai Nielsen. 2010. "Measuring Diaspora Identity Among Liberians in the United States." Presented at the Annual Meeting of the Southern Political Science Association. Atlanta, GA.

Reiche, B. Sebastian. 2011. "Knowledge Transfer in Multinationals: The Role of Inpatriates' Boundary Spanning." *Human Resource Management* 50 (3): 365–89.

Reuveny, Rafael, and Quan Li. 2003. "Economic Openness, Democracy, and Income Inequality." *Comparative Political Studies* 36 (5): 575–601.

Riddle, Liesl. 2008. "Diasporas: Exploring Their Development Potential." *ESR Review* 10 (2): 28–35.

Riddle, Liesl, George A. Hrivnak, and Tjai M. Nielsen. 2010. "Transnational Diaspora Entrepreneurship in Emerging Markets: Bridging Institutional Divides." *Journal of International Management* 16 (4): 398–411.

Riddle, Liesl, and Jennifer Brinkerhoff. 2011. "Diaspora Entrepreneurs as Institutional Change Agents: The Case of Thamel.com." *International Business Review* 20 (6): 670–80.

Riddle, Liesl, and T. Nielsen. 2011. "Policies to Strengthen Diaspora Investment and Entrepreneurship: Cross-National Perspectives." *Realizing the Development Potential of Diasporas*, 230–52. New York: United Nations Library.

Rodríguez-Montemayor, Eduardo. 2012. "Diaspora Direct Investment Policy: Options for Development." Policy Brief No. IDB-PB-183, Inter-American Development Bank, Washington, DC.

Rolfe, Robert J., David A. Ricks, Martha M. Pointer, and Mark McCarthy. 1993. "Determinants of FDI Incentive Preferences of MNEs." *Journal of International Business Studies* 24 (2): 335–55.

Ronnas, Per. 1992. *Employment Generation Through Private Entrepreneurship in Vietnam*. Geneva: International Labour Organization.

Rosenfeld, Bryn, Kosuke Imai, and Jacob N. Shapiro. 2016. "An Empirical Validation Study of Popular Survey Methodologies for Sensitive Questions." *American Journal of Political Science* 60 (3): 783–802.

Royston, Patrick. 2004. "Multiple Imputation of Missing Values." *Stata Journal* 4 (3): 227–41.

Royston, Patrick. 2009. "Multiple Imputation of Missing Values: Further Update of ice, with an Emphasis on Categorical Variables." *Stata Journal* 9 (3): 466–77.

Rudra, Nita. 2002. "Globalization and the Decline of the Welfare State in Less-Developed Countries." *International Organization* 56 (2): 411–45.

Rudra, Nita. 2008. *Globalization and the Race to the Bottom in Developing Countries: Who Really Gets Hurt?* Cambridge: Cambridge University Press.

Rugman, Alan M. 1981. *Inside the Multinationals: The Economics of Internal Markets*. New York: Columbia University Press.

Ryan, Louise. 2007. "Migrant Women, Social Networks and Motherhood: The Experiences of Irish Nurses in Britain." *Sociology* 41 (2): 295–312.

Ryan, Louise. 2009. "How Women Use Family Networks to Facilitate Migration: A Comparative Study of Irish and Polish Women in Britain." *History of the Family* 14:217–31.

Ryan, Louise. 2011. "Migrants' Social Networks and Weak Ties: Accessing Resources and Constructing Relationships Post-Migration." *Sociological Review* 59 (4): 707–24.

Ryan, Louise, Rosemary Sales, Mary Tilki, and Bernadetta Siara. 2008. "Social Networks, Social Support and Social Capital: The Experiences of Recent Polish Migrants in London." *Sociology* 42 (4): 672–90.

Safran, William. 1991. "Diasporas in Modem Society: Myths of Homeland and Return." *Diaspora* 1:83–99.

Sako, Mari. 1992. *Prices, Quality, and Trust: Inter-Firm Relations in Britain and Japan*. Cambridge: Cambridge University Press.

Samovar, Larry A., Richard E. Porter, and Nemi C. Jain. 1981. *Understanding Intercultural Communication*. Belmont, CA: Wadsworth Publishing.

Sana, Mariano. 2005. "Buying Membership in the Transnational Community: Migrant Remittances, Social Status, and Assimilation." *Population Research and Policy Review* 24 (3): 231–61.

Saxenian, AnnaLee. 2006. *The New Argonauts: Regional Advantage in a Global Economy*. Cambridge, MA: Harvard University Press.

Scheve, Kenneth F., and Matthew J. Slaughter. 2001. "Labor Market Competition and Individual Preferences over Immigration Policy." *Review of Economics and Statistics* 83 (1): 133–45.

Schiller, Nina Glick, and Georges E. Fouron. 1999. "Terrains of Blood and Nation: Haitian Transnational Social Fields." *Ethnic and Racial Studies* 22 (2): 340–66.

Schilling, Melissa A., and Corey C. Phelps. 2007. "Interfirm Collaboration Networks: The Impact of Large-Scale Network Structure on Firm Innovation." *Management Science* 53 (7): 1113–26.

Schotter, Andreas, and Paul W. Beamish. 2011. "Performance Effects of Mnc Headquarters—Subsidiary Conflict and the Role of Boundary Spanners: The Case of Headquarter Initiative Rejection." *Journal of International Management* 17:243–59.

Schulte, Bettina. 2008. "Second Generation Entrepreneurs of Turkish Origin in Germany: Diasporic Identity and Business Engagement." *COMCAD Arbeitspapiere—Working Papers*. Bielefeld: Center on Migration, Citizenship, and Development.

Seawright, Jason, and John Gerring. 2008. "Case Selection Techniques in Case Study Research a Menu of Qualitative and Quantitative Options." *Political Research Quarterly* 61 (2): 294–308.

Sebastian Reiche, B. 2006. "The Inpatriate Experience in Multinational Corporations: An Exploratory Case Study in Germany." *International Journal of Human Resource Management* 17 (9): 1572–90.

Shain, Yossi. 2002. "The Role of Diasporas in Conflict Perpetuation or Resolution." *SAIS Review* 22 (2): 115–44.

Shain, Yossi. 2007. *Kinship and Diasporas in International Affairs*. Ann Arbor: University of Michigan Press.

Sheffer, Gabriel. 1986. *Modern Diasporas in International Politics*. Sydney: Croom Helm.

Sheffer, Gabriel. 2003. *Diaspora Politics: At Home Abroad*: Cambridge: Cambridge University Press.

Shi, Weiyi. 2013. "Risky Business? A Firm-Level Analysis of Chinese Outward Direct Investments." Presented at the Annual Meeting of the International Political Economy Society. Claremont, CA.

Shi, Weiyi. 2014. "State Preference, Policy Distortion, and Outbound FDI: Firm-Level Evidence from China." Working Paper, University of California, San Diego.

Shouten, Fredreka, and Alan Gomez. 2013. "Tech Companies Driving the Lobbying on Immigration." *USA Today*. Available at http://www.usatoday.com/story/news/nation/2013/04/29/tech-companies-lobbying-immigration-facebook-family-visas/2121179

Sinclair, Michelle, and Joseph Galaskiewicz. 1996. "Corporate-Nonprofit Partnerships: Varieties and Covariates." *New York Law School Law Review* 41:1059–98.

Soehl, Thomas, and Roger Waldinger. 2012. "Inheriting the Homeland? Intergenerational Transmission of Cross-Border Ties in Migrant Families." *American Journal of Sociology* 118 (3): 778–813.

Solinger, Dorothy J. 1989. "Urban Reform and Relational Contracting in Post-Mao China: An Interpretation of the Transition from Plan to Market." *Studies in Comparative Communism* 22 (2): 171–85.

Sommer, Elena, and Markus Gamper. 2018. "Transnational Entrepreneurial Activities: A Qualitative Network Study of Self-Employed Migrants from the Former Soviet Union in Germany." *Social Networks* 53: 136–47.

Szulanski, Gabriel. 1996. "Exploring Internal Stickiness: Impediments to the Transfer of Best Practice within the Firm." *Strategic Management Journal* 17 (S2): 27–43.

Taylor, J. Edward. 1992. "Remittances and Inequality Reconsidered: Direct, Indirect, and Intertemporal Effects." *Journal of Policy Modeling* 14 (2): 187–208.

Transparency International. 2010. "The Georgian Taxation System—An Overview." Tbilisi, Georgia: Transparency International.

United Nations. 2000. *World Investment Report*. United Nations Commission on Trade and Development.

United Nations, Department of Economic and Social Affairs. 2013. "Trends in International Migrant Stock: Migrants by Destination and Origin."

Uzzi, Brian. 1996. "The Sources and Consequences of Embeddedness for the Economic Performance of Organizations: The Network Effect." *American Sociological Review* 61 (4): 674–98.

Vaaler, Paul M. 2008. "How Do MNCS Vote in Developing Country Elections?" *Academy of Management Journal* 51 (1): 21–43.

Vaaler, Paul M. 2011. "Immigrant Remittances and the Venture Investment Environment of Developing Countries." *Journal of International Business Studies* 42 (9): 1121–49.

Van Buuren, Stef. 2007. "Multiple Imputation of Discrete and Continuous Data by Fully Conditional Specification." *Statistical Methods in Medical Research* 16 (3): 219–42.

Vernon, Raymond. 1971. *Sovereignty at Bay: The Multinational Spread of U.S. Enterprises*. New York: Basic Books.

Vertovec, Steven. 2009. *Transnationalism*. New York: Routledge.

Viswanatha, Aruna. 2016. "J. P. Morgan Settlement Lays Bare the Practice of Hiring

Princelings." *Wall Street Journal*. Available at https://www.wsj.com/
articles/j-p-morgan-to-pay-264-million-to-end-criminal-civil-foreign-corrup
tion-cases-1479398628

Wahba, Jackline, and Yves Zenou. 2012. "Out of Sight, Out of Mind: Migration,
Entrepreneurship and Social Capital." *Regional Science and Urban Economics* 42
(5): 890–903.

Walker, Markus. 2016. "EU Officials Call for Urgent Action on Migration, Security."
Wall Street Journal. Available at http://www.wsj.com/articles/eu-officials-call-
for-urgent-action-on-migration-security-1453377608

Wang, Dan. 2014. "Activating Cross-Border Brokerage Interorganizational Knowledge Transfer Through Skilled Return Migration." *Administrative Science Quarterly* 60 (1): 133–76.

Wang, Miao, and M. C. Sunny Wong. 2009. "What Drives Economic Growth? The
Case of Cross-Border M&A and Greenfield FDI Activities." *Kyklos* 62 (2): 316–
30.

Weidenbaum, Murray, and Samuel Hughes. 1996. *The Bamboo Network: How Expatriate Chinese Entrepreneurs Are Creating a New Economic Superpower in Asia*.
New York: Free Press.

Wellhausen, Rachel L. 2013. "Investor-State Disputes: When Can Governments
Break Contracts?" *Journal of Conflict Resolution* 59 (2): 239–61.

Wernerfelt, Birger. 1984. "A Resource-Based View of the Firm: Ten Years After."
Strategic Management Journal 5 (2): 171–80.

Wibbels, Erik. 2006. "Dependency Revisited: International Markets, Business Cy-
cles, and Social Spending in the Developing World." *International Organization*
60 (2): 433–68.

Wierzbicki, Susan K. 2004. *Beyond the Immigrant Enclave: Network Change and Assimilation*. El Paso, TX: LFB Scholarly Publishing.

Williamson, Oliver E. 1975. *Markets and Hierarchies: Analysis and Antitrust Implications*. New York: Free Press.

Wong, Sze Sze, and Wai Fong Boh. 2010. "Leveraging the Ties of Others to Build a
Reputation for Trustworthiness Among Peers." *Academy of Management Journal* 53 (1): 129–48.

Woolcock, Michael, and Deepa Narayan. 2000. "Social Capital: Implications for
Development Theory, Research, and Policy." *World Bank Research Observer* 15
(2): 225–49.

World Bank. 2016. Global Bilateral Migration Database. Available at http://data.
worldbank.org/data-catalog/global-bilateral-migration-database   (accessed
May 15, 2016).

World Bank. 2016a. "Doing Business: Measuring Business Regulations." Available
at http://www.doingbusiness.org/custom-query (accessed May 15, 2016).

World Bank. 2016b. "World Development Indicators." Available at http://databank.
worldbank.org/data/reports.aspx?source=world-development-indicators (accessed May 15, 2016).

Ye, Min. 2010. "Ethnic Investors vs. Foreign Investors: The Impact of Diasporas on

Economic Liberalization in China and India." Annual Meeting of the American Political Science Association. Washington, DC.

Ye, Min. 2014. *Diasporas and Foreign Direct Investment in China and India*. Cambridge: Cambridge University Press.

Yli-Renko, Helena, Erkko Autio, and Harry J. Sapienza. 2001. "Social Capital, Knowledge Acquisition, and Knowledge Exploitation in Young Technology-Based Firms." *Strategic Management Journal* 22 (6–7): 587–613.

Zaheer, Srilata. 1995. "Overcoming the Liability of Foreignness." *Academy of Management Journal* 38 (2): 341–63.

Zak, Paul J., and Stephen Knack. 2001. "Trust and Growth." *Economic Journal* 111 (470): 295–321.

Zimmermann, Klaus F. 1995. "Tackling the European Migration Problem." *Journal of Economic Perspectives* 9 (2): 45–62.

Zucker, Lynne G. 1986. "Production of Trust: Institutional Sources of Economic Structure, 1840–1920." *Research in Organizational Behavior* 8:53–111.

INDEX

Abkhazia, 72, 144–45
Aguas, Nina, 1–2, 14
altruism, 58, 142
Aquino regime, 73
Aroyo regime, 73
assimilation, 6

balikbayan, 83
Bangladesh, 14–15
bankruptcy, 109
brain drain, 13–14, 16, 150, 158
bribery, 10–11
business strategies: diaspora-affiliated firms
   and, 61–63, 78–80, 136, 162; diasporans as
   transnational brokers and, 25–26, 60–61,
   150; foreign firms and, 25–26, 79–80, 136

charitable donations, 54–58, 122, 132–34,
   218n54
Chevron Philippines, 125–27
China, 2, 53
circular migration, 14–15. *See also* returnees
Citibank, 1–2
conflict: in Georgia, 71–73; migration and, 12;
   profitability and, 62, 68, 130, 141–47, 152,
   180, 218n57, 223n8. *See also* violence; war
contract enforcement: credit and, 109–10;
   diaspora-affiliated firms and, 17, 101–2,
   107–10; diasporans and, 101–2; diasporans
   as transnational brokers and, 25–26, 48; foreign firms and, 17, 25–26, 101–2, 109–10;
   Philippines and, 73–74; social ties and, 48,
   67, 86
corporate social responsibility, 59, 126, 222n2,
   222n4, 222n7
corruption, 10–11, 23, 38, 48, 75–76, 116
Council of British Medical Associates, 13
credit: contract enforcement and, 109–10;

diaspora-affiliated firms and, 18, 62, 101–2,
   108–13, 123–24, 142, 151–52; diasporans as
   transnational brokers and, 1–2, 18, 28, 67,
   102, 123–24; foreign firms and, 18, 101–2,
   108–13, 123–24, 142, 151–52; loan sharks
   and, 109; micro-credit movement, 15; in the
   Philippines, 1–2, 123–24, 142; social ties
   and, 18, 28, 67, 101–2, 127
credit reporting agencies, 109–10
cultural fluency, 24, 27, 34–36, 53, 125, 161,
   216–17n27

Department of Energy, 125
developing countries: brain drain and, 12–14,
   16; budgets of, 11; civil conflict and, 68; corruption in, 29, 38; definition of, 219n9; development in, 11; diaspora-affiliated firms
   and, 3, 18–19, 127–28; diasporans and, 3,
   27, 39, 63–64, 147, 149–50, 157–58; emigrants of, 223n2; emigration increases and,
   12–16, 18–19; FDI into, 5, 7–12, 26–29, 50;
   foreign firms and, 18–19, 100, 127–28, 147,
   153–54; globalization and, 59, 138–39; information access and, 29; investments in, 3–
   5, 11, 18–19, 39, 57–59, 68–69, 100, 127–28,
   154–55; liability of outsidership and, 29;
   nepotism and, 38; policy influence and, 87;
   political risks and, 7, 18–19, 22, 27, 29, 87,
   147, 156; promotion of diasporan investments and, 18–19; public health of, 11; remittances and, 5–7, 14–16, 56, 71, 135, 150,
   158, 214–15n22, 214n19; resources of, 27;
   social ties and, 26–29, 37–38, 42
diasporans: capabilities of, 65, 150, 160; cultural fluency and, 39, 46; definition of, 2, 5–
   6, 83; developing countries and, 39; downsides of hiring, 16–17, 54–55, 121–22;
   education of, 11, 52–54, 155, 218n50;

253

Printed and bound by CPI Group (UK) Ltd, Croydon, CR0 4YY

23/04/2025

14660943-0001